the development

of an

american culture

Edited, with an introduction,
by

STANLEY COBEN

Department of History
University of California, Los Angeles

LORMAN RATNER

Department of History
Herbert H. Lehman College
of the City University of New York

PRENTICE-HALL, INC., Englewood Cliffs, New Jersey

Current printing (last digit):
10 9 8 7 6 5 4 3 2 1

13-207266-1

Library of Congress catalog card number:
69-17484

Printed in the United States of America

Prentice-Hall International, Inc., London
Prentice-Hall of Australia, Pty. Ltd., Sydney
Prentice-Hall of Canada, Ltd., Toronto
Prentice-Hall of India Private Ltd., New Delhi
Prentice-Hall of Japan, Inc., Tokyo

contents

iii

introduction:
culture,
history,
and the history
of culture

The idea of culture stands as one of the central concepts in modern social science. Developed largely by anthropologists in the early twentieth century from nineteenth century German and to a lesser extent British and French origins, the concept has become the basis for what a few theorists argue already is a science of culture. Certainly a distinct body of thought seems to be developing, fostered both by an abundance of theoretical speculation and by the collection and comparison of data from hundreds of different cultures and subcultures. Scholars in every social science and in some of the humanities have contributed to this development—archeologists, art historians, social and intellectual historians, sociologists, and philosophers have taken part—although anthro-

1

pologists continue to play the most important role. Even certain economists, sociologists, and political scientists with practical rather than
theoretical objectives have become part-time culturologists, as they observed that massive injections of capital, technological assistance, or
military force, failed to bring about desired changes in non-industrial
societies. Historians increasingly find the concept useful as they widen
their field of inquiry and attempt to understand the lives of ordinary
people.

For over a century, the various meanings given to the term culture by
social scientists have existed in rather ambiguous tension with a humanistic usage connoting an ideal standard of intellectual, artistic, and
moral cultivation. The English poet and essayist Matthew Arnold
popularized the latter definition with his famous statement in 1869 that
culture consisted of "a pursuit of total perfection by means of getting to
know, on all matters which most concern us, the best which has been
thought and said in the world. . . . Sweetness and light are the main
characters [of culture]." Although Arnold's usage persists today, and
traces of it have even found their way into this volume, the broader
anthropological meaning seems to us one of the most fertile ideas available to historians, and it is around that concept that this book is organized.

Social scientists who have attempted to define culture recently seem
to agree that the essence of the idea now lies in its implication of a set
of distinctive patterns of and for behavior, prevalent among a group of
human beings. This meaning differs more than generally is realized from
the definition usually considered the origin of the word's use in the
modern anthropological sense, given by British anthropologist Edward
B. Tylor in 1871: "that complex whole which includes knowledge, belief,
art, law, morals, custom, and any other capabilities and habits acquired
by man as a member of society." To Tylor, then, culture was an ag-
gregate in which each of many aspects was of nearly equal importance.
Specialists a century later, however, increasingly regard culture as an
abstraction defying exact definition, a largely unverbalized and implicit
code for communication among individuals who must, at certain points,
synchronize their disparate lives. Furthermore, certain factors now are
considered far more significant than the rest.

To modern theorists, culture is a system which makes possible a high
degree of both uniformity and diversity among individuals in a society.
The shared knowledge of behavior patterns imposes uniformity of action
and style. However, the same shared perceptions also enable individuals
with a variety of different motives to meet in thousands of standardized
relationships involving detailed mutual expectations, ranging from the
most intimate marital relationships to formal business dealings. Anthony
F. C. Wallace, an anthropologist who specializes in the connection between culture and individual personality, declares: "Society is as Rousseau

intuited, built upon a set of continually changing social contracts made possible by human cognitive equipment. Culture can be conceived as a set of standardized models of such contractual relationships."

In studying culture—or anything else—selected factors are, as anthropologist Edward Sapir wrote, "intrinsically more valuable, more characteristic, more significant" than the rest. The most important cultural phenomena, the most inclusive, and those crucial for cultural integration, are related to what frequently is termed style. Like culture itself, style is a word that has become difficult to define precisely. However, few scholars—including historians—doubt that cultures do differ in style, and if these differences are identifiable we should be able to describe them.

Our view, reflected in this book, is that the primary elements in cultural style are ideas and values. The problem of deciding which ideas and values are "intrinsically more valuable, more characteristic, more significant" in any single culture, or at any time in that culture's history, is another that may always elude attempts to achieve exact measurement. Nevertheless, a sampling and weighing process does go on in the scholar's mind, affected always by his own cultural bias, which perhaps can be overcome to a large extent, and by his peculiar personal interests in certain kinds of ideas and activities, which probably cannot. This sampling and weighing process, then, remains an art; accuracy is made possible only by the high level of sensitivity and critical judgment developed by some practitioners, and by years of careful study of the cultures they analyze.

Discrepancies exist in the extent to which members of a society share the prevailing cultural tendencies. These tendencies everywhere can be traced to factors like age, sex, and class. In the United States our authors found unusually wide variations ascribable to racial differences, especially to the forced 200-year immigration of Africans who then were held as slaves. During certain periods, cultural variations in the United States can be traced to distinctions between urban and rural life, and between geographical areas, most dramatically between North and South in the decades preceding the Civil War.

The problems posed for our authors by the simultaneous existence in the United States of numerous and diverse subcultures has been settled, although not solved, by their decision to devote primary attention to the dominant ideas and values. These exercised decisive influence over the development of American institutions and public policies. They also penetrated almost every subculture, permeating most of them over a period of generations. Undeniably, United States historians have paid insufficient attention to influences running in the other direction, as well as to the effects of the subgroups upon each other. However, the authors decided that only certain of these relationships should be explored carefully in this volume.

The difficulty of dealing not only with a variety of complex subcultures, but with a great range of personality types within these groups, as well, currently leaves most social scientists and historians who consider the task, filled with despair. Possibly these problems will remain insoluble until we can describe both subcultures and personality types, and their interactions, more precisely, perhaps with the aid of more sophisticated quantitative techniques than commonly are used now.

Meanwhile, the culture concept provides historians with an extremely valuable intellectual tool for dealing with certain types of questions and material. Consider for example one of the historians' most perplexing questions: to what extent do individuals—especially those most influential—affect history, and to what extent do they act as agents of the culture? In one of the classic works in cultural history, *Jackson, Symbol of an Age*, John William Ward demonstrated that impressions of President Andrew Jackson held by large segments of the American electorate were closer to certain popular ideas, peculiar to the time and crucial to American culture in that period, than they were to Jackson's actual career and character. Although he was admirably suited to act as symbol for his age, Jackson would have been created under a different name if he had not existed; such was the condition of American life in 1828, Ward argues. Ward carries his analysis further in an essay in this volume. It must be granted that some individuals have exercised at least a slight influence over major historical events and tendencies; but in the history of a culture these individuals are as likely to be intellectual or religious leaders as they are to be politicians.

A related problem is the question of whether, in general, history can be understood best in terms of long-term cultural processes. Philip Bagby, one of the most thoughtful and persuasive of the historians who have taken the extreme cultural view, declared in 1958: "History is most likely to become intelligible if individual historical events are seen as instances of cultural regularities and our inquiries are pursued on the level of culture."

On the other hand, the vagaries of history occasionally have a drastic effect upon a culture. Certainly American culture was altered by variation in geographical habitat, as occurred when the early settlers from Europe reached the North American wilderness; also by contact with members of other cultures: for example the Indians, the slaves from Africa, and the millions of immigrants from semi-feudal European and Mexican peasant societies. Nevertheless, our authors—encouraged by the editors—tended to write within a framework akin to Bagby's. Major historical events and epochs are described primarily in terms of cultural processes. Similarly, intellectual and artistic creations, ranging from novels to a President's State of the Union message, are examined as products of the culture as well as individual expressions.

The overarching problem in the writing and study of cultural history

—incorporating those already mentioned—lies in the nature of the fundamental relationship between a culture and its history. In this interrelationship the two seem always to be working upon each other, the culture
giving broad historical movements their form; history reinforcing, modify-
ing, and occasionally even transforming the culture. Cultural history
provides a context and a perspective in which both culture and history
are illuminated. It also brings the two together, an act of considerable
importance that still takes place too infrequently. Alfred L. Kroeber, an
anthropologist whose contributions to culture theory are monumental,
declared toward the end of his life, "When we now proceed to consider
systematically the sciences of man as a whole or of human behavior as
they are sometimes called, there would appear to be two considerations
that cannot be omitted: first, the historical approach and second, the
concept of culture."

From time to time some of the most fertile minds in the historical
profession have expressed an appreciation similar to Kroeber's of the
reciprocal importance of history and culture. The annual meeting of the
American Historical Association in 1939 was devoted principally to papers
emphasizing "the study of history from the standpoint of the total culture. Three main topics are being treated: the technique of cultural
analysis and synthesis, the cultural role of ideas, and cultural conflict
and nationality groups." Unfortunately, the program was arranged so
haphazardly, and the choice of scholars from other disciplines was so
consistently inappropriate, that the meeting and the book of essays that
issued from it probably set back the progress of cultural history. Furthermore, as John Higham remarked, "A good part of the profession . . .
was antagonized by the obeisant attitude that most of the reformers
evinced toward their sister disciplines." Subsequently, American historians
have made sporadic appeals for more sophisticated cultural history, and
a handful of brilliant studies—such as Ward's on Jacksonian America,
and William Taylor's *Cavalier and Yankee*—are consistently offered as
evidence that the approach has a bright future.

In the essays that follow, all written for this book, our authors have
not attempted to provide a comprehensive survey of the national culture
or cultures in the period they treat. They have tried rather to explore
periods during which important aspects of American culture became
significant—or at least obvious—concentrating usually on the groups most
involved in these changes. Although the essays speak for themselves, and
most are too complicated to be summarized satisfactorily, a few of the
threads that run through them should be noted.

In the opening chapter Alden Vaughan describes the scattered European outposts of the mid-seventeenth century, separated not only by
distance and a terrible communications system, but also by loyalties to

different segments of European society, especially different religious groups. In the seventeenth century, Vaughan concludes, centrifugal forces seemed stronger than the centripetal, a variety of cultures appeared to be developing, and a real possibility existed that the English North American colonies would succumb to Balkanization. This process was checked, Vaughan implies, largely by the similarity of the experiences colonists underwent in the new world, and by a rough similarity in the aspirations they developed. Internal migration, non-English immigration, a religious pluralism enforced from London, and a tightening of the British imperial system, swung the balance decisively toward cohesion, and ironically, toward a nationalistic movement for independence.

Robert Middlekauff is concerned with the meaning of the symbols that aroused popular enthusiasm during that independence movement. In important respects, he finds, the Revolution resembled a Protestant revival, a struggle for true Christian liberty, with America serving as the instrument of Providence. Tom Paine mobilized popular support for the rebels in an otherwise ambiguous situation by identifying King James with the Pope. As a consequence of symbols connected with the American Revolution, "the culture was explicitly pledged to a political process that took its power and its limits from the people." The Revolution itself became the primary symbol of a promise and a prophesy that "pervaded every attempt of the revolutionary generation to understand what it had done."

The crucial egalitarian and pluralistic elements in American culture flourished despite a powerful counterattack after the Revolution from conservative Protestant clerical and political leaders. These still hoped, early in the nineteenth century, for "a stable commonwealth evolving in an orderly manner under the restraining hands of a paternalist government allied openly with established religious institutions." W. David Lewis describes the reforms instituted during this period by men basically conservative, if not reactionary, who made the most concerted attempt in American history to impose from above a single value system for American culture. Responding to the rapid political changes and social upheaval associated with the Revolution, motivated largely by doubts and fears, and by a yearning to preserve the certainties of the past, they attempted to provide psychological substitutes for the aristocratic and religious barriers to change that existed in older cultures. Recognizing the futility of trying to arrest the growth of egalitarian democracy in every sector of the society, the conservatives made an effort instead to inculcate within Americans respect for order and propriety. A large number of reform movements originated as part of this effort; "civilization" was promoted on the western frontier regions, and religious revival movements were launched intentionally.

Although vestiges of the counterrevolution survived—in the form of rigid Sabbath observance, and hostility to such frivolous activities as card playing, dancing, horse-racing, and the drinking of alcohol—the crusade itself failed miserably. Even the revivals became infected with unorthodox ideas. On some issues, evangelical Protestant sects joined Catholics and non-English immigrants in defeating the conservative reformers. Despite deflections here and there the culture continued to evolve on its egalitarian, pluralistic course.

The fervent popular beliefs that doomed the conservative reaction are abstracted by John W. Ward from the political speeches and essays of the period 1820–1850. Few contemporary authors speculated about the philosophical bases of America's unique form of government. The first to attack the problem explained that all "the chief speculators" of the day "were in merchandise and real estate." Ward explores the political rhetoric of the era in search of the hidden logic that will disclose "what uncommon hopes motivated the politics of the age of the common man." For that period, at least, when the level of political consciousness in most men was high, Ward asserts, politics is an excellent guide to cultural values.

At the heart of these implicit beliefs Ward finds a widespread contempt for all human authority, an antagonism to established organizations that bordered on anarchy. Fundamental law, for most Americans, existed not in the Constitution, but in nature. Its true interpretation could be found not in the decisions of judges, but in the will of the popular majority. The form of the United States government, so in accord with divine will, determined the citizens' character, and their culture. It was widely believed that because of this ideal political form, and the intrinsic moral equality of all white men, it was unnecessary for Americans to plan for the good society. Divine favor and political subservience to the will of the infallible majority would guarantee success in the long run.

Carl Degler examines the subcultures most responsible for the swift disruption of these pleasant myths. Millions of Negro slaves in the South did not share basic elements of the dominant culture. And largely because of the presence of these Blacks, a regional culture developed in the South different in important respects from the North and West, which came increasingly to resemble each other.

The Southern ideal life style—essentially that of the country gentleman freed by slaves from any form of manual labor—seemed so unlike the Northern style, at least to Southerners, that planters who pushed their slaves hard in an effort to increase profits were referred to contemptuously as Southern Yankees. Even the burgeoning romantic nationalism of the mid-nineteenth century could not overcome these cultural disparities, and in the face of world-wide hostility to its "peculiar institution" the Southern states seceded and attempted to form a society that could ward off the threats to its unique culture.

During the Reconstruction era the Revolutionary ideal of the fundamental equality of all men finally was applied to Blacks. Degler traces the partially successful attempts to assimilate the former slaves through the Reconstruction period and into the present. "In cultural terms," he concludes, "the ending of Radical Reconstruction meant that the United States was not to be a unified homogeneous nation, but a federation of regions still, in which each section should be free to pursue its own social patterns."

The belief that Christianity and democracy were related formed the vital core of the progressive effort to revitalize American society early in the twentieth century. This same belief had sustained the faith of the Jacksonians almost a century earlier. Many of the peculiarities of the Progressive Movement, Clyde Griffen finds, can be attributed to the predominantly white, middle-class, Protestant native-born leadership whose value system included important vestiges from an earlier society. The reformers described by Griffen were not the only group involved in the progressive movement, as he observes; but they supplied most of the leaders, and they gave the crusade its dynamic spirit.

Even more remarkable than the progressives' tendency to confuse, or at least to blend, Christian and democratic ethics, says Griffen, was their certainty that complicated economic and social problems could be reduced to simple moral questions for which Christianity had clear answers. This touching optimism, this faith in the efficacy of Protestant middle-class paternalism, was hardly the stuff from which a radical reform movement could be made. Nevertheless, the progressive spirit did unify a wide spectrum of reformers with different interests in support of specific measures. Griffen suggests that the Communist revolutions in Europe and the Red Scare of 1919–1920 in the United States frightened the Christian reformers, perhaps with a sudden vision of what a too literal reading of the social gospel might lead to. During the 1920's, moreover, the intensity of religious commitment decreased among the urban middle classes. The progressive spirit then largely dissolved, and the reform movement lost its essential cohesion.

Historians have noted that the generation that came of age just before, during, and just after World War I—in the cities of Europe even more than in the United States—seemed in important respects to be a different breed than their elders. Loren Baritz, reviewing the intellectual crisis of the 1920's, presents an interpretation of what may in the future appear to have been an advanced stage of cultural disintegration; or could, conceivably, be instead the beginning of a cultural re-synthesis.

The inherent pluralism of American society, hidden temporarily by the progressive crusade, reappeared in full force after World War I. Baritz observes that the intellectual and artistic elite were not the only critics of the direction in which the United States was moving. Their opponents were no less adamant. A provincial newspaper editor, complaining of the huge number of unassimilated immigrants in the country, declared that this undigested urban lump was forcing its own immoral standards—including drunkenness and Sabbath breaking—upon the rest of the United States. "They govern our great cities . . . ; the great cities govern the nation; and foreign control or conquest could gain little more, though secured by foreign armies and fleets." The Imperial Wizard and Emperor of the Ku Klux Klan announced in the mid-1920's that his organization would battle Jews, Catholics, Negroes, and intellectuals, and return power in the country to the "not overly intellectualized, but entirely unspoiled and not de-Americanized average citizen of the old stock."

According to Baritz, the Klan, prohibition, and immigration restrictions all were evidence of the temporary victory of Americans with rural and small town origins. The village, he asserts, "was in virtual control of America's public life during the Twenties, and the dismay of the writers and artists cannot be fully understood in any other context." The intellectuals, and other urbanites, struggling with problems of modern life of which provincial Americans seemed altogether unaware, found the situation grotesque. It was this attitude that led F. Scott Fitzgerald to write (from Paris), "Can you name a single American artist except James and Whistler (who lived in England) who didn't die of drink?"

The Great Depression, and then the World War, Baritz asserts, which gave all Americans concrete objectives and tasks, did not solve but temporarily obscured this peculiarly modern anguish. He concludes: "With peace and returning affluence, with skirts rising again and traditional morality declining again, those now old questions re-asserted themselves."

Just when there seemed a possibility that American culture might fly apart from the violence of its various internal conflicts and contradictions, the terrible depression that began in 1930 promoted a deceptive return of cultural community and cooperation. Warren Susman describes the eruption of literary sentimentalizing about "the people," the gigantic effort to document in art, reporting, social science, and history the national life and values. New communication forms—pictorial magazines, the radio, and motion pictures—also played a part in creating an impression of coherence. Above all, the popularization of the concept of culture itself reinforced a social order that had been deteriorating rapidly, and helped create a desire to participate somehow in the community among those who might otherwise have encouraged revolt. Perhaps because of this desire for commitment and the pervasive idea of culture, Susman suggests, the dominant mood of the period, even among intellectuals, was not rebellion but acquiescence in established social and economic structures.

By mid-century it was almost a ritual among social scientists to proclaim that conformity now occupied a dominant place in the life style of most Americans. The pressure of the 1930's had been reinforced by the celebration of conventional beliefs and actions that accompanied mobilization for World War II and the Cold War. Furthermore, large organizations exercised inordinate influence on the culture as well as over the economy of the United States. Members of these large organizations—universities as well as corporations and government agencies—the social scientists reported, tended to act as though conformity was their most important task. Furthermore, and this seemed to depress the investigators most, these middle and upper middle-class groups probably were molding future generations of acquiescent organization men and women in their suburban housing developments.

Cushing Strout is skeptical about the accuracy of these sad commentators. He finds popular sociology a bit deficient in historical perspective; and he dismisses as pretentious pessimists those philosophers like Herbert Marcuse who blend varying portions of Hegel, Marx, and Freud to diagnose the tragic "alienation of modern man." Strout believes that a historical analysis of changes in social scientists' perceptions of the United States provides more valuable insight into the present state of American culture than does a summary of contemporary views. However, Strout uses recently published work by psychologists and sociologists, as well as political scientists and novelists, in his survey.

Strout starts his review with Alexis de Tocqueville, the perceptive French visitor whose warning during the 1830's of a coming "democratic despotism" in the United States, has served the social scientists so very well. He ends with Tocqueville also; for modern critics, he believes, over-impressed with the temporary "mindless cult of moderation for which the Eisenhower Administration was a historical symbol," ignore the more favorable aspects of the French aristocrat's great description and prophecy. For example, Tocqueville believed that Americans would counter the growth of oligarchic power and protect their civilization by cultivating "the art of associating together." This art appeared, when Strout wrote his essay, to be suffering somewhat from disuse. But he, at least, expected it to revive in response to what Tocqueville called "that salutary fear which makes men keep watch and ward for freedom."

Strout, a bold as well as a creative spirit, completed his essay well in advance of the other contributors. His experience is a lesson in the perils as well as the glory of writing contemporary history. Before his chapter could be set in type, the urban ghettos erupted, violent rebellion broke out on the major college and university campuses, President Johnson committed the nation to a large-scale war in Vietnam that polarized public opinion, and young Americans moved dramatically into the country's politics. Sporadic anarchy in the cities stimulated demands for repressive reactions. Although Strout insists that crucial elements in

American society continue to "keep watch and ward for freedom," he acknowledges now that the emphasis others have put upon Tocqueville's long-range fears for America may not have been misplaced. In a postscript added to his essay shortly before publication Strout declared: "We are all Cassandra's now. . . ." Thus the writing of contemporary cultural history blends into autobiography.

ALDEN T. VAUGHAN

Columbia University

societies apart: america in the seventeenth century

To Europeans of the early seventeenth century the likelihood seemed remote that America one day would hold people from scores of disparate heritages living in general, if tenuous, harmony. To the European, and also undoubtedly to the aborigine—soon to be forced aside by history's largest migration—the emergence of an American civilization seemed improbable. Instead, the pattern of the future appeared to be clusters of transplanted people *in* America. For until late in the century the most obvious characteristic of American society was its fragmentation—not only geographical, but political, ethnic, and religious as well.

The reasons are clear enough. There were, in the first place, differences among the North American colonies that derived from the variety of national origins. Unlike the colonization of Central and South America which from the beginning was almost exclusively Spanish, white settlement north of Mexico was international. At various times during

12

the century, five European powers owned settlements along the Atlantic coast: the Dutch at New Netherland from 1609 to 1664 and again briefly in the 1670's; the Swedes in the Delaware Valley from 1638 to 1655; the French in Canada and the Mississippi Valley after 1608 and at various times in Maine and northern New York; the Spanish in Florida as early as 1521; and, most significantly, the English after 1607 in a semicontiguous chain of outposts stretching from Maine to the Carolinas. The area east of the Appalachians held a checkerboard of national spheres of settlement, of overlapping claims and rival interests. There was good reason to fear, as J. H. Plumb has pointed out, that North America would succumb to Balkanization.[1]

Such a possibility stemmed only in part from the variety of nationalities; equally important was the disunity within the British sphere. Instead of a single colony in the New World, England had several, and, unlike their European neighbors, the English colonists rarely joined hands in common cause. More often they bitterly debated their rights, religions, and boundaries. At the same time, each English colony looked to the mother country for protection, supply, and guidance, thus reducing the needs and opportunities for intercolonial cooperation. Furthermore, as the national unity of England temporarily succumbed to a segmentation of its own, and the religious-political factions of seventeenth-century England spawned similar factions in America, each colony in British America gave allegiance to a different faction in the homeland. The mother country did possess a few men like John Smith and Richard Hakluyt who were interested in English colonization *per se*, harboring no preference for any colony so long as it was English. But most promoters, adventurers, and settlers had far narrower vision: their loyalties were restricted to some one segment of English society for which they sought an exclusive outpost in the New World. Each party hoped its own brand of religion or political theory would some day gain supremacy throughout the British dominions; in the meantime each asked to be left alone in its New World haven. And in order to be free to chart its own course—as well as to get necessary supplies and additional immigrants—a colony needed powerful friends back home. To such friends, and to sympathetic elements in the general population, each colony appealed. Thus the Catholics of Maryland looked for help from English Catholics; New England tracts were directed primarily at England's Puritan community; Quaker merchants sought commercial ties with their religious brethren in the mother country. During most of the century the Anglicans of Virginia had the easier task of appealing for spiritual and material help from the dominant religious and political power in England, although

[1]John R. Alden, *Pioneer America* [*The History of Human Society*, J. H. Plumb, ed.] (New York, 1966), p. xxiv.

even the Virginians found themselves allied to a minority faction during the 1640's and 50's. And as the conflicts at home became increasingly bitter during England's *siècle terrible*, the English outposts in America in turn drew still further apart. The centrifugal forces seemed stronger than the centripetal.

Yet partly because of changes taking place in Europe and partly because of the realities of life in the New World, the disunity of the American colonies would last less than one hundred years. While American society was sharply segmented in the seventeenth century, it was also developing the characteristics that would one day reverse the trend of mutual exclusiveness; parochialism would in the end give way to more insistent tendencies toward social and political integration. But until the dawn of the eighteenth century, the dynamics of fragmentation plagued British America.

I

With the proclamation of the second charter of Virginia in 1609, England embarked on a policy of establishing private settlements that could limit admission as they saw fit. To Englishmen of the seventeenth century this seemed only natural, for it was in keeping with the prevalent European understanding of the prerogatives of a privately sponsored community. Nor did it seem odd that in the charter itself the crown would mandate a fundamental restriction on settlement: "we should be loath, that any person should be permitted . . . that we suspected to affect the Superstitions of the Church of *Rome* . . . but such, as first shall have taken the Oath of Supremacy."[2] Virginia was to be an English colony, but not a colony for all Englishmen. Still, for almost two decades Britain's first colony remained a truly national enterprise. Private investors cooperated with the crown in the administration of the colony, Puritans worked side by side—though not always peacefully— with Anglicans, and noblemen as well as gentlemen, yeomen, and laborers helped carve an English outpost in the wilderness.

Until 1620 it was conceivable that the Virginia Company of London would expand its holdings and impose on all British settlement a homogeneous political pattern—much as took place in the French and Spanish possessions—yet one that, unlike New France and New Spain, would find room for the whole spectrum of British life. The almost defunct Virginia Company of Plymouth, which held title to the northern half of England's New World claim, had failed to plant a permanent colony

---

[2]Henry Steele Commager, ed., *Documents of American History* (6th ed., New York, 1958), p. 12.

despite temporary success in 1607 at the Sagadahoc River in Maine; absorbtion of the Plymouth Company's title by the London Company would have consolidated England's territories under a single corporation. But the rise of religious and political strife in England, the settlement of New England by Puritan factions (under the newly created Council for New England), and the dissolution of the Virginia Company itself soon ended such a prospect. With the revocation of Virginia's third charter in 1624 and its replacement by a royal structure, the die was cast for British colonization in the seventeenth century. Henceforth colonies were established piecemeal, some by private corporations, some by one or more proprietors; and the authority extended to companies and proprietors varied widely. So too did the size and viability of their territorial assignments, for the boundaries were often contradictory and frequently overlapped the territories held by other nations. The home government, however, rarely seemed to care, for throughout most of the seventeenth century the Crown, and briefly the Commonwealth, stepped into colonial affairs only to revoke a charter or impose an occasional imperial policy. Otherwise each colony was on its own.

The new tone in British settlement was rapidly reflected in Virginia. With the shift in leadership that accompanied the repeal of its charter, Virginia became almost exclusively Anglican in theology and royalist in imperial politics. At the same time, the colony continued to strengthen tendencies it had had under corporate leadership: representative government based on county units, an economy rooted in the raising and exporting of tobacco, a social structure that increasingly emulated the English gentry, and most portentous for the future of American culture, a labor system centered on Negro slavery.

Any free man, regardless of national origin, was welcome to join this New World outpost so long as he abided by the colony's social and political premises and took an oath of allegiance to the English sovereign; servants and slaves were admitted with the proviso that their masters be responsible for their outward conformity. Everyone else was decidedly unwelcome. Hence Englishmen who still held to the Church of Rome continued to avoid Virginia, and a sporadic effort to purge neighboring Maryland of its Catholic influence remained a pet project of many Virginians throughout the century. No more welcome were Puritans—whether from New or old England made no difference—for to Anglican royalists their countrymen of the Puritan persuasion represented a threat to the foundations of society, treason against church and state. If the Virginia colony had no Bishop Laud to harry the Puritans out of the land, it did have a governor "and some other malignant spirits" in full sympathy with such a policy. The few Puritans who, during the Commonwealth years, put Virginia's exclusiveness to the test soon wearied of harassment and moved on to New England or to Maryland, their departure hastened by an act of the legislature requiring the governor to oust all religious nonconformists.[3]

During the Commonwealth period, Virginians had cause to be concerned for their future position: persistent rumors told of a Cromwellian plan to force the royalist colony into palpable loyalty to the Commonwealth, but it never came to pass—nor is there any evidence that the Lord Protector considered it seriously. On the other hand, the English Civil War encouraged thousands of Anglican royalists (including the forebears of George Washington) to migrate to Virginia; thus at the time of the Restoration the population of the colony was as homogeneous as ever, a condition conducive to continued separateness. By the end of the century, Virginia was, as it had been since the 1620's, almost entirely English in ethnic composition, Anglican in theology, royalist in sympathy, and economically dependent on the export of tobacco—with the corollary phenomena of ruralism and inheritable bondage.

Maryland, no less than Virginia, wished to stand apart, but for somewhat different purposes. The object of George Calvert and his son Cecilius was essentially defensive: to create a colony where Catholics could worship without fear of molestation. In a militantly Protestant empire, Catholics could hope for no more. Exclusion, had it been considered at all, would have invited attack; it was much wiser and more in keeping with the liberal taste of the proprietor to maintain equality in worship, government, and landholding.[4]

From its founding in 1634, the Catholic colony was open to Protestants. Although the Calvert charter made the proprietors "absolute lords" of Maryland, their coreligionists formed a numerical minority (though not a minority of the leaders) in the first expedition to the new colony. Accordingly, the proprietors prohibited religious controversy, and not surprisingly when such controversy eventually developed the Protestants, not the Catholics, were to blame. When the Protestant majority meted out harsh punishment to Catholics during the turbulent 1640's, the second Lord Baltimore countered with that curious milestone on the road to religious liberty, the Act of Toleration. Proposed by the Catholic proprietor, passed by the Protestant legislature, and enforced sporadically by the mixed population, the Act had equal parts of modern toleration and medieval bigotry. The complete freedom of worship it

3[Edward Johnson], *Johnson's Wonder-Working Providence, 1628–1651* [*Original Narratives of Early American History*, J. Franklin Jameson, ed.] (New York, 1910), p. 265. On Virginia's treatment of Catholics see Andrew White, "A Relation of the Colony of . . . Maryland. . . ," Peter Force, *Tracts and Other Papers Relating Principally to . . . the Colonies in North America. . .* (4 vols., Gloucester, Mass., 1963), IV, number XII, esp. 17, 43–44.

4Charles M. Andrews, *The Colonial Period of American History*, II (New Haven, Conn., 1936), 276–81.

extended to all Trinitarians was juxtaposed with the mandatory death penalty for all blasphemers and outspoken non-Trinitarians.[5] Fortunately, the full penalty of the law was never applied. In any event, before the century ended the proprietor renounced the Church of Rome and endorsed proscriptions against the Catholics. Maryland had failed to become the Catholic haven its founders intended. It remained, however, a society quite distinct from its colonial neighbors. Although it emulated the plantation society of adjacent Virginia it remained a far more open—and turbulent—community. Its religious diversity was responsible in part, but also important were the growth of coastal ports, a greater variety of crops, and proximity to the Quaker colonies of the Delaware Bay. Moreover, Maryland and Virginia were almost constantly at odds. For much of the century they wrangled over title to Kent Island in Chesapeake Bay, and during the times of crisis, such as Virginia witnessed in 1675 and Maryland in 1689, neither colony proved a comfort to its neighbor. To the casual observer, at least, the Chesapeake colonies might as well have belonged to rival empires.

Significantly different in purpose and character from Virginia and Maryland were the Carolinas. Although officially one colony throughout the seventeenth century, the ink was barely dry on the charter of 1663 before settlement below Virginia centered on two widely separate areas. In the southern portion, Charles Town (later Charleston) emerged as the nucleus of a cosmopolitan community based on slave labor, large plantations, an active Indian trade, and an urban center of business and social activity. Settlers poured into the region from England, the West Indies, and most conspicuously from France after Louis XIV resumed persecution of the Huguenots in 1685. In 1700 Charleston boasted 2000 inhabitants and there were another 3000 in the vicinity. By that date the economic and social patterns of the region were clearly established. So too was the region's lack of identification with the Albemarle Sound area to the north. There settlers from Virginia had spilled across the border into the rugged pine country and turned to the production of naval stores, hemp, and tobacco. North Carolina, as it would soon become known, showed few similarities to the Charleston area: no larger towns emerged, few plantations were established, slavery languished, and the ethnic composition remained predominantly English-Anglican.[6]

Neither section of the Carolinas quite fulfilled the proprietors' hopes for abundant revenue, nor did either abide long by the Fundamental

---

[5]H. Shelton Smith, Robert T. Handy, and Lefferts A. Loetscher, *American Christianity: An Historical Interpretation with Representative Documents*, I (New York, 1960), 35–39.

[6]M. Eugene Sirmans, *Colonial South Carolina* (Chapel Hill, N. C., 1966), Part I.

Constitutions of Anthony Ashley Cooper and his philosopher-physician John Locke. Their attempt to impose a rigid social hierarchy on the Carolinas came to nought in the free air of the New World. What emerged instead was a bipolar colony in which the two centers had little contact with each other and where the attitudes and experiences they did share—such as resistance to proprietary prerogatives, Indian troubles, religious jealousies—did not result in a common cause. In many respects the Carolinas epitomize the centrifugal temper of the seventeenth century. Long before 1700 it was clear to all that the two regions of Carolina were entirely separate colonies, a fact officially acknowledged early in the next century by the creation of the royal colonies of North and South Carolina.

By the end of the seventeenth century, then, four English outposts had been planted in the southern latitudes. They resembled each other very little, and probably no visitor suspected that in another century and a half they would lead an attempt to form a separate nation. For as Carl Bridenbaugh has pointed out, there was no South in the colonial period; the settlements carved out of the old London Company grant had many latent similarities, but they neither acknowledged nor sought any intercolonial ties.[7]

While the South was clearly not a section in the seventeenth century, New England was. The qualities that mark a section—strong similarities in institutions, aspirations, attitudes, and often, though not necessarily, in ethnic background—were abundant in New England. Throughout the century it was common to speak of "Boston in New England" and to designate a resident of any one of the Puritan colonies as a "New Englander." Whether or not that term encompassed Rhode Island was always debatable. In point of fact the people who settled in the smallest colony differed from those in Massachusetts, Plymouth, Connecticut, and New Haven in theology only, and not always fundamentally even there. However, that in itself was a reflection of the seventeenth century's penchant for fragmentation: even in highly homogeneous New England there took root a colony of anti-Puritans—"Rogue's Island" as the Puritans were fond of calling it. When in 1643 the four Congregational colonies formed a Confederation of New England for purposes of defense and mutual aid, Rhode Island was not invited to join.

To most New Englanders of the seventeenth century, the central feature of their society was its religion. Many, perhaps most, had come to the New World primarily because of dissatisfaction with the orthodoxy of England, and they had no intention of traveling three thousand miles in vain. Certainly their leaders were of this mind, and leaders and

---

[7]Carl Bridenbaugh, *Myths and Realities: Societies of the Colonial South* (Baton Rouge, La., 1952).

followers showed their determination by creating a society that could resist both internal and external threats. In Plymouth and Connecticut no less than in Massachusetts Bay and New Haven Colony, church and state formed a close partnership. Like any partnership, this one involved occasional overlaps of effort and interest, and the proper function of each partner is almost impossible to describe with accuracy. Yet the broad outlines of the "New England Way" are clear enough: the colonies of New England (excluding for the most part Rhode Island and New Hampshire) would be a Bible-centered community in which all actions must—insofar as human frailty permitted—accord with God's rules for civil and religious society. Winthrop thought of it as "a Citty on a Hill" to which the eyes of European heretics and Indian heathens alike would turn—at first, perhaps, with skepticism but in the end with admiration.[8]

The Puritans assumed that in order to carry out their religious and social experiment it must rest in the hands of those who had conceived it and, later on, of heirs whose commitment to its success was equally devoted. This required that anyone who threatened the basic character of the community be excluded. Hence the Massachusetts law of 1637 forbidding strangers to remain in any town for more than three weeks without explicit approval from the magistrates. In defending the regulation, Winthrop argued that "if the peace of our cohabitation be our owne, then no man hath right to come into us, etc., without our consent. . . . We may lawfully refuse to receive such whose dispositions suite not with ours and whose society (we know) will be hurtful to us." A few years later Nathaniel Ward, self-styled "Herald of New England," put the same sentiment more bluntly when he observed that dissenters from the New England had "free Liberty to keep away from us, and . . . be gone as fast as they can, the sooner the better." Those who tarried or, worse still, insisted on preaching their own brand of religious or political philosophy, were forcibly expelled. So discovered Roger Williams in 1636, the Antinomians in 1638, and the Quakers in the 1650's and 60's. The lesson was also impressed upon such lesser known but equally representative non-Puritans as Thomas Morton in 1628 and again in 1630, John and Samuel Browne in 1629, and Philip Ratcliffe in 1631.[9] These people were deemed dangerous, for reasons theological, social, or political, to the survival of the experiment and were therefore sent away, though not necessarily with bitterness. (The classic example of amity in the face of expulsion is the role of John Winthrop in aiding Williams to

---

[8]Massachusetts Historical Society, *Winthrop Papers* (5 vols., Boston, 1929–1947), II, 295.

[9]*Ibid.*, III, 423; Nathaniel Ward, *The Simple Cobbler of Aggawam in America* (London, 1647; reprinted Boston, 1843), p. 3; Nathaniel B. Shurtleff, ed., *Records of the Governor and Company of the Massachusetts Bay in New England* (5 vols.; Boston, 1853–1854), I, 51–54, 74–75, 88, 196.

escape to another part of New England rather than be shipped back to England. Winthrop and Williams remained close friends, despite their theological differences, and after the death of the Massachusetts governor in 1649 his eldest son continued to be a frequent correspondent of the Rhode Island heretic.) Similarly, a Massachusetts ordinance of 1647 forbade entrance to Jesuits unless shipwrecked or on diplomatic or business errands. Visiting clerics such as Father Gabriel Druilletes, who in 1650 was entertained by John Eliot and other Puritan spokesmen, were welcome guests so long as they made no attempt to settle or to proselytize among the New Englanders.[10]

While New England, then, shared with the other colonies a desire to remain aloof from the rest of British America, it applied this preference more consciously and more extensively than did the other American settlements, directing its resentment of interference against the government of the mother country as well as against individuals from Europe or from sister colonies. Only Massachusetts built a fort to defend itself against British efforts to revoke its charter. Only Connecticut hid its charter rather than relinquish it to royal envoys. Only the New England colonies withheld cooperation from the Andros regime. And, perhaps most significantly, only a New England colony decided that it was better to hang returned exiles than to incarcerate them until the next ship left for England. In the execution of the Quakers, the Puritan fathers carried to its logical but frightening conclusion the theory of exclusion to which all American colonies tacitly subscribed. The horror of its own actions left Massachusetts stunned; fortunately for all settlers it also marked the high point of the theory itself.

A further obstacle to eventual unity among the British colonies was the presence in their midst of a Dutch territory. Until its conquest in the 1660's by Richard Nicolls, New Netherland posed a formidable physical and cultural barrier between the English settlements in New England and the more southerly colonies. Even after the Treaty of Westminister brought *de jure* English control, New York's predominantly Dutch culture continued to separate the northern and southern spheres of British influence. Eventually the colony of New York would become almost as Anglicized as its neighbors, but in the seventeenth century Dutch flavor remained strong in language, law, architecture, local polity, and religion. Having been conquered rather than created, the British colony of New York did not owe its early development to English factionalism. It did, however, have a heritage almost as inimicable to colonial unity. While from the start the Dutch had welcomed immigrants of diverse ethnic groups, spokesmen for the Dutch Reformed

[10]Shurtleff, *Records of Massachusetts Bay*, II, 193; Reuben Gold Thwaites, ed., *The Jesuit Relations and Allied Documents* (73 vols., Cleveland, Ohio, 1896–1901), XXXVI, 87–95.

Church tried hard to preserve a semblance of religious purity. Backed by Governor Peter Stuyvesant and the burgomasters of New Amsterdam, Reverends Johannes Megapolensis and Samuel Drisius urged the Directors of the Dutch West Indian Company to prohibit migration into the colony by Jews and Christian clergymen of non-Reformed persuasions. Letters to the Classis in Amsterdam warned of attempts by several religious sects to hold public services; the Classis in turn voiced dismay at the idea of a Jewish synagogue "for the exercise of their blasphemous religion." Nor were the civil and ecclesiastical rulers of New Netherland sympathetic to the early Quaker settlers; they were imprisoned, fined, and banished. Under the Duke's Laws of 1665 freedom of worship was granted to all Christians, but in practice it was a limited freedom which did little to encourage immigration by religious minorities. Despite New York's broad ethnic diversity (which included clusters of Frenchmen, Swiss and Sephardic Jews in addition to the Dutch and English groups), its religious diversity proved almost as limited as Boston's: in 1687 only four faiths were practiced in New York City— Dutch Reformed, Lutheran, French Calvinist, and Anglican—and the Anglicans had to share quarters with the Dutch church until late in 1697.[11] Furthermore, the earlier Dutch pattern of feudal estates along the Hudson and the presence of a large and powerful Indian confederacy in the Mohawk Valley kept Englishmen from flocking to the newly acquired colony. Of course there were exceptions. Robert Livingston, for example, had qualities and aspirations ideally suited to the time and place; he gladly settled in New York after a brief sojourn in New England.[12] Others would follow, but in such sparse numbers that New York retained its Dutch character until well into the eighteenth century.

During the latter half of the colonial period Pennsylvania rivaled New York as the most cosmopolitan colony. However, Pennsylvania's claim to religious, ethnic, and economic variety rests primarily on its performance in the eighteenth century, not the seventeenth. Until 1700 Penn's proprietorship contained a few thousand Quaker farmers surrounding a small but growing Quaker village, a village which in twenty-five years would have a population greater than New York's. In part this growth was due to the sincere toleration of the Quakers toward newcomers, whatever their faith; in still larger part it was due to the changing English understanding of the role of colonial societies. By the

---

[11]J. Franklin Jameson, ed., *Narratives of New Netherland, 1609–1664* (New York, 1909), pp. 391–402; Smith, Handy, and Loetscher, *American Christianity*, pp. 59–78; Wayne Andrews, ed., "A Glance at New York in 1697: The Travel Diary of Dr. Benjamin Bullivant," *New-York Historical Society Quarterly*, XL (1956), 62. On intolerance see *A Narrative of a New and Unusual American Imprisonment ...* [1707], reprinted in Peter Force, *Tracts and Other Papers ...*, IV, number IV.

[12]Lawrence H. Leder, *Robert Livingston, 1654–1728, and The Politics of Colonial New York* (Chapel Hill, N. C., 1961), Chap. I.

last quarter of the seventeenth century it had become axiomatic that each colony must open its doors to all law-abiding Englishmen (but not to lawbreakers, as the New England friends of the regicides found out), and that expulsion or mistreatment for reasons of religion would not be tolerated by the mother country. Yet if the Quakers in Pennsylvania, Delaware, and western New Jersey made no effort to resist the new mood of England—for in fact they benefited from the toleration it accorded them—they did hope to keep their colonies under Quaker control. Theirs, after all, was "a Holy Experiment," and Penn meant by that much the same as Winthrop had with his "citty on a hill." The Quaker political faction and the Quaker proprietor retained effective control until mid-eighteenth century, and relinquished it then only after a bitter struggle.

II

A society is often unaware of the forces that bind its members most closely together. Such certainly was the case in the seventeenth century where few Americans knew or cared about the characteristics they held in common with any but their immediate colonial neighbors. But to the historian looking backward, one of the most striking features of early America is the similarity of its immigrants.

This is especially true in the realm of religion. British Americans could, to be sure, argue heatedly and interminably over the relative merits of "Grace" and "Works," yet we can now see—as they could not then—that their entire debate took place within a remarkably solid consensus. Most early immigrants were Protestants (in 1700 probably 95% of the inhabitants of British North America claimed affiliation with Protestant denominations; Roman Catholics numbered only a few thousand, Jews even less), and a majority belonged to the Church of England or its offshoots.[13] In fact, much of the century's religious conflict occurred because Englishmen on neither side of the Atlantic could agree as to the exact dogma of the Church, and various sects emerged on the basis of their minute differences, in defiance of their substantial similarities. Thus disagreement over the proper age for baptism led to the formation of one church, while disputes over the appropriateness of clerical garments helped create another.

Neither could they agree on many details of church polity. Prominent in the debates of seventeenth-century Anglo-Americans were organizational concepts: hierarchy, synod, presbyters, episcopacy, congrega-

---

[13]In the absence of reliable statistics, estimates of religious distribution are at best educated guesses, based on contemporary materials that suggest the religious composition of each colony.

tions. Yet throughout the century most Americans practiced an effectual congregationalism or something approaching it. In Anglican Virginia, local vestries selected clergymen and determined parish policy without the aid of vicars or bishops or archbishops; even the Roman Catholics of Maryland worked without a hierarchy. The same was true of New York's Dutch Reformed Church, which got along without an American classis. The Quakers in Pennsylvania and elsewhere, who in a sense had no formal church structure, did have silent Assemblies of "God's People" with disciplinary supervision from monthly, quarterly, and yearly meetings. If they had no "hireling clergy" they did have religious spokesmen. Too, the Presbyterians and Congregationalists had almost identical polities: the former had separate congregations under loose supervision from superior authorities; the latter had theoretically independent congregations which in fact were under rather close scrutiny from snyods, associations, and each other. From Massachusetts to South Carolina, ecclesiastical organization had become a predominantly local and quasi-democratic affair.

More important, the common heritage of Calvinist and Lutheran precepts made most Americans view the fundamentals of Christianity in much the same light. Almost all were Trinitarians and most adhered, at least nominally, to a belief in predestination and salvation only through the Grace of God. At the same time, the Protestant majority enjoyed a binding tie in its repulsion at the Church of Rome's version of Christianity.

While most Americans remained unaware of their basic similarity in theological thought and organization, they were probably also unaware that they had come from the same class of English society. Seventeenth-century Americans brought with them from Europe a deep consciousness of class distinctions, rife with implications for social and political inequity, and the settlers would have been aghast to be told that they were essentially of the same class. Of course they were aware that there were very few nobles among them, and they must also have realized how few paupers there were. (It mattered little that tens of thousands of new Americans arrived under indentures which assigned them to temporary servitude, for that condition rarely lasted longer than four or five years and most of the ex-servants soon became self-employed.) Almost instinctively, American colonists knew that within every New World colony there existed from the outset an array of class distinctions in which the gentry cherished their social superiority, the yeomen jealously guarded their independence, and the "meaner sort" paid grudging honor to their betters. Not that in America everyone kept his station; if he had there would have been no need for such sumptuary laws as the Bay Colony passed in 1658, admonishing "men or women of mean condition [who] take upon them the garb of Gentlemen by wearing gold or silvar lace, or buttons, or points at their knees, or . . . walk in great boots, or women of the same ranke, [who] wear silk or tyffany hoods or scarfs. . . ."[14] On the other hand, very little social distinction separated the highest from the lowest in seventeenth-century America. Among the emigrants to America were no prominent church officials, very few noblemen, and only scattered representatives of the more prosperous gentry. Thus the social structure was free from the massive weight of tradition, of overwhelming political privilege, and vast ranges of wealth. By the eighteenth century the narrowness of social and economic range would disappear: in Virginia and South Carolina where a burgeoning slave population and a few mammoth estates emerged, in New York where a few landed aristocrats and merchants contrasted sharply with the lot of tenant farmers, and in New England where a handful of merchant families achieved handsome fortunes and social influence. But throughout the first century of colonization the relatively narrow range of social-economic classes helped to bind the American colonists closer together.

Narrowness of class distinctions would have meant little had it not been accompanied by social mobility—the result of exceptional economic opportunities, open to every free man. Some colonists were of course aware of the unparalleled opportunities before them and perhaps sensed the implications that opportunity held for all white Americans, although the full impact was probably not evident until the following century when Franklin and Crèvecoeur elevated mobility into a philosophical system. Rather, most seventeenth-century colonists saw only that in their own immediate locality there existed a world of opportunity not known in the mother country. Men grew rich who had before been only comfortable, and poor men became property owners. Moreover, they also came to have many of the prerogatives that accompanied property ownership: the right to vote and to hold office. The exercises of political privileges, in turn, helped to keep down class barriers.

Equally unrecognized but equally important in forming a basic tie among American colonists was their similarity of outlook on a number of aspects of their society. Most Americans, for example, had brought in their cultural baggage a preference for life as they had known it in small English towns, cities, or countryside. As Sumner Chilton Powell and others have shown, there was usually more than one precedent to follow, and the patterns that emerged in America were not exact reproductions of old England: there was adaptation, experiment, blending, and discarding in the social laboratory of the New World.[15] Still, almost every-

---

[14] *The Colonial Laws of Massachusetts, reprinted from the Edition of 1660, with the Supplements to 1672* (Boston, 1889) , p. 123.

[15] Sumner Chilton Powell, *Puritan Village: The Formation of a New England Town* (Middletown, Conn., 1963); Darrett B. Rutman, *Winthrop's Boston* (Chapel Hill, N. C., 1965) ; Philip J. Greven, Jr., "Family Structures in Seventeenth-Century Andover,

thing that did emerge was fundamentally English: the forms of land ownership and cultivation, the system of government and the nature of laws and legal procedures, the choices of entertainment and leisure-time pursuits, and a thousand and one other aspects of colonial life. At heart this was an English land. In 1700 probably 70% of the settlers in British North America were English, 20% Scotch, Irish, or Welsh, 5% Dutch, and the rest divided among several European nationalities. While there were a few pockets of non-English settlement—Dutchmen in New York, Swedes in the Delaware Valley, Frenchmen in Charleston, and Germans in Pennsylvania—they were conspicuous exceptions to the dominant pattern.

Being English meant more than a cultural bond; it provided as well the condition for a powerful ingredient in molding the American people into a nation—a common enemy. England's seventeenth-century New World outposts may have been unfriendly to each other, but at least they saw common cause in the need to resist encroachment by Spaniards, Frenchmen, or Dutchmen. In the 1600's, there were abundant opportunities for rallying against a national foe: against the French in the 1620's, against the Dutch in the 1650's, 60's and 70's, against the French again in the 1680's and 90's. And always there was fear of attack from the Spanish lands to the south. While it is impossible to measure with any precision the impact of international rivalry on the colonial mind, it undoubtedly helped to create a sense of American unity and self-consciousness. It also helped to insure a continuing dependence on the mother country, a condition that has too often caused historians to overlook the parallel trend of intercolonial cohesion.

Similarly, American unity was bolstered by another persistent enemy, the American Indian. Most colonies had been founded partly (so at least the promotional literature proclaimed) in order to convert the heathen to Christianity. Before long that part of the venture had proved hopeless and the red man emerged in the end as a mortal foe; it came to that in Virginia as early as 1622, in New Netherland in 1643, and in New England by 1675. Despite many instances of friendly relations between the Europeans and the American aborigines, the cultural gap proved too wide to cross in the seventeenth century, and much of the white population viewed the Indians with suspicion, scorn, and fear. Such an attitude was not necessarily held by colonial leaders, and it was rarely held by colonial clergymen (contrary to their supposed contempt for the heathen), but it increasingly characterized the bulk of English colonists, especially on the frontier where the irresponsible elements of both white

---

Massachusetts," *William and Mary Quarterly*, 3 ser. XXIII (1966); John J. Waters, "Hingham, Massachusetts, 1631–1661: An East Anglican Oligarchy in the New World," *Journal of Social History*, I (1967–68).

and red races often clashed far from the reach of Indian or English authorities.   Stirred by stories of wilderness massacres, scalpings, and torture, the colonial mind increasingly lumped all red men together and designated them "enemies of his Majesty" against whom all British colonies must unite.   Thus another unconscious link was forged in the lengthening chain of intercolonial ties.

At the same time, the colonists were unconsciously forming common ideas about their relationship to the Empire.   Ostensibly every seventeenth-century Englishman who moved to America retained his attachment to king and country.   And no doubt the majority continued to do so.   Yet quite obviously most of the Englishmen who migrated to the New World were unhappy with conditions at home.   In America the migrants became exposed to the non-English elements that increasingly entered British America, resulting in a slow dilution of cultural Englishness. Furthermore, there soon developed conflicts of interest which made the colonists less grateful to the mother country.   The contest over the Massachusetts charter and later over the Andros regime, the squabble over the tobacco tax in Virginia, and the series of Acts of Trade and Navigation that were enacted in the second half of the seventeenth century are cases in point.   None of these episodes tore the imperial fabric.   To many colonists they were simply domestic spats and most colonists perhaps gave them no thought at all, but each episode made clear to a growing number of the Americans that the home government was a rival as well as a friend and protecting power.   Except for the few who held positions within the imperial bureaucracy, the colonists seemed increasingly ready to question the wisdom and righteousness of the imperial administration. The widespread resistance to the Dominion of New England and the vehement reactions in Maryland, New York, and New England to the Glorious Revolution reflect the political awareness of colonial America.

In character as well as in outlook, Americans of the seventeenth century probably had more in common than they themselves realized. They were not a cross section of Englishmen but rather a very special breed: the hardy variety that pulled up stakes and risked the dangers of ocean voyage to plant new homes in the wilderness.   The qualities that Oscar Handlin found among the "uprooted" of the nineteenth century apply in large measure to the men and women of the seventeenth-century American colonies.   But at least one difference is central: the special challenge that the first immigrants faced was more physical than cultural.   If the adjustment was not intrinsically more difficult than that of later centuries, it demanded, at any rate, a particular kind of men and women: young, adventurous, energetic, optimistic.   They had to have the initiative and grit to embark on a three-thousand-mile voyage, fraught with danger, to reach a land where hardship vied with opportunity as the most characteristic feature.

Those very hardships, however, created an unconscious bond between the first Americans, English and non-English alike.   The perils of the voyage were real enough; thousands died on the ships that safely navigated the Atlantic, while scores of vessels foundered without survivors. To be sure, second and third generation Americans escaped the danger of the trip, but they knew keenly of it from relatives and friends or from awaiting the arrival of still other immigrants.   And the ocean crossing was merely the first step; there followed hazards more perilous still.

During the first years both men and nature seemed to conspire against survival itself.   Most dramatic was the threat of Indian warfare.   From the earliest days of exploration and settlement Indian arrows and tomahawks claimed scattered victims among the newcomers.   Then in 1622 the massacre of three hundred Virginia settlers on a single afternoon made it clear that even long-established communities were susceptible to attack. But the lesson bore repeating, as Virginians themselves discovered in 1644, the Dutch in 1641 and 1663, the Carolinians in 1671, and New Englanders in 1675.   In some areas, particularly along the frontiers of Maine and the Carolinas, Indian raids remained a common occurrence well into the next century.   By 1700 perhaps five thousand colonists of British America, including the former Dutch colony, had been slain by Indian foes.

Others had fallen to less personal enemies, for the environment of the New World could be as treacherous as it was bountiful.   Partly from the natural hazards of the land and partly from physical weakness enhanced by the voyage, the mortality rate in the early stages of colonization was frightening.   Well remembered are the losses of the first winter at Jamestown when 63 of 105 perished, and the first winter at Plymouth—52 of 101, while in Massachusetts scurvy took scores of "the poorer sort of people" in the months following the arrival of the Winthrop fleet.   Nor was the American environment any respecter of persons: William Bradford's wife drowned within a week of the *Mayflower's* arrival, Governor Carver of Plymouth Colony succumbed to disease during the winter of 1620–21, and less than a month after his arrival in Massachusetts Bay, Governor Winthrop recorded in his journal that "my son Henry Winthrop was drowned at Salem."   Before the year was out Winthrop had also recorded the deaths, probably from typhus, of Lady Arbella Johnson and her husband Isaac, of the Reverend Francis Higginson, and of Edward Rossiter, one of the Colony's magistrates.[16]   Almost every seventeenth-century plantation suffered comparable losses, and in some cases the high mortality rate lasted long beyond the first years.   So discouraging were the hardships and so dim the prospects that some colonies witnessed periods

---

[16]Winthrop, *Journal*, I, 51–53; John Winthrop to John Winthrop, Jr., 9 Sept. 1630, in Massachusetts Historical Society, *Winthrop Papers*, II (Boston, 1931), 314.

of heavy emigration, especially Virginia, where a combination of departures and death by disease and Indian massacre left a population of only 1,275 in 1624, despite the arrival of over four thousand persons since 1618.[17]

III

Out of the similarity of experiences, outlooks, and aspirations of the first white Americans came a society that had enough internal homogeneity to overcome concomitant tendencies toward permanent separation. This development of a sense of community became stronger as intercolonial migration and the increase in non-English arrivals broke down old patterns of self-isolation and aided in the diffusion of a common American culture, a culture at once distinctively American and increasingly intercolonial.

In large part the integration of British America stemmed from a new attitude toward religious exclusiveness and its corollary, religious intolerance. During the second half of the seventeenth century there grew rapidly in England, and somewhat less rapidly in America, the belief that the only solution to the constant mayhem of religious controversy was a form of toleration that allowed dissenters from the majority faith to practice their beliefs openly, provided they did not try to undermine the state. One by one the colonies relaxed their strictures—both legal and social—against the immigration of dissenters, while some colonies, most notably South Carolina and Pennsylvania, permitted recruitment of newcomers whose religion did not coincide with the majority's. Thus there slowly emerged a new kind of religious pluralism in which groups of differing faiths were separated not by colonial boundaries but by town or neighborhood lines—or by no geopolitical lines at all. By the end of the seventeenth century, the denominational maps of Pennsylvania, New York, and Maryland resembled patchwork quilts, and no colony was without sizable minority enclaves.

The most remarkable change in religious demography took place in New England. With the quasi-liberal policies of Charles II and James II, and the more truely liberal by-products of the Glorious Revolution, the Puritan colonists could no longer oust with impunity those who agitated for Presbyterian church polity or Anglican worship. Continuing pressure from non-Puritans in old and New England brought almost complete disintegration of the Massachusetts Bible Common-

17Wesley Frank Craven, *The Southern Colonies in the Seventeenth Century* [*A History of the South*, Wendell Holmes Stephenson and E. Merton Coulter, eds.] ([Baton Rouge, La.] 1949), pp. 138, 146–47.

wealth during the last quarter of the seventeenth century. By 1680 the Anabaptists were numerous enough to have their own church buildings, and under Governor Edmund Andros' Dominion of New England, Anglican services were held in South Meetinghouse from 1685 until King's Chapel opened in 1688. By early in the next century Boston had houses of worship for Quakers, Presbyterians, and French Calvinists as well as for Congregationalists, Episcopalians, and Baptists.[18]

The breakdown of religious exclusiveness also had important political implications. In Massachusetts non-church members had been allowed local political privileges in 1649; in 1664 they became eligible for the colony-wide franchise as well, largely because of pressure from the mother country. Under the new charter of 1691 all religious restrictions were prohibited. Elsewhere religious limitations on political participation diminished in practice if not in law, although the trend was not without exceptions. In Maryland, for example, Roman Catholics actually lost ground: early in the eighteenth century Maryland's legislature and proprietor, now an Anglican, disfranchised Catholics on the assumption that "if Papists should continue to be allowed their vote . . . it would tend to the discouragement and disturbance of his Lordships Protestant government."[19]

Soon after the Restoration, the mother country had taken other steps to end colonial exclusiveness. The Royal Commissioners sent to investigate the New England colonies in 1664 saw more than mere recalcitrance. They saw also the factionalism that pervaded the colonies. The upshot was the creation of a union of the northern colonies which would break down tendencies toward mutual exclusiveness at the same time that it promoted greater imperial control. The Dominion of New England was fated to perish with the Stuart monarchy, but it is significant that post-Dominion Massachusetts was no longer an exclusively Puritan commonwealth. Gone was the religious restriction on freemanship, gone the Puritan monopoly on religious polity, gone the fiction—valid enough at one time—that the shareholders and officers of the corporation *owned* the colony. The charter had been laid to rest; Massachusetts and the other New England settlements were now purely civil dependencies, nothing more, nothing less. Significant also in the shift away from fragmentation was the absorption, promoted by the imperial government, of

[18]Dates of church buildings are given on the map of Boston by John Bonner in 1722, and subsequent revisions. The 1722 map is reprinted in Walter Muir Whitehill, *Boston, A Topographical History* (Cambridge, 1959), p. 23. Although there were no Roman Catholic churches before the nineteenth century, some practicing Catholics may have lived there as early as 1687. See *Report of a French Protestant Refugee*, (Brooklyn, 1868), p. 30.

[19]*Abridgement and Collection of the Acts of the Assembly of the Province of Maryland* (Philadelphia, 1759), p. 197.

two New England colonies by their larger neighbors: New Haven by Connecticut in the 1660's, and Plymouth by Massachusetts in 1691.

Elsewhere the empire had also tightened as the century progressed. The first step had come as early as 1624 with the revocation of the Virginia charter, but the trend is more clearly reflected in the progressive decline of powers granted in proprietary charters. The Calverts in 1632 received almost limitless authority over Maryland; less was allowed to the New Jersey and Carolina groups in the 60's and 70's; by William Penn's day the proprietorship was curbed by restrictions which made clear that Crown and Parliament considered Pennsylvania a British dependency, open to all loyal subjects and an integral part of the imperial scheme. The Quakers tried hard to maintain dominance in their colony, and they did manage to give it a Quaker tone, but the mother country would not have allowed the "Holy Experiment" to become a second New England. Thus the very purpose of colonization had changed during the century; the apartness enjoyed for varying periods by Maryland, Virginia, Massachusetts, and Connecticut was no longer possible, regardless of the dedication of colonial leaders or the intentions of their followers. It was in large measure then, England, rather than America, which made exclusiveness impossible and inaugurated instead a trend toward colonial intercourse that would one day become a stepping stone to nationhood.

As the century of the colonization gave way to the century of revolution, it was still too early to speak of American nationalism; too early to call the American "a new man." It was not too soon, however, to see that an amalgam was being created in which the men and women of the British colonies were beginning to look on themselves as people of a unique society: a society at once deeply British and yet not entirely British. By the end of the seventeenth century, the society of Colonial America, despite significant regional variations, had nonetheless a solid core of shared characteristics. Most, if not all, of the colonies had a strongly English cast to their ethnic composition, most had political institutions that permitted a remarkable degree of autonomy and representation, and all shared a fairly well-defined relationship to the homeland. At the same time the bulk of Americans could identify with each other on the basis of common attitudes rooted in the similarity of their backgrounds and experiences. The people of the several colonies differed sharply on a number of matters of great importance to them, but what we can see now better than they could then is that their differences were, from the start, more of form than substance and that, as the eighteenth century approached, the grounds for their differences gradually diminished. By 1700 a consensus of sorts had been reached on most matters that had separated the colonies throughout the previous century—a consensus that proved a necessary precursor to Revolutionary America.

ROBERT MIDDLEKAUFF

University of California, Berkeley

the ritualization
of the
american
revolution

Shortly after the United States Senate convened for the first time in April, 1789, it engaged in one of those farces which have enlivened its proceedings ever since. The Senate held in its hands the inaugural address of the President, and it believed that it had to reply. Framing the response proved less troublesome than sending it with proper address to the President. What was he to be called anyway? Vice-President Adams, presiding energetically over the Senate, plumped for "His Highness the President of the United States and Protector of their Liberties." Over in the House of Representatives, James Madison averted his gaze from this pseudo-monarchism and quietly addressed the House reply "to George Washington, President of the United States." The Senate eventually agreed that republican simplicity was the only appropriate guide and adopted the practice of the House, but not until it had listened to the Vice-President's pleas for giving the President high sounding titles and not until it had coaxed the House into sending representatives to a Conference Committee which thrashed about and decided nothing. The only title that emerged from this episode was tagged to John Adams, thereafter celebrated as His Rotundity.[1]

John Adams appears ridiculous in this episode: his insensitivity to the American revulsion against anything smacking of monarchy was monumental. But in his concern for form, his feeling that even a simple republic required conventions and symbols, he was sound. Americans had felt this need for a very long time, and acutely, ever since they began resisting Parliamentary attempts to tax them in 1764.

Almost all people have experienced at various times the need to express their values and intentions in some sort of forms—especially in symbol and ritual. The need seems to be an essential part of human nature, related to aesthetic and even religious concerns. Ritual and symbol permit expression of the highest values and they satisfy impulses for order in relationships among human beings and their ideals.

The formalism of social movements may have several uses, of course. In primitive social movements—that is in premodern and preindustrial movements, form assumes a far more important role than content, at least in providing the essential unity holding participants together. The failure of a medieval king to be crowned and anointed in the correct ritual-way might seriously compromise his claims to the allegiance of his subjects, and today in many religious groups baptism, or any sacramental observance including marriage, that is not celebrated according to prescribed form lacks authority. Baptism is of course an initiatory rite in many Christian groups—by it men are admitted to the church, or as one group of Congregationalists used to insist, by it their membership was confirmed. Besides bringing men together, a joint act of worship, or any ritualistic act performed in a group, may impart a sense of community, a kind of emotion common to the group, and may discipline it and give it a sense of purpose. Symbols may contribute similar kinds of emotion, summing up in themselves the leading desires and impulses of a group. For more than a century in the American colonies, the church building, from the New England meeting house to southern Gothic churches, must have performed this function, evoking the most important values and aspirations of its members.[2]

Apart from religion, colonial life was not especially rich in symbol and

[1]For a good brief account of this affair see Irving Brant, *James Madison: Father of the Constitution, 1787–1800* (Indianapolis and New York, 1950), pp. 255–57.

[2]The paragraph owes much to E. J. Hobsbawn, *Primitive Rebels* (New York, 1963), pp. 150–74.

ritual. Politics began in factions and remained factionalized until the Revolution was well advanced. If they opposed the representatives of the Crown, colonial factions had to tread a narrow line between legitimacy and disloyalty, a situation which discouraged the invention of formalistic observance. Membership in the Empire supplied all the forms British subjects could ask for anyway—a King still carrying a faint whiff of divine origin, a structure of administrative officials all conscious of their place in the apparatus of empire, and the conventions regulating the relationship of crown and commons. If the factions organized themselves along other lines, as in Rhode Island where Ward's opposed Hopkins's and where force, knavery, and nastiness probably repelled any attempts at ritualization, the transitory character of the groups never permitted symbolic forms to develop.[3]

Where organization intruded into other areas of colonial affairs ritualization of function appeared only casually. Merchants joined one another in colonial cities but interest overruled everything else; guild and artisan organizations developed late in the colonial period and assumed a few of the forms marking comparable nineteenth-century organizations. The absence of guilds seems startling; as pale as they are, modern unions in the United States have succeeded in perpetuating a more colorful ritualistic life. The difference in styles lies partly in the differences in class. Eighteenth-century artisans in cities were usually aspiring merchants and often engaged in some kind of mercantile activity. Though this activity was usually only a sideline that contributed to their main efforts, it blurred their economic interests and they experienced difficulty in locating themselves socially. Their lack of a clear sense of identity inhibited the ritualistic expression so characteristic of guilds in the next century, which usually were composed of members beset with no such doubts.[4]

Not even the violence that filled colonial life supplied much ritual. There were rebellions before the Revolution in all the colonies, but none aimed at independence, or at separation from Britain, and none lasted long enough to develop their own forms. Rather almost all clung to the fiction that they represented legitimacy and its forms. Rebels uniformly professed loyalty to Britain—and believed it. A profession of loyalty imposed the use of a ritual already long established, as in

[3]For the Ward-Hopkins contest, see David S. Lovejoy, *Rhode Island Politics and the American Revolution, 1760–1776* (Providence, R. I., 1958) and Mack Thompson, "The Ward-Hopkins Controversy and the American Revolution in Rhode Island: An Interpretation," *William and Mary Quarterly*, 3d Ser., 16 (1959), 363–75.

[4]For information about artisans see Carl Bridenbaugh, *The Colonial Craftsman* (New York, 1950) and *Cities in Revolt: Urban Life in America, 1743–1776* (New York, 1955).

Nathaniel Bacon's "Manifesto," which proclaimed that the Rebellion of
1676 in Virginia aimed "at his Majesties Honour and the Publick
good."[5]

Of all the crude social movements in the colonies preceding the
Revolution, only the revivals—and in particular the Great Awakening—
created their own ritualism. Revivals of religion depend upon meetings
and even the simplest of these meetings usually offered a ritualized
performance which created relationships between revivalist and listeners,
among the participants themselves, and hopefully between the initiates
and some higher being. The first such gatherings began in New England
as a communal exercise in renewing the church covenant. After a brief
sermon by the minister explaining what was required of the church, the
members were asked to rise silently as a token of their devotion. This
simple ceremony held possibilities for extension which did not escape the
ministers who soon enlisted the congregation and then nonmembers as
participants; sermons grew more hortatory and the purpose of the ritual
assumed larger proportions. By the time of the explosions of the 1740's a
highly structured ritual had developed, the climax of which saw the mass
undergo conversion, an initiation which sealed them to God and to one
another. The progress of awakening enthusiasm from community to
community also followed a ritualistic path, with a minister making his
way from one community to the next, holding meetings, confronting the
Devil and his agents, and bringing the populace to the faith.

The Revolutionary movement that began in the 1760's and that
carried through to independence displayed many of the characteristics of
a revival. It was larger and more complex, of course, and it was defined
primarily by its substantive issues. (The Revolutionary movement was
value-oriented, to use the jargon of sociologists, in a way the Great
Awakening was not.) Before 1776 the movement gained its cohesion at
the top, in particular from groups which took a name rich with symbolic
meaning, the Sons of Liberty. The Sons had a variety of tactical objectives throughout this period: at times they simply wished to force the
resignation of crown officials—the Stamp Distributors in 1765, for example. As they grew in sophistication they managed boycotts and joined
merchants and artisan groups in enforcing non-importation agreements.
They also collected arms, drilled their followers in military tactics, and
prepared for war. All these activities contributed to resistance against
Parliamentary measures of imperial reform and to the development
of a revolutionary tradition.[6]

The Sons chose to develop resistance, and to create a revolutionary
tradition in still other ways: most importantly by ritualizing the move-

[5]Robert Middlekauff ed., *Bacon's Rebellion* (Chicago, 1964) p. 20.
[6]For the Sons of Liberty and their activities see Edmund S. and Helen M. Morgan,
The Stamp Act Crisis: Prologue To Revolution (Chapel Hill, N. C., 1953).

ment against Britain and giving it symbolic expression. Here their activities approached in technique those of the revivalists. Just as the revivalists did, the Sons of Liberty depended upon the public meeting. Although these meetings occurred in various places, the favorite spot up and down the Eastern Seaboard came to be the vicinity around a "liberty tree," or in many cases, a "liberty pole." The first tree seems to have been designated the representative of liberty on August 14, 1765. The place was near the Boston Common, the tree a stately elm, and the occasion an attempt to bring Andrew Oliver to resign his Stamp Distributorship. Oliver gave up his office, and the tree gained the fame that was to make it an emblem of liberty—and the model for dozens of others in all the colonies.[7]

There is no need to pause too long over the meaning of the liberty tree or the liberty pole as a symbol. By themselves they symbolized freedom and worked the strong emotions of resistance to attempts to subvert freedom. The historical origin of the poles doubtless was the maypole of English country life (perhaps the first to appear in America was at Merrymount in Plymouth Colony). The maypole had served first as the emblem of the lower classes' disaffection from their social betters, and it soon took on the obvious sexual connotations which a later, Freudian influenced age has seen in it. (The sexual significance of the liberty tree was suggested long before Freud; Joel Barlow in the eighteenth century It was to be illuminated by several hundred lamps, and on its sides were to it was even more important for meanings, one suspects, than the Americans were aware of. The Liberty Tree in Boston, for example, was usually adorned with effigies of the Devil and his local repesentatives, the assorted officials of the Crown.[8] The confrontation intended may have been good against evil, the tree of course representing the forces of good. At the grand celebration of the repeal of the Stamp Act in the spring of 1766, the symbolism was even more explicit. A large obelisk of oiled paper was to decorate the tree (it burned up before it could be placed). traced the liberty tree to phallic symbols common to ancient mythologies.) As a symbol the liberty tree expressed a subtle meaning dependent upon the context in which it was used. In part what was attached pictures of the tree, with an angel hovering over it, and an eagle in the branches.[9]

Any Protestant would have recognized the meaning of this tableau: the struggle between imperial and colonial powers was the age-old conflict of the forces of dark and light. Good was arrayed against evil in

[7]Arthur M. Schlesinger, "Liberty Tree: A Genealogy," *New England Quarterly*, 25 (1952), 435–58.

[8]*Ibid., passim*; Esther Forbes, *Paul Revere and the World He Lived In* (Cambridge, Mass.), pp. 101–2.

[9]Forbes, *Revere*, pp. 115–17.

the American resistance to illegal taxation. The theme was honestly felt in a culture that still retained its Protestant cast and that instinctively thought of politics, as of all else, in moral terms. Something of the same meaning surely was implicit in the series of ceremonial burials of liberty poles which occurred in the 1760's and the 1770's. The religious significance of this ceremony is plain; the ritualized manner of the performance, with truth, liberty, and evil taking allegorical forms, could not escape anyone.

Numerology was employed in much the same way, for example, in the episode of the Massachusetts circular letter. Sent by the Massachusetts Assembly in 1768, the circular letter called the attention of the other colonial assemblies to the Townshend Acts. Its phrasing and tone were moderate but the Grafton ministry thought it seditious and saw in it an opportunity to smash the colonial opposition. The ministry ordered the Massachusetts assembly to rescind the letter and the Governor to dissolve them if they refused. They refused, of course. The vote was 92 to 17, and the Sons of Liberty under Sam Adams' tutelage began to celebrate the glorious 92 and to execrate the cowardly 17. At this time John Wilkes in England was trying to stay in the House of Commons; his slogan was "45," the number of the issue of his newspaper which the English government had suppressed. The Sons of Liberty in Boston sent him two turtles, one weighing 45 pounds, the other 47 pounds, for a total of 92 pounds—the number synonymous with patriotism in Massachusetts. The number 92 was celebrated in other ways too: Paul Revere fashioned a silver punch bowl, dedicated to the "Immortal 92," and engraved with slogans and symbols, among them "Wilkes & Liberty," and "No. 45." Here the technique—which may seem strained today—may have derived from the Protestant fascination with eschatological numerology which sometimes expressed the opposition of good and evil in numbers.[10]

Even the simple act of wearing homespun as a part of the boycott of British goods, which seems devoid of any motive except economic coercion, was freighted with Protestant concern. The use of homespun

---

[10]See Arthur M. Schlesinger, *Prelude to Independence: The Newspaper War On Britain 1764–1776* (New York, 1958), pp. 36–37 and the newspapers cited there. The Sons of Liberty in Petersham trimmed the town's Liberty Tree so that 92 branches remained. In South Carolina, the number 26 was celebrated because 26 members of the Assembly defied the Governor and passed resolves supporting the Circular Letter. For an example of Protestant numerology see Elisha Rich, *The Number of the Beast Found Out By Spiritual Arithmetic* (Chelmsford, Mass., 1775). Rich says (on p. 23) of the Antichrist: "Observe, that although it [Antichrist] numbers so many: yet the number seven, or sevens is never once brought into the reckoning, but it lacks one of that number by which GOD would have the true CHURCH distinguished from the false. For the BEAST comes to six hundred and sixty six, but not seven or sevens, and so the Beast lacks one in each number."

was one part of the general repudiation of English corruption, and the resolve to wear it was testimony in favor of purity in thought and action. The Association, the large-scale boycott and nonimportation agreement adopted by the First Continental Congress in 1774, pledged Americans to a wholesale reform: "we will, in our several stations encourage frugality, economy, and industry, and promote agriculture, arts and the manufactures of this country, especially that of wool; and will discountenance and discourage every species of extravagance and dissipation, especially of horse-racing, and all kinds of gaming, cockfighting, exhibitions of shews, plays, and other expensive diversions and entertainments; . . ."[11] In this context homespun became emblematic of Protestant values.

The Congress also called upon Americans to repent and reform before invoking divine aid against the British government. It suggested that Parliament's oppression was punishment for the Americans' sins, and could be lifted only by an act of national self-purification. This theme was also featured in countless sermons of the 1760's and 70's. Such preaching employed a device much older than the colonies; utilized in the Revolutionary situation, it explained current griefs and offered a way out of them.[12] In a peculiar way this sort of ritualization, playing on old, conventional themes in a familiar tone, probably offered some reassurance. The problems, it implied, only seemed new—in reality they were the old ones of good against evil; their form was new but the old remedies were sure. All in all, this was a masterful, if instinctive, formulation of Revolutionary affairs.

If the revivalistic impulse contributed so much to the Revolutionary movement and if Protestant values inescapably found expression there, so also did Protestant expectations about the future of America. Although the American sense of order curbed "enthusiasm," there were unspoken millennial hints in American Revolutionary thinking. Any revolution rests on the assumption that things can be made better—this one seemed to Americans to forecast the New Jerusalem, the new heavens and the new earth of the thousand years. Despite their concern for property and taxes, the Americans were not what their fathers called "carnal chiliasts," seekers only of earthly abundance. Their utopianism was in some measure a response to the evils they perceived in English

---

11Samuel E. Morison, *Sources and Documents Illustrating The American Revolution, 1764–1788* (2nd ed. Oxford, Eng., 1953), p. 124. Since this essay was written, Edmund S. Morgan's, "The Puritan Ethic and The American Revolution," *William and Mary Quarterly*, 3d Ser., 24 (1967), 3–43 has appeared which provides an excellent discussion of the relationship between Protestant values and the revolutionary movement.

12Perry Miller, "From the Covenant to the Revival," in *Religion in American Life: American Religion*, James Ward Smith and A. Leland Jamison, eds. (4 vols., Princeton, N. J., 1961), I, 326–34.

life, bribery in politics, decadence in manners, and infidelity in religion, and hence they were committed to a general reformation of morals and institutions.

Politics, more than anything else, demanded reform and it began with the resistance to Parliamentary measures and royal officials in the 1760's. Americans hesitated for years about open attack on the monarchy but that reluctance vanished early in 1776 with Thomas Paine's *Common Sense*. With his delicate ability to read public sentiment, Paine sensed that the monarchy was a kind of image, or idol, for Americans, and his role was that of the iconoclast. He played the part with great skill, treating the monarchy as a remnant of heathenish and Jewish superstition which had been transformed into modern despotism. His conclusion must have seemed obvious in this context: monarchy was the enemy of freedom in religion as well as in politics, "For monarchy in every instance is the Popery of government."[13]

The Revolutionaries' concern for reform had yet another source: evangelical Protestantism, which had been preoccupied with social reformation as a fulfillment of history—thus the calls for Americans to attain a purified society, with simple and sinless institutions. In this millennial state, bliss would be enjoyed as long as purity and simplicity lasted. Even the "life, liberty, and pursuit of happiness" of the Declaration of Independence gained resonance in this context of millennial expectation.

During the period before independence, millennialism proved to have great allegorical utility which could be elaborated and extended as the conflict with the English government developed. At the beginning of the Revolutionary movement the Americans applied the symbols of millennialism to specific men and measures. By the end in 1776, when American purposes had expanded from resistance to independence, they gave these millennial symbols broader, even typological meanings. Such development can be seen by comparing sermons preached in 1766 with those of 1776. For example, on February 14, 1766, a sermon was preached around the Liberty Tree in Boston in which the doctrine was inspired by the thirteenth chapter of Revelation, "where the wolves of our day are so plainly pointed out. . . ."[14] This chapter describes two terrible beasts: the first, with seven heads and ten horns, the preacher

[13]Thomas Paine, *Common Sense and the Crisis* (Garden City, N. Y., 1965), p. 22. Americans in New York City carried out another kind of iconoclasm when they pulled down an equestrian statue of George III in Bowling Green in 1776. Had there been more such statues, there surely would have been more such iconoclasm. For similar episodes in the French Revolution see the account by Stanley J. Idzerda, "Iconoclasm During the French Revolution," *American Historical Review*, 60 (Oct., 1954), 13–26.

[14]*A Discourse, Addressed To The Sons of Liberty, At A Solemn Assembly, Near Liberty-Tree in Boston, February 14, 1766* (Providence, R. I., 1766), p. 3.

asserted "sets before our eyes the wicked Earl of Bute." The seven heads represented the offices he held; the crowns on them indicated that he was royally appointed; the horns he soon fixed on the heads of "honester men." This beast continued in power for forty-two months and so, by the calculation of the minister preaching this sermon, did Bute. The second beast had two horns, like a lamb, and spoke like a dragon; this monster was George Grenville, whose mark was the Stamp Act. Thus the crisis of the Stamp Act was treated as an old prophetic scheme: the beast, or the Antichrist, and its creation, the Stamp Act, opposed Christ and his own, the Americans in the wilderness. This design appeared clear to all a month before the Stamp Act was repealed. The end of the prophecy could not be doubted; just as the beast was slain so also would the Stamp Act be killed.[15]

How this symbolic representation could be extended to give larger meaning may be seen in a sermon preached in New York almost exactly ten years later, in January, 1776. In this sermon the American struggle with Britain was completely absorbed into Biblical prophecy. It pictured the church in the American wilderness with the emphasis on God's commitment to America, where the church, and Christian liberty, would survive. It was an optimistic statement identifying the American cause with "the Protestant cause in general." The "American quarter of the globe," it announced, is reserved by Providence for the church, free of tyranny and free to enjoy "right of rule and government, so as not to be controll'd and oppressed by the tyrannical powers . . . represented by the Great Red Dragon." The war of Britain upon America was described as a war on God, and God's support of America was not doubted: "we have incontestible evidence, that God Almighty, with all the powers of heaven, are on our side. Great numbers of Angels no doubt, are encamped round our coast, for our defense and protection. Michael stands ready, with all the artillery of heaven, to encounter the dragon, and vanquish this black host."[16] As in 1766, victory awaited the powers of good: the good in the New World where liberty "has been planted. . . . These commotions and convulsions in the British empire, may be leading to the fulfillment of such prophecies as relate to his [the Devil's] downfall and overthrow, and to the future glory and prosperity of Christ's church."[17] In this formulation the purpose of the American struggle had been broadened so as to coincide, in defense of Christian liberty, with the final epic conflict with sin.

This exalted expression of the meaning of the war with Britain spoke

15The quotations are in the *Discourse*, pp. 4–5.

16Samuel Sherwood, *The Church's Flight Into The Wilderness: An Address on the Times Containing Some Very Interesting and Important Observations on Scripture Prophecies* (New York, 1776). The quotations are from pp. 18, 24, 46n.

17*Ibid.*, p. 49.

to the deepest impulses in Americans. It defined liberty and union in Christian terms; it reconciled the defense of property with the defense of good (they were inseparable, it suggested). It posed the struggle in the terms most congenial to Americans—in moral terms, with America serving as the instrument of Providence. In the next eight bloody years, it invested sacrifice with Christian meaning and thereby released those energies of Americans which would sustain them to the end of the war.

Independence did not bring Americans to a repudiation of these old Protestant values, but it did begin a fresh tendency towards a secular culture. Historians of religion in America have taught us that secularization in America began in the seventeenth century, perhaps almost simultaneously with its founding. Secularization, they urge, expressed itself institutionally: in church organization that saw laymen progressively assume authority in discipline, management of church affairs, and even in the definition of doctrine; and in the altering of church-state relationships in favor of the voluntary principle. Secularization also expressed itself in values: in the decline of traditional piety or its conversion into ethical and humanitarian impulses; and in the indifference which found men taking their definitions of life's purposes and concerns from authorities other than religion—reason and science, business and politics.

The Revolution contributed to this process by redirecting American energies and by wrenching American thought and feeling into some new forms. The ritualization of the Revolution helped to create, but more importantly to express, new values, for their sources lay, to a large extent, outside the forms themselves.

With independence, the Revolution itself became a symbol, evocative of a complex tradition of liberty and sacrifice. Perhaps in the incantations to American sacrifices during the war lies the strongest link to the Protestant past, with its emphasis on sin and affliction. As a symbol, the Revolution was celebrated through the means of other symbols and an intricate ritualization drawing on the familiar devices of meetings, holidays (the Fourth of July was preeminent), medals, paintings, statues, and hero-worship. A part of this process was plainly deliberate and self-conscious. Thus in ordering medals struck in France, Congress declared their purposes to be "grateful to the illustrious personages for whom they are designed, worthy the dignity of the sovereign power by whom they are presented, and calculated to perpetuate the remembrance of those great events which they are intended to consecrate to immortality,' "[18] During the Confederation period fifteen medals were authorized by Congress commemorating such events as the evacuation of Boston

[18]Julian Boyd ed., *The Papers of Thomas Jefferson* (17 vols. to date, Princeton, N. J., 1950–), XVI, 53.

by the British, the surrender of Burgoyne at Saratoga, the engagements at Stony Point, Cowpens, Eutaw Springs, the capture of Major André, and the victory of the *Bonhomme Richard* over the *Serapis.*

Although medals and meetings espoused a simple patriotism calculated to strengthen national feeling, they also presented the Revolution as an event having transcendent meaning. No doubt the connection between this conception of the Revolution and the remnants of the eschatological vision lie here. The connection may be seen in a proclamation of 1776 commemorating the Battle of Lexington which stated, "'from this day will be dated the liberty of the world.'" In the same year a Massachusetts minister compared the robust liberty in Revolutionary America to other benighted parts of the world where it was "'gasping for life.'" America's Revolution was described in 1780 as being in the service of such less happy areas: "'Our contest is not merely for our own families, friends, and posterity, but for the rights of humanity, for the civil and religious privileges of mankind.'" And David Ramsey, the historian of the Revolution, who watched its course, agreed with foreign opinion that the Revolution marked a new age in history.[19]

The Revolution as a symbol of promise and prophecy pervaded every attempt of the revolutionary generation to understand what they had done. This tendency is especially apparent in the symbolic meanings attached to the Union. Although after 1776 the Union remained "elusive in its form and function," it commanded emotional and intellectual attachment as the means for the American experiment.[20] There was resistance to this concept, of course, and opposition to what it meant when it was translated into power relationships in government. Those who persisted in seeing the Union as America's hope wished to strengthen it, and those who valued the states or other local authority opposed attempts to add to its power. Advocates of state sovereignty proved as fully aware of the connections of form and function as any devotee of the Union. In 1783 the freeholders of Fairfax County, Virginia, expressed their fears about the encroaching Union, thus "We like not the language of the late address from Congress to the different States [urging that Congress be given powers to tax], . . . The very style is alarming. . . . Forms generally imply substance."[21] This last point—"Forms imply substance"—probably put the matter too strongly for the exponents of the Union. Their conception, the prevailing one, was of the Union as a

19The quotations and the citation from Ramsey are from Wesley Frank Craven, *The Legend of the Founding Fathers* (New York, 1956), pp. 59–60.

20Paul C. Nagel, *One Nation Indivisible: The Union in American Thought, 1776–1861* (New York, 1961), p. 15.

21Quoted in Alpheus Thomas Mason, *The States Rights Debate* (Englewood Cliffs, N. J., 1964), p. 22.

means by which Revolutionary ends might be achieved, not as an end in itself. In the most frequently used language the union was the "foundation," the "tie," the "bounds," the "remedy" for political diseases—it was not an end, nor an absolute. As a means the Union would ensure happiness and peace. It would, in Hamilton's phrase, serve as a barrier to faction and insurrection; Madison in the Tenth Federalist conceived of it as an agency by which the worst effects of political faction might be controlled. Useful in domestic politics, it would serve American interests abroad by focusing power, which had been tending to fragment among the new states, against European enemies.[22]

For some Americans the Union evoked the Revolution's dedication to the principle of democratic consent as the basis of government. After all, the early resistance to Britain rested on the right of men to be taxed only by political bodies in which their representatives sat, and the Constitution, in the procedure by which it was drafted and ratified and in its substantive commitment to popular interest and the general welfare, institutionalized a broadly-based government. Other Americans resisted these propositions and urged that the States alone could be relied upon both for the protection of rights and as the mechanisms through which popular consent should be registered. But in either case the culture which explicitly pledged to a political process that took its power and its limits from the people.

Form did not control substance in 1789 when the new government commenced its operations, and would not begin to until the great romantic outpouring of the nineteenth century when a secular cult would grow up around the Union. In the eighteenth century, as a symbol, the Union was unavailable to those who would have made it the basis for a secular ideology because it was still imprecise in meaning. Yet even though it was an inexact symbol, and seemingly invited only experimentalism, the Union contributed to secularization, as indeed it expressed it. For its very character as a means opened the way to new centers of thought and purpose. It permitted, for example, the development of a national politics. In time such new purposes would find ritualized expression.

Yet a Protestant culture survived the Revolution intact, committed to traditional purposes and means but also, in a subtle way, liberated from them, and prepared for further revolutionary change. With disestablishment accomplished in several colonies and threatened in all, the church as an institution seemed less self-contained and more dependent upon popular desires if it were to perpetuate itself. By itself, this new condition of financial precariousness did not impose a greater sensitivity

---

[22]For language describing the Union I have relied on *The Federalist*; see in particular numbers 2–10, 39, 84.

to secular purposes. But considered with the strengthened authority of laymen and the increased authority of the national state, disestablishment inevitably resulted in renewed secularization. Revivals would break out again at the end of the century, but despite their familiar incantations to original sin and human depravity, Protestantism would have to accommodate itself increasingly to nonreligious values.

The proclivity to see things in moral terms persisted; it is one of the enduring American characteristics. Many of the old symbols survived too, with undiminished evocative capacity, though they were susceptible to fresh interpretations. The liberty tree, for example, took on meanings defined more by politics than by morals. The problems of the society offered further promise of secularization—especially the need to ease sectional tensions. And the questions surrounding the national government's role in economic life, which would receive a neomercantilist resolution under Hamilton's careful tuition, carried the state far away from any religious issues.

The ritualization of the Revolution in the eighteenth century remained faithful then to revolutionary values, clarifying and expressing them. Revolutionary experience itself was so evocative of the colonial past, and still so promising of the future, that in some measure it acted to check for a time the extravagant ritualization of the intense sense of American destiny and the absolutist conceptions of America which would appear in the nineteenth century. Yet by the end of the Revolution, ritualistic and symbolic expression had taken on an ambiguous character, still indebted to the past and yet holding promise of development.

JOHN WILLIAM WARD

Amherst College

jacksonian democratic thought: "a natural charter of privilege"

When, in 1834, George Bancroft remarked on the need for a book which described the nature of American democracy, a correspondent replied that "no dependence can be placed upon any treatise that has yet appeared which professes to discuss [the business of government.] You must draw upon your own resources, you must think—and think alone."[1] Similarly, Orestes Brownson thought no American had produced a "work on politics of the slightest scientific value."[2] And when Harper and Brothers brought out George Sidney Camp's *Democracy* in 1841, the

[1]W. S. Wait to Bancroft, October 15, 1834, cited in Arthur Schlesinger, Jr., *The Age of Jackson* (Boston, 1948), p. 309.

[2]*The United States Magazine and Democratic Review*, XIII (1843), 129.

publisher drew attention to the curious fact that it was the first book "the express design of which is to elucidate the democratic *theory*."[3] Camp, in his own introduction, dwelt at length on the anomaly that "in a democratic country, where self-government has been successfully exercised by the people for nearly three-quarters of a century" there was no literature on democracy to which one might refer "the young democratic disciple."[4] There was no *"connected and philosophical exposition of the peculiar theory of democratic government,"* insisted Camp, and the result, he pointed out, was that Americans "journey on, living in the rich experience and practical enjoyment of democratic freedom, but in the entire and reckless indifference to its abstract principles."[5]

Camp tried to account for the dearth of theoretical interest in America's triumphantly successful practise by observing, with mild wit, that the "chief speculators" of the day were "in merchandise and real estate." Camp thought "political opinions seem to have retrogaded since the Revolution"; the majority of "educated" men in the United States did not, he believed, understand the nature of freedom or "the maxim of the natural equality of mankind." Having won independence, with a continent to conquer and a nation to make, Americans were content "with the practical results" of their political system, hardly inclined to the "patient study of its abstract nature." We have been "all action," said Camp. "There has been no room for the thinker; he has been jostled to one side."[6]

Yet Camp's own book suggests it was not simply the activism of a practical people on the make which discouraged intellectual speculation in the business of politics. At one point Camp observed, "Government, like religion, is essential to our happiness, and was designed by the Author of our being for universal use; it is a proof of the justice and propriety of a scheme of government, as it is of the genuineness of a religious system, that it may be easily and universally comprehended."[7] "Nothing," he wrote, "can be more simple than the theory of republican government. It may be readily comprehended by the plainest minds; it appeals to the first maxims of common-sense observation, and the universal principles of morals."[8] If, as Camp had it, the chief merit of the American system of politics was that it needed no philosopher, it is hardly surprising that it did not get one. The limits of plain minds and the first maxims of common sense do not define resources which promise to sustain intense speculation. Yet the curious result has been to make

[3]George Sidney Camp, *Democracy* (New York, 1841), p. iii.

[4]Camp, *Democracy*, p. 10.

[5]Camp, *Democracy*, pp. 12–13.

[6]Camp, *Democracy*, pp. 14–15.

[7]Camp, *Democracy*, p. 89.

[8]Camp, *Democracy*, p. 88.

speculation on Jacksonian political thought a risky enterprise.   There is an implicit logic, an unstated argument, which defines the assumptions of American democratic political thought of the early nineteenth century, assumptions which contemporaries took to be nothing more than the common sense of the matter.   One must make that hidden logic explicit in order to catch a glimpse of what uncommon hopes motivated the politics of the age of the common man.

Further, the similarity Camp saw between religion and democracy suggests a way of looking at the political thought of Jacksonian America. Politics is many things, but before it can be any of the particular activities one normally associates with it, politics necessarily involves an expression of the cultural values which make politics possible at all. Camp thought that Christianity and democratic liberty "flourish best on the same soil" because of "strong points of similarity between them." Not only were both universally true and easily understood by all men everywhere, but because both rested on self-evident general principles, both were hostile to "precedent or authority."   Both "inculcated the same contempt for human authority, the same regard for the poorer and humbler classes, the same disregard of merely adventitious and accidental circumstances, the same paramount authority of principle."   And, although both had "for their basis the law of benevolence," both, Camp pointed out, "have borne the reproach of being disorganizing and anarchical."[9]

For Camp, the similarities between Christianity and democracy proved that both were true.   For us, the similarities suggest also the pervasiveness in his time of a common way of apprehending the relation of the individual to society.   The question of that relation, the relation between the one and the many, is always and inevitably a matter of politics, but the answer to the question involves more than politics.   It involves the values of the general culture of which politics is but one expression.[10]   Michael Chevalier the French Saint-Simonian who had visited and written about the United States before Camp published his book, had this in mind when he said of the United States, "Under the influence of Protestantism and republicanism, social progress has been achieved by pushing the process of division to its extreme, that is, individualism; for Protestantism, republicanism, and individualism are

---

[9]Camp, *Democracy*, pp. 180–81.

[10]Sidney Verba has used the term "political culture" to denote the "psychological orientation to politics."   See his essay, "Comparative Political Culture," in *Political Culture and Political Development*, eds., Lucian Pye and Sidney Verba (Princeton, N. J., 1965).   I refer rather more simply to the expression of the general values of the culture in the idiom of politics.   See Talcott Parsons, *The Social System* (Glencoe, Ill., 1951), pp. 126–27, and especially the introduction to Parsons, *et. al., Theories of Society* (New York, 1961).

all one." Chevalier, along with his fellow countryman, Tocqueville, had observed the centrifugal impulse in American society, the extremity of division in which "individuals have cut themselves off from each other," but his observation did not stop with what Camp termed "the reproach" of seeing nothing but disorganization or anarchy.[11] Chevalier recognized that in the United States, Protestantism, republicanism and individualism were simply different aspects of a comprehensive system of values. Despite "the process of division," each derived its sanction from the good of society. Or, to put it another way, the discovery of assumptions which underlie Jacksonian democratic thought may lead to a better understanding of the political thought of the time but leads also to a problem which lies beyond politics and finds its answer only in the values of the general culture.

I

In 1824, Andrew Jackson received a plurality of the popular and electoral vote in a four-cornered race for the Presidency, followed by John Quincy Adams, William Crawford, and Henry Clay. Since no candidate had a majority, selection devolved on the House of Representatives where choice, according to the provision of the Constitution, lay among the three leading candidates. Clay, now excluded as a candidate, threw his political influence behind Adams, and after Adams became President he named Clay his Secretary of State, placing him in the office which to that time had been the conventional stepping-stone to the Presidency. Immediately, Jacksonian partisans raised the cry of a corrupt bargain between Adams and Clay and began the campaign which was to bring Andrew Jackson to the White House in 1828.

It was against this background that Jackson decided, in his first message as President to Congress, to catechize the legislative branch on the principles of democratic government. In the course of his message he laid bare the major assumptions of his democratic faith and provides us with a characteristic statement of "the first principle" of Jacksonian democracy, *"the majority is to govern."*[12]

When Jackson asserts the rule of the majority to be the first principle of "our system," he is on uncertain historical ground. True, even Alexander Hamilton, who was not greatly enamored with the prospect of rule by the people, defended the principle as primary, but the Constitu-

---

[11] Michael Chevalier, *Society, Manners and Politics in the United States,* trans., ed., and with an introduction by John William Ward (New York, 1961), p. 356; the first American edition of Chevalier's book was in Boston in 1839.

[12] James D. Richardson, *A Compilation of the Messages and Papers of the Presidents, 1789–1907* (n.p., 1908), II, 448.

tion to which Jackson appeals is not a document devised to implement a thoroughgoing domination by the majority in politics. Jackson, in saying it does, seems to verge toward the tyranny of the majority which so concerned Tocqueville in his analysis of an equalitarian society. But as one watches the development of Jackson's argument, one sees him avoid in an astonishing way the power of the majority which seems at first to be the conclusion toward which he is moving.

"To the People," said Jackson, "belongs the right of electing their Chief Magistrate." Neither the electoral college nor the House were ever meant to frustrate the people's choice. "Experience proves," as for Jackson it clearly did in 1824, "that in proportion as agents to execute the will of the People are multiplied there is danger of their wishes being frustrated. Some may be unfaithful; all are liable to err. So far, therefore, as the People can with convenience speak, it is safer for them to express their own will."[13] So Jackson spoke for the obliteration of "all intermediate agency" in the election of the President.

The premise of Jackson's message is a trust in the will of a virtuous and competent people. But agents trusted with the power of translating the will of a virtuous people into reality will inevitably be corrupted by that power: "There are, perhaps, few men who can for any great length of time enjoy office and power without being more or less under the influence of feelings unfavorable to the faithful discharge of their public duties . . . . they are apt to acquire a habit of looking with indifference upon the public interests, and of tolerating conduct from which an unpracticed man would revolt. Office is considered as a species of property, and government rather as a means of promoting individual interests than as an instrument created solely for the service of the people."[14]

The negation of Jackson's premise is the corruption of the will of a virtuous people by the selfish instincts brought into play by power. At this point in his message, Jackson stands at the edge of the world of practical politics. He has already summarily solved the theoretical problem of identifying the People. The People are the majority of the people. If the People could act directly, there would be no problem because there would be no need for refractory intermediate institutions. The problem arises because the People must rely on agents, the body of legislators, to translate their will into reality; but, by that very fact, "corruption" and a "perversion of correct feelings and principles" threaten constantly to divert government from its "legitimate" ends and "make it an engine for the support of the few at the expense of the many."[15]

13Richardson, *Messages and Papers*, II, 447.
14Richardson, *Messages and Papers*, II, 448–49.
15Richardson, *Messages and Papers*, II, 449.

Having identified the will of the people with the will of the majority outside the institutions of government, Jackson's task becomes, then, to show how it is possible to pattern the institutions of government so the governors are made responsible to the power which creates them. In other words, if the seductions of power threaten constantly to make the political state the enemy of the general society, then the first job of politics is to circumvent the danger.

Jackson's solution is, however, to deny the very antithesis he has just developed; that is, he tries to obliterate the distinction between the government and the people. "The duties of all public officers are, or at least admit of being made, so plain and simple that men of intelligence may readily qualify themselves for their performance; and I can not but believe that more is lost by the long continuance of men in office than is generally to be gained by their experience."[16] So Jackson spoke for limited tenure in elective offices and rotation in all appointive offices. Later generations would stigmatize the principle by remembering it only as the "spoils system." It is true that, under the tutelage of professional politicians like Martin Van Buren who saw the need and the advantages of party organization, Jackson recognized the uses of patronage in building a national political party, but Jackson's rejection of a trained and experienced class of legislators and civil servants was, much more importantly, a species of reform.

Jackson's solution to the paradox of politics, the corruption of the selfless will of the people by the power necessary to instrument that will, was no less than to try to dismiss the need for politics at all, that is, to abolish the distinction between the People and the government. If power corrupts, then America was in the happy state of having no need for power. Jackson could say so only on the assumption that the work of government was essentially so plain and simple that the average intelligent man could do the job. The assumption of simplicity made it possible to reject the need for training and experience, to dismiss the existence of a governing class, and to argue that the people could act directly by being rotated through the offices of government and performing the simple tasks which were the legitimate ends of government. The task of government was to see to the minimal preservation of law and order and to leave the business of society "to flow in those channels to which individual enterprise, always its surest guide, might direct it."[17] The danger of the tyranny of the majority vanishes in a world where each individual is busy about his own business.

The abortive dialectic, the refusal to attempt a synthesis which would resolve the antithesis between the will of a virtuous people and the

[16]Richardson, *Messages and Papers*, II, 449.
[17]Richardson, *Messages and Papers*, II, 449.

corruption of political power, was not Jackson's alone. It suffused the political thought of the period. Jackson's message comes at the beginning of his tenure of office. At the end of that tenure, in 1838, the *United States Magazine and Democratic Review*, founded to advocate the "high and holy DEMOCRATIC PRINCIPLE which was designed to be the fundamental element of the new social and political system created by the 'American experiment,' " introduced itself to the public with a presentation of the nature of that democratic principle.[18] The argument of the "Introduction" to the *Democratic Review* is longer and more ambitious than Jackson's *obiter dicta* to the Congress, but the underlying structure of the argument is precisely the same. Because the article is an attempt to present a reasoned account of the democratic faith, it becomes involved in a crucial dilemma concerning the relation of the individual to society and points, by its solution, to the vital source of a democratic faith which staked its all on the self-sufficiency of the single individual.

The author of the "Introduction" to the *Democratic Review*, presumably John L. O'Sullivan, who was part owner and political editor of the magazine, begins on a characteristic Jacksonian note. His task is the "purification" of the democratic creed "from those corruptions" which have prevented its glorious tendencies. He proclaims his "abiding confidence in the virtue, intelligence, and full capacity for self-government, of the great mass of our people, our industrious, honest, manly, intelligent millions of freemen." The premise, put with somewhat greater rhetorical flourish, is the same as Jackson's in his message to Congress: the people are virtuous and capable, but somehow corruption has entered the populist heaven.

"We are opposed," O'Sullivan continues, "to all self-styled 'wholesome restraints' on the free action of the popular opinion and will, other than those which have for their sole object the prevention of precipitate legislation." To assure that the speed with which the popular will is translated into action is deliberate enough, O'Sullivan accepts "the expedient of the division of power, and by causing all legislation to pass through the ordeal of successive forms; to be sifted through the discussions of coördinate legislative branches with mutual suspensive veto powers." O'Sullivan speaks, of course, of what we call the system of checks and balances, the ordering of the institution of government into separate departments which check each other, but he does not mean to say that such a system of countervailing power is to act against the will of the people, only against other departments, and he stresses his point

---

[18]*United States Magazine and Democratic Review*, I (October-December, 1837), 1. Although carrying the date "October-December, 1837," the first volume was actually published in January, 1838; see the publisher's "Note" at the front of the first volume.

immediately. "Yet all should be dependent with equal directness and promptness on the influence of public opinion; the popular will should be equally the animating and moving spirit of them all, and ought never to find in any of its own creatures a self-imposed power, capable (when misused either by corrupt ambition or honest error) of resisting itself, and defeating its own determined object. We cannot, therefore, look with an eye of favor on any such forms of representation as, by length of tenure of delegated power, tend to weaken that universal and unrelaxing responsibility to the vigilance of public opinion, which is the true conservative principle of our institutions."[19]

O'Sullivan has here compressed an extremely long and complicated problem in American constitutional thought into a short statement. There are many issues lurking in his few words. One is the uneasy tension between the "true" conservatism of responsiveness to public opinion and the acceptance of institutional arrangements which will prevent "precipitate" legislation: the latter strategy implies that public opinion is sometimes hastily wrong. But beneath such obvious problems lies a much more complex one. Two different and opposed traditions in the history of American constitutional thought coexist awkwardly in O'Sullivan's paragraph.

From the beginning, there have been in American political thought two implicitly antithetical views of the nature of a proper constitution. One places emphasis on the form of government created by a constitution, on the institutional arrangement of the organs of government; that is, responsibility on the part of the government is to be achieved by setting up a certain kind of government with power distributed throughout the various parts in order to check undue power by any one particular branch in the whole, finely articulated, self-regulating system. A good constitution is one which sets up a specific form of government. The other view of the nature of a proper constitution places emphasis on the process by which constitutions are made, and unmade, and insists that the true check on the power of government, or on any one or all of the particular, institutionalized branches of government, lies in the power of the people outside the doors of the government. Here, a good constitution is not so much a form of government as the effectiveness of the process by which the people out of government are constantly able to discipline government by exercising the inalienable power which ultimately sanctions all governments.

In the first, the language of the constitution which creates the government is the will of the people. Having spoken once, the people are excluded, except through the unwieldy amendment process, from speaking again, and the organ of the government which is given the final say on the meaning of the constitution which embodies the will of the people is that department of government most removed from the people in their electoral capacity, the Supreme Court. In the second, the will of the people is always vital and alive, always potent. The people never exclude themselves from exercising the power which is always, by definition, invested in them: changing or abolishing the present form of government. Other than revolution, of course, the only way the people can act in such a sovereign capacity is through what O'Sullivan refers to as "public opinion," and it was to give institutional structure to the amorphous shape of public opinion that political parties came into being in our national politics. The first strain of constitutional thought, the emphasis on constitution as institutional form, is best associated with the name of John Adams; the second, the emphasis on constitution as process, the process by which people constitute and control government, is best associated with the name of Thomas Jefferson.

Even so brief a description of what lies behind O'Sullivan's compact statement hardly enters the thicket in which his acceptance of both the division of power and the will of the people outside the government lands him. But there is not much more reason to develop the duality which is part of the tradition of American constitutionalism other than to name it in order to dramatize the stark simplicity of O'Sullivan's avoidance of the subtle and sophisticated political terms of his problem. Both versions of constitutionalism raise difficult problems concerning the relation of the single individual to society. In one, the will of the actual, empirical, living individual is somehow supposed to be represented in the order of government created by the language of the constitution; in the other, the will of the individual is somehow supposed to be represented by the will of the majority of his equal fellows in society. O'Sullivan recognizes that either view of politics will land him in a dilemma concerning the uninhibited freedom of the individual. He sees in any check on the will of the people the danger of rule by a minority; he is also uneasy about the extinction of minority rights under rule by the majority. If pushed to choose, he will pragmatically accept the lesser evil of majority rule but asks, "Have we but a choice of evils? Is there, then, such a radical deficiency in the moral elements implanted by its Creator in human society, that no other alternative can be devised by which both evils shall be avoided, and a result attained more analogous to the beautiful and glorious harmony of the rest of his creation?"[20] The tone, of course, suggests surely not.

O'Sullivan answers his own rhetorical question by pointing out that "it is under the word *government*, that the subtle danger lurks." Like Jackson, rather than pursue the problem he has defined, O'Sullivan

[20]*Democratic Review*, I, 5.

proceeds to abolish it. "All government is evil, and the parent of evil. A strong and active democratic *government*, in the common sense of the term, is an evil, differing only in degree and mode of operation, and not in nature, from a strong despotism." If government presents the dilemma of the power of a minority in office on one hand, or the tyranny of the majority outside of office on the other, the dilemma is to be avoided by denying the need for government. "The best government is that which governs least."[21]

The reason O'Sullivan gives seems, at first glance, perverse: "No human depositories can, with safety, be trusted with the power of legislation upon the general interests of society. . . . Such power must be perpetually liable to the most pernicious abuse, from the natural imperfection, both in wisdom of judgment and purity of purpose, of all human legislation." So sour a view of human nature leads O'Sullivan to the drastic conclusion that "government should have as little as possible to do with the general business and interests of the people." Since the general interests of the people define the whole business of government, nothing is left when O'Sullivan finishes but a bare administrative state: "the administration of justice, for the protection of the natural equal rights of the citizen, and preservation of social order."[22]

As one follows O'Sullivan's argument with its distrust of "human depositories" and its assertion of the "natural imperfection . . . of all human legislation," one wonders what ever happened to that great mass of "industrous, honest, manly, intelligent millions of freemen" who, at the outset, provided support for his buoyant faith in democracy. There are, rationally, two views of human nature which will support a dismissal of the power of government. Anarchism can, logically, find a basis in two different and opposed views of human nature. One is optimistic: the people are so honest and manly they need no government. The other pessimistic: people are so naturally depraved that, whatever the other inconveniences, none of them had best be trusted with the power of ruling. O'Sullivan seems to be having it both ways, arguing for the abolition of government from two antithetical conceptions of human nature. But his position is a bit more sophisticated than such blatant self-contradiction. His premise is, like Jackson's, "an abiding confidence in the virtue, intelligence, and full capacity for self-government, of the great mass of our people." The accent falls on "self-government." As long as the virtuous, manly, American democrat has only his own interests in hand, there is no cause for hesitation or doubt. But give him power and he will, all too humanly, read his own interests as the general interest and become "selfish and tyrannical . . . vigilant, persevering,

21*Democratic Review*, I, 6.
22*Democratic Review*, I, 7.

and subtle in all the arts of deception and corruption." It is the power made possible by the awful power of legislation "by which human nature has been self-degraded."[23]

To repeat, then: the same dialectic, or aborted dialectic, provides the structure for both Jackson's few words and O'Sullivan's long article. Both subscribe to the thesis of the will of the people by power. The synthesis, or better, the absence of a synthesis, is astonishingly simple: there is no need for power, for government. Do away with it.

II

The key words in the political vocabulary of the period of the early nineteenth century were "simple" and "corruption." Not only were the principles of democracy simple enough to be easily and universally comprehended, but the practise of democracy, the duties of public officers, involved tasks so simple that they could be entrusted to the average citizen for their execution. Jacksonian political thought can best be understood as an attempt to celebrate the capacity of a virtuous people by insisting that the intricacies of government were essentially so plain and simple that there was no need to admit a distinction between the governors and the governed. The result was to abolish the distinction between government and society, to deny the problem of politics by refusing to define a general interest at all. Society was no more than the sum of individual interests. Corruption was to be avoided by denying any individual, or group of individuals, power over others. Leave each man free from external restraint and the good society would emerge spontaneously and unbidden.

In discussing a political movement so thoroughly dedicated to the denial of power, historians ever since have been bemused by Jackson's vigorous Presidency. He was one of our few "strong" presidents. Nearly every important issue Jackson confronted in office led to an enlargement of the powers of the office of the President. His extensive use of the veto power, his removals from office, his veto of internal improvements in the Maysville Road Bill, his attack on and destruction of the Second U.S. Bank, and his assertion of Federal supremacy over the threat of nullification in South Carolina: all these major actions demonstrated the variety of sources of power at the disposal of the Chief Executive. After Jackson and because of Jackson, the Presidency was a far more potent element in the system of organized power we call the government.

Yet whatever consequences Jackson's Presidency had for the expansion of the power of the office, Jackson's whole intention was to strip government of power. He may have acted powerfully to achieve his ends, but his ends were negative in the sense of attempting to deny positive power to the national government. The rationale underlying removals from those offices within the power of the President's appointment was to destroy the possibility of the existence of a corps of permanent professionals who would have a vested interest in the offices of government. The veto, by definition, was to prevent action by the legislative branch. The Maysville Road veto was to get the national government out of the business of internal improvements within the particular states. The attack on the Bank was to separate the government from the business of banking as well as to see to it that the government did not create an artificial monopoly in a trade which, the Jacksonians thought, should be open to entry and competition like any other business. The only positive action Jackson took on a major issue was the elemental one of preserving the Union, the nation itself, against the threat of dissolution into the petty principalities of the separate states.

The paradox of Jackson's administration appears whenever power is used to destroy power. In acting to whittle away the power of the national government, Jackson greatly enlarged the power of his office and schooled subsequent presidents on the potent dimensions of their place in government. Analogies are always dangerous, but the Jacksonian program does bear analogy to the communist theory of the dictatorship in behalf of the proletariat where, ideally, the power of the state is seized and used with intense vigor in order to realize the harmonious society, free from social conflict, in which the state then withers away because it has achieved its mission. One is, of course, rightly uneasy with the analogy because there is a basic difference between Marxist ideology and Jacksonian democratic ideology. For the Marxist, the ideal community in which the free development of each individual is compatible with the development of all individuals is to be arrived at, to be won, only at the end of the unfolding of history. A disciplined group seizes the power of the state to create the conditions in which the state is unnecessary. What remains after success is what the Jacksonians dreamed of: simple administration of a few essentials. But for the Jacksonians, as for all classical liberals, the ideal community was to be recovered. The ideal society of individuals free from external restraint was to be the premise of history, not its conclusion.[24] The world was not to be made simple and harmonious. It *was* simple and harmonious. The job of government was negative in the sense that it need not act to create the good society; it needed only keep a sharp eye on and check those who might corrupt the good society.

[24]For further discussion of the point, see my article, "Mill, Marx, and Modern Individualism," *Virginia Quarterly Review*, XXXV (Autumn, 1959), 527–39.

In the history of American political thought the Jacksonians are rightly placed in the Jeffersonian tradition of strict construction of the Constitution. If only Americans would remain true to the wisdom of the founding fathers, if only Americans would resist the seductions of power, public or private, if only Americans would purify their system from the corruptions which tend to stain it, then American Democracy would last "through countless ages of the future."[25] The accent has persisted in American politics: looking nostalgically backward to a golden past, Americans press energetically into an auspicious future. But the animating source of the Jacksonian faith was not simply the fundamental law of a man-made political constitution; it was no less than a cosmic constitutionalism, a belief in a fundamental law which pervaded all reality, natural and social, which was made not by man but which was there in the very structure of the universe, and which would manifest itself inevitably if man did not pervert it by his actions.

"Afford but the single nucleus of a system of administration of justice between man and man," O'Sullivan argued in support of his principle of freedom from the coercive power of the state, "and, under the sure operation of this principle, the floating atoms will distribute and combine themselves, as we see in the beautiful natural process of crystallization, into a far more perfect and harmonious result than if government, with its 'fostering hand,' undertake to disturb, under the plea of directing, the process. The natural laws which will establish themselves and find their own level are the best laws. The same hand was the Author of the moral, as of the physical world; and we feel clear and strong in the assurance that we cannot err in trusting, in the former, to the same fundamental principles of spontaneous action and self-regulation which produce the beautiful order of the latter."

This was the "principle" which constituted the Jacksonian "point of departure": "This is the fundamental principle of the philosophy of democracy, to furnish a system of administration of justice, and then leave all the business and interests of society to themselves, to free competition and association—in a word, to the VOLUNTARY PRIN- CIPLE." What had worked so well in religion would work just as well in all areas of social life. If government refused to intervene, if government were "sifted and analyzed down to the lowest point of simplicity consistent with the preservation of some degree [!] of national organization," then the result would be "the best possible result of general order and happiness."[26]

In O'Sullivan's argument, the imagery of the perfect crystal is Newtonian. When he writes that the principle of freedom from government "is borrowed from the example of the perfect self-government of the

[25]*Democratic Review*, I, 1.
[26]*Democratic Review*, I, 7.

physical universe, being written in letters of light on every page of the great bible of Nature," he is reading from a different book of nature than, say, his contemporaries, Emerson and Thoreau. But he is with them in believing that the utmost freedom for each individual is a "great moral truth," and, even more importantly, he is with them in believing that spontaneous action and self-regulation by each member in society is the only and proper road to the good society.[27]

Alfred North Whitehead has written that "every philosophy is tinged with the coloring of some secret imaginative background, which never emerges explicitly into its train of reasoning."[28] The secret imaginative background which made it possible for Jacksonian political philosophy to come to the astonishing conclusion that America had no need for politics was a fervent belief in a fundamental law in the universe, a cosmic constitutionalism, which made it unnecessary for man to plan for, create, and achieve the good society. Further, this fundamental law was reached by the "instinctive perception" of the mass of the people.[29] Once man was freed from the "artificial institutions" of society, he would "walk abroad through the free creation in [his] own majesty.' "[30] As George Sidney Camp put it, "a republic is not so correctly a form of government as it is the supremacy of principle. Forms of government have been, for the most part, only so many various modes of tyranny. Where the people are everything, and political forms, establishments, institutions, as opposed to the people, nothing, there and there only is liberty; such a state, and such a state only, constitutes republican government, the fundamental principle of which is not a human invention, but results from the leaving untrammelled by human devices the just and natural relations of man to man."[31] No less than with Transcendentalism and Protestant Evangelical Revivalism, the secret spring of the political faith of the early nineteenth century lay in the trust that the ideal society was to be reached by turning away from the actual institutions of society and allowing the "just and natural" relations of man to man to appear.

III

Democratic thought of the early nineteenth century has many curious turnings. The constant celebration of the People and the instinctive wisdom of the average man seems to point toward what Tocqueville

[27]*Democratic Review*, I, 8.

[28]Alfred North Whitehead, *Science and the Modern World* (New York: Signet edition, n.d.), pp. 49–50.

[29]*Democratic Review*, I, 13.

[30]*Democratic Review*, I, 11.

[31]Camp, *Democracy*, pp. 161–62.

called the "tyranny of the majority," an egalitarian populism in which the many run roughshod over the one. But the conclusion turns out to be a world in which power, even the power of the many, disappears and in its place we have the happy concourse of the individual wills of manly, independent American Democrats acting on the "natural moral principles" infused into them by their creator for their own "self-development and self-regulation."[32] Similarly, the ideology of simplicity would seem to imply a sociology of simplicity, that is, a relatively uncomplicated social world of self-sufficient individuals living in a providentially determined and easy harmony one with another. But that is not the conclusion reached.

At one point in his exposition of the democratic principle of freedom from the restraint of government, John L. O'Sullivan speaks with an "honest, manly contempt" of "the pretensions of those self-styled 'better classes' to the sole possession of the requisite intelligence for the management of public affairs." He bases his contempt, first, on the pragmatic ground that the "general diffusion of education" in the United States makes the requisite intelligence available to all classes of men. Then, however, he goes on to say: "As far as superior knowledge and talent confer on their possessor a natural charter of privilege to control his associates, and exert an influence on the direction of the general affairs of the community, the free and natural action of that privilege is best secured by a perfectly free democratic system, which will abolish all artificial distinctions, and, preventing the accumulation of any social obstacles to advancement, will permit the free development of every germ of talent, wherever it may chance to exist, whether on the proud mountain summit, in the humble valley, or by the wayside of common life."[33] As always in Jacksonian rhetoric, the critical words here are "natural" and "artificial." If the organization and institutions of society do not confer on some an "artificial" advantage, such as legislative charters which grant a favored position in the market, there will still be privilege, but it will be a "natural" charter of privilege to wield power, to "control" one's associates and direct the affairs of the community. Having wiped the social slate clean of artificial lines of distinction, the American Democrat begins an anxious race to prove he is naturally a good deal more equal than his fellows.

George Sidney Camp, in his definition of liberty as that society in which the people are everything and "political forms, establishments, institutions" nothing, was careful to avoid the suggestion that those who held his view were "levellers." On the contrary, as he insisted more than once, "Republicans do not contend for the annihilation of social distinc-

[32]*Democratic Review*, I, 11.
[33]*Democratic Review*, I, 4–5.

tions"; "Republicans are . . . for distinctions and inequalities."[34] Camp thought "the 'I'm-as-good-as-you principle' " was not correctly understood. "When we say that all men are by nature equal," he explained, "we mean nothing more than that all are by nature equal in their moral attributes—equally moral and accountable beings—and, therefore, equally entitled to the regulation of their own conduct, as that is the basis of moral accountability; therefore, all by nature equally entitled to exercise their own government, privately and publicly, socially and politically."[35] But there would still be "just distinctions" among men. "If one man has a more inventive genius, a more comprehensive prudence, a more enlarged experience, a more scrupulous integrity than another, what is the natural, I may say, the inevitable consequence, from the possession of such superior qualities? He possesses superior power and influence." He has, in O'Sullivan's words "a natural charter of privilege"; as Camp put it, not "from the arbitrary force of circumstances, or the coercive power of human laws."[36] "Nature" would, by "her own means, effect the same harmony of ranks and orders in society which she has so successfully achieved in the vegetable and animal creation." So, a republican government was to achieve "the proper divisions of rank and grade in society" by leaving "the matter entirely to the regulation of itself." It was by assuming the moral equality of all men and then leaving them to their own devices that "you increase, as much as human means can, the force of [a man's] moral motives and the energy of his active powers."[37]

In a chapter devoted to "Aristocratic Society in America," Camp pointed out that there was, properly speaking, no aristocracy in the strict sense of government by the few in the United States; he preferred not even to use the word to describe American society but did so, grudgingly, since it was "in use." If by aristocracy, however, one meant, in the more general sense of the word, "discrimination of ranks in society," there was nothing in democracy incompatible with the notion, "so long as that discrimination is voluntarily made by individuals." Democracy has borne the "obloquy of cherishing a levelling spirit and aiming at agrarian measures" but this was, one "cannot too often repeat, a mistaken notion as to the kind of equality that a democracy demands, which is not an equality in the circumstances, but an equality in the rights of mankind. In utterly repudiating all distinction in political rights, it admits freely of every other distinction, to the most absolute and unqualified extent. It destroys arbitrary and fictitious, to make room for real rank."[38]

[34]Camp, *Democracy*, pp. 133, 136.
[35]Camp, *Democracy*, p. 133.
[36]Camp, *Democracy*, p. 135.
[37]Camp, *Democracy*, p. 136–38.
[38]Camp, *Democracy*, pp. 220–21.

It is a commonplace in the history of political ideas to draw a sharp distinction between equality and liberty. To maintain the equality of all men implies an abridgement of the liberty of some men; to allow the liberty of all men implies an eventual inequality between some men. Democratic political thought of the early nineteenth century attempted to yoke the two, to maintain what analytically may seem a contradiction, by confining the notion of equality to the political dimension of life on the ground that it created the greatest possible liberty in the social dimension of life. Whether the political and social dimensions can be so neatly isolated one from the other can reasonably be doubted, but the Jacksonian notion ran that if each individual was made equal before the law, and if organized power in the form of governmental intervention in the society did not create artificial advantages, then each individual was set free to make what he could of himself. If, at first glance, the democratic thought of the time seems to offer the ideal of a simple, naturally harmonious society, at second glance, it reveals an intensely busy, competitive society.

To a later generation, accustomed to the assumption that a rough degree of social and economic equality must exist to make democracy a viable form of government, it is hard to catch the accent of political idealism in early American democratic thought. The argument did not run that economic and social conditions create a certain kind of personality which, in turn, makes possible a characteristic form of government. Quite the opposite. The form of government, rather than an epiphenomenon of the material base of society, was itself the dynamic source of change which transformed the rest of society. "The liberty that republics afford to all men of every rank of governing themselves," asserted Camp, "elevates their characters, and qualifies them for self-government. The elevation which this freedom confers on people of the lowest station, stimulates to a degree of self-improvement."[39] Freedom would create the personality appropriate to the conditions of freedom and, as a by-blow, release the energies which would lead to self-improvement and industrious activity.

The notion was a common one. Frederick Grimke, in the best single contemporary book on the political thought of the period, *Consideration Upon the Nature and Tendency of Free Institutions* (1848), pointed out that "even in America we can discern a well-defined line between the higher and lower orders of men. Free institutions do not obliterate the distinctions; on the contrary, they are eminently favorable to the accumulation of wealth in private hands, since they add to the natural gift of some, the further advantage of opportunity, and the protection of a system of laws which is equal and invariable in its operation. It is like

---

39Camp, *Democracy*, p. 141.

the addition of a new faculty to some men." Grimke, speaking out of the tradition of Lockean faculty psychology, is making an extravagant analogy here. Free institutions create new personalities by calling into being new "faculties" among men. The result is that "the resolute, the enterprising, and the industrious, move forward with rapidity."[40] Grimke argued that "the principle of equality may very well be recognized as the rule among men as citizens—as members of a political community, although as individuals there may be very great and numerous inequalities between them. The utmost which the citizen can demand is that no law shall be passed to obstruct his rise, and to impede his progress through life. He has then an even chance with all his fellows. If he does not become their equal his case is beyond the reach of society, and to complain would be to quarrel with his own nature."[41] Free institutions had the double merit of stirring men into activity and then refusing to intervene to erase the natural distinctions which would arise. Government was to be limited in its activity to that of umpire in an equal contest on an open field because of the belief that "the improvement of our condition, whether intellectual or physical, depends infinitely more upon our own independent exertions, than upon all other circumstances put together."[42]

IV

The appropriate symbol for the political thought of the early nineteenth century would be Janus, the god who faces both ways, looking backward and forward. With one face, early democratic thought looks backward in time to a simple order of society, free from the unnecessary institutions which corrupt the arcadian world of independent individuals related one to another only through the moral order in which each participates. With the other face, it looks forward to a busy, competitive, expansive society in which energetic individuals are constantly on the make. Yet, despite the different worlds which each face looks upon, in each the solitary, self-reliant individual stands at the center of the social order.

In his "Farewell Address" to the American people on March 4, 1837, Andrew Jackson spoke to the great mass of the people who constituted his following and for whom he had acted: "The planter, the farmer, the mechanic, and the laborer all know that their success depends upon their

---

[40]Frederick Grimke, *Considerations Upon the Nature and Tendency of Free Institutions* (Cincinnati and New York, 1848), p. 459.

[41]Grimke, *Free Institutions*, p. 53.

[42]Grimke, *Free Institutions*, p. 459.

own industry and economy and that they must not expect to become suddenly rich by the fruits of their toil. Yet these classes of society form the great body of the people of the country; they are the bone and sinew of the country—men who love liberty and desire nothing but equal rights and equal laws, and who, moreover, hold the great mass of our national wealth, although it is distributed in moderate amounts among the millions of freemen who possess it."[43] It was for a world defined by these millions of simple, hard-working folk that Jackson had restricted government to its limited tasks, attacked artificial monopolies of wealth, and resisted "extravagant schemes" of governmental action. Speaking to them directly, Jackson's last counsel as their leader was to say, "If you are true to yourselves nothing can impede your march to the highest point of national prosperity."[44] The worth of the Constitution, Jackson thought, was "in the security it gives to life, liberty, character and property."[45] To the conventional trinity, Jackson added "character." If the great mass of manly, independent American Democrats, acting for themselves, were not seduced by the expectation of becoming "suddenly rich," if the people did not "withdraw their attention from the sober pursuits of honest industry,"[46] then a pure and simple government would be sufficient for a pure and simple people.

But they were a people, in Jackson's words, pressing forward in the "march to the highest point of national prosperity." There are many ironies in American history, but surely one of the most massive is that the ideal of a simple, uncomplicated society based solely upon the character of men strong enough to remain true to their best selves found its most persuasive political voice at precisely the moment we have come to name the "take-off period" of economic and industrial growth, the full emergence of a society committed to wealth and power. The hero of that enterprise, too, was a self-reliant man. "Ours is a country," wrote Calvin Colton, speaking for the Whigs, in 1844, "where men start from an humble origin . . . and where they can attain to the most elevated positions, or acquire a large amount of wealth, according to the pursuits they elect for themselves. No exclusive privileges of birth, no entailment of estates, no civil or political disqualifications, stand in their path; but one has as good a chance as another, according to his talents, prudence or personal exertions. This is a country of self-made men, than which nothing better could be said of any society."[47] The enigma which lies at the

43Richardson, *Messages and Papers*, III, 305.
44Richardson, *Messages and Papers*, III, 294.
45Richardson, *Messages and Papers*, III, 297.
46Richardson, *Messages and Papers*, III, 302.
47Calvin Colton, *The Junius Tracts*, VII (1844), 15.

heart of the political thought of the early nineteenth century is whether the American Democrat it had in view was the self-sufficient character of Emerson's ideal and Jackson's rhetoric or the self-made man on the make, desiring only a natural charter of privilege which would not impede his march to great wealth. Or was he one and the same person?

W. DAVID LEWIS
State University of New York at Buffalo

the reformer as conservative: protestant counter-subversion in the early republic

One of the most striking features to be observed in the history of American reform movements is the great diversity of ideas and impulses by which reformers have been impelled. It is sometimes tempting, however, to lose sight of this fundamental complexity and think of reformers in terms of stereotypes. At one extreme is the selfless humanitarian, willing to brave any danger for a worthy cause. At the other is the deluded fanatic or impractical dreamer, creating all sorts of difficulties for sensible persons who must bear the burden of managing affairs in an inevitably imperfect world. Or there is the reformer who acts as the conscious or unconscious agent of selfish interests. However valid such facile impressions may be in individual cases, they can seriously distort the past if carelessly applied, for human motives are seldom—if ever—simple. This is as true in evaluating the influence of religion upon reform, with which this essay is primarily concerned, as it is in other cases.

In examining the history of reform movements, therefore, it is well to analyze the influence of specific impulses and beware of hasty generalizations. Yet, if it is dangerous to oversimplify the aims and motives of reformers, it is also desirable and fruitful to look for common ideas and traditions which have been shared by like-minded persons, or for recurrent impulses at work in a particular nation or culture over extended periods of time. Perhaps more deeply than most people, reformers are strongly influenced by what is going on around them. Indeed, it is because they perceive—or think they perceive—certain conditions or trends with abnormal clarity that they are impelled to take part in various ameliorative causes. In view of this receptivity, it is logical to suppose that the existence of broad patterns of thought or climates of opinion in given historical eras will be reflected in the activities and pronouncements of individual reformers, each manifesting in his own way certain paramount ideas or concerns of the time in which he lives. This approach does not deny the existence of diverse aims and motives in any period, nor overlook continuities between one era and the next. It merely suggests that some impulses may appear more strongly in certain historical contexts than in others.

Like various other historical phenomena, reform movements can be seen to occur in cycles, each of which manifests a characteristic pattern. For example, some periods have been deeply affected by a concern for the individual, while others show the influence of organic group-consciousness.[1] Similarly, some eras display a strong receptivity to change, while others reveal a desire for stability and order. This essay lends support to the views of recent scholars who have seen that reform efforts can stem from what are customarily called "conservative" impulses as well as from what might be considered "liberal" or "radical" ones.

Cyclical trends are observable in the reform movements which flourished in antebellum America. The era of the American Revolution, for example, manifests the impact of closely associated impulses. The idea of natural rights had obvious applications in various areas of life, as did the doctrine that all men are created equal, with its corollary that

---

[1]For an interesting analysis in this regard see John L. Thomas, "Romantic Reform in America, 1815–1865," *American Quarterly*, XVII, 4 (Winter, 1965), 656–81. The cyclical view of American history, especially in political matters, is perhaps most closely associated with the work of the late Arthur M. Schlesinger, Sr.; see particularly his book *Paths to the Present* (New York, 1949), pp. 77–92. However, Schlesinger's book *The American As Reformer* (Cambridge, Mass., 1951), as well as Alice Felt Tyler's *Freedom's Ferment: Phases of American Social History to 1860* (Minneapolis, 1944), suffers from a tendency to see reformers only in a "liberal" perspective, without realizing that "reformer" and "conservative" are not necessarily antithetical terms. The same deficiency exists in the Introduction to Henry Steele Commager's book of source materials entitled *The Era of Reform, 1830–1860* (Princeton, N. J., 1960), except that the "liberal" view does happen to fit that particular three-decade period better than it does some other eras.

artificial distinctions among human beings are wrong. The full implications of these concepts were not quickly or completely translated into action, but their influence was clearly evident in measures taken to separate church and state, to abolish primogeniture and entail, and to outlaw slavery.[2] Reforms like these also drew upon the ideas of eighteenth-century rationalists who demanded an end to social practices based upon mere superstition and credulity or blind reverence for the past. In addition, this era witnessed the flowering of a religious and humanitarian outlook that had been gaining strength in England among members of the Society of Friends, the followers of John Wesley, and the associates of the noted Anglican minister Dr. Thomas Bray. Exemplified in the work of such men as the great prison reformer John Howard, this type of Christian concern provided much of the impetus for efforts in America by men like Thomas Eddy and Episcopal bishop William White to improve the treatment of criminals and the mentally ill.[3] And although strong conservative trends were evident during the 1790's, the outbreak and progress of the French Revolution inspired sympathetic Americans to struggle for a wider application of civil liberties and to intensify their efforts for such objectives as women's rights and equal educational opportunities for the poor.[4]

Turning from the late eighteenth century to the decades just before the Civil War, one can observe various similarities in the reforms that flourished during these two eras, as well as equally important differences. Certainly a deep concern for human equality helped motivate the antislavery efforts of men like William Lloyd Garrison and the feminist crusade of Elizabeth Cady Stanton and Susan B. Anthony. The struggle for free public education carried on by such leaders as Stephen Simpson, Horace Mann, and Robert Rantoul, Jr. can be seen in part as a logical extension of principles espoused in an earlier day by Thomas Jefferson, and the activities of Dorothea Dix on behalf of the insane and other social deviates remind one of previous efforts by such men as Thomas

---

[2]J. Franklin Jameson, *The American Revolution Considered as a Social Movement* (Princeton, N. J., 1940), pp. 21–26, 37, 83–91 and *passim*. In his article, "The American Revolution Considered as a Social Movement: A Re-Evaluation," *American Historical Review*, LX, 1 (October, 1954), pp. 1–12, Frederick B. Tolles points out that the significance of such reforms can be exaggerated, especially because some of the institutions which were abolished or attacked were of only vestigial importance by the time of the Revolution. Nevertheless, it is pertinent to note that some of these changes were effected only after protracted struggles in the states involved. See for example Merrill Jensen, *The New Nation: A History of the United States During the Confederation, 1781–1789,* Vintage ed. (New York, 1965), pp. 131–36.

[3]See especially W. David Lewis, *From Newgate to Dannemora: The Rise of the Penitentiary in New York, 1796–1848* (Ithaca, N. Y., 1965), pp. 1–28.

[4]Eugene Perry Link, *Democratic-Republican Societies, 1790–1800* (New York, 1942), *passim*, particularly pp. 156–74.

Eddy. The fact that Eddy belonged to the Society of Friends suggests another similarity between the two periods, for Quakers like James and Lucretia Mott, Dr. Thomas Kirkbride, and Richard Vaux were active in pre-Civil War attempts to free the slave, elevate the status of women, improve the treatment of the mentally ill, and provide better care for prisoners.[5] Yet the reform activities of the late antebellum period also show the impact of new influences, like romanticism, transcendentalism, Christian perfectionism, anarchism, and utopianism, which were either totally absent or at best weakly felt in the late eighteenth century. Nor are these differences surprising, for the dynamic, mobile, and rapidly growing America of the 1840's and 1850's was hardly the same as the young republic which had existed two generations before.

In the broadest sense, however, the reform currents of the Revolutionary era and the late antebellum period were similar in that they revealed strong impulses to question previous ways of doing things, to experiment with radical ideas, and to welcome social change. But reformers are not always so receptive to the unfamiliar. As scholars like Clifford S. Griffin and Charles I. Foster have shown, they can be animated by doubts and fears as well as by hopes, by desires to preserve as well as propensities toward change, by yearnings for the past as well as visions of the future.[6] The existence of reform cycles dominated by such

[5] Citations from the vast literature on the abolitionist movement in general and Garrison in particular would be superfluous here, but for a useful general survey see Louis Filler, *The Crusade Against Slavery, 1830–1860* (New York, 1960). For varying points of view on the female rights movement, see Eleanor Flexner, *Century of Struggle* (Cambridge, Mass., 1959); Robert E. Riegel, *American Feminists* (Lawrence, Kansas, 1963); and Andrew Sinclair, *The Better Half: The Emancipation of the American Woman* (New York, 1965). Selections from the writings and speeches on free public education by Simpson, Mann, and Rantoul can be conveniently found in George E. Probst, ed., *The Happy Republic: A Reader in Tocqueville's America* (New York, 1962), pp. 419–39. On the activities of the Motts, Kirkbride, and Richard Vaux, see Ira V. Brown, *Pennsylvania Reformers from Penn to Pinchot* (University Park, Pa., 1966), pp. 7, 31, and 34. Vaux was the son of Roberts Vaux, an important penal reformer of the late eighteenth and early nineteenth centuries.

[6] The works toward which attention is chiefly directed here are Clifford S. Griffin, *Their Brothers' Keepers: Moral Stewardship in the United States, 1800–1850* (New Brunswick, N. J., 1960), and Charles I. Foster, *An Errand of Mercy: The Evangelical United Front, 1790–1837* (Chapel Hill, N. C., 1960). See also Griffin's article, "Religious Benevolence as Social Control, 1815–1860," *Mississippi Valley Historical Review*, XLIV, 3 (December, 1957), pp. 423–44. I greatly admire Griffin's work, but believe that the social control motivations he describes are less helpful for understanding reform developments after about 1830 than they are for explaining prevailing tendencies prior to that time. Foster, it seems to me, shows acute perception in ending his study in the 1830's, which I regard as a decade of transition into a period dominated by new reform impulses. Although my essay had been substantially completed before the appearance of a book of readings on pre-Civil War reform recently published by David B. Davis, I concur with the implications of his statement that "Few subjects

impulses is readily understandable, for periods of marked change and upheaval lead naturally to desires for a return to stability and order. The influence of such desires can be observed by examining in detail the period between the Revolutionary era and the onset of the Jacksonian age.

During the closing years of the eighteenth century, a number of Protestant clergymen and lay leaders launched a vigorous effort to overcome forces of immorality, infidelity, and instability which they believed to be widespread throughout the United States. The existence of a relatively large number of books and articles by recent and contemporary historians who have studied this phenomenon makes it possible to examine the movement in detail and to assess its importance in the development of American culture. Viewed in one perspective, it can be seen as a stage in the long and sometimes painful process of adjustment that took place as church and state were separated in a democratic society. In yet another light, it illustrates the influence of mingled hopes, doubts, and fears fostered by the rapid internal development of a young nation striking out on new political, social, and economic paths. And it helps illuminate the long-range impact of certain moral and religious beliefs deeply imbedded in America's colonial past.

To be properly understood, therefore, this movement must be seen in a broad cultural perspective. This poses problems, for it must be acknowledged at the outset that the relationship of religion to social reform is a subject surrounded by potential pitfalls. It is deceptively easy, for example, to assume a crudely functional position which makes religious ideas and practices mere tools in the hands of self-interested groups or classes, and to ignore the possibility that the religious life possesses an inner vitality of its own. As David B. Davis has pointed out, "the great object of American revivalists from Jonathan Edwards to Billy Graham has not been to perfect society but to save men's souls by arousing them to full awareness of their involvement in sin."[7] And Sidney Mead has reminded us that, in a modern world deeply permeated by scepticism on religious matters, it is misleadingly tempting to impute ulterior motives to people who, in an age of belief, were capable of actions stemming from a sincere and overpowering "experience of God."[8]

---

in American history are in such need of rigorous analysis as the interrelationship of specific reform movements and the transition from an evangelical drive for social control to a romantic and humanitarian crusade for liberty, uplift, and social justice." See Davis, ed., *Ante-Bellum Reform* (New York, 1967), Introduction, p. 9. Like Davis, I also recognize the conceptual inadequacies of terms like "conservative," "liberal," and "radical" in analyzing reform movements, but I have no better ones to propose.

[7]Davis, *Ante-Bellum Reform*, Introduction, p. 6.

[8]Sidney E. Mead, *Nathaniel William Taylor, 1786–1858: A Connecticut Liberal* (Chicago, 1942), pp. 58–9.

On the other hand, it would be completely unrealistic to maintain that religious and secular ideas have existed in sealed compartments and exerted no influence upon one another. The Gospel emphasis upon loving one's neighbor has been a potent source of reform ideas, as has the Quaker conviction that all men possess a share of the divine "inner light" which can be reached and nurtured in the worst of human beings. In another vein, the Judaeo-Christian concept of a just God has periodically inspired victims of oppression, whether individually or in groups, to rebel against conditions that seemed plainly at variance with Biblical precepts. Christian millennialism has also had an important bearing upon reform. Ernst Troeltsch has indicated that a belief in the imminence of Christ's return weakened the desire of the early church to rectify earthly conditions which were soon destined to pass away; he has also shown that a far different result was produced in later times by a belief that men could prepare the way for the second coming by establishing, so far as lay within their ability, a secular order consistent with the Savior's teachings.[9]

For a proper understanding of reform efforts by American Protestants in the late eighteenth and early nineteenth centuries, however, it is especially pertinent to note the impact of influences associated with New England Puritanism. Calvinist in theology, Puritans believed in an all-powerful and all-sovereign God who before time began had arbitrarily predestined certain individuals to salvation and others to eternal damnation. Although it was difficult to determine who belonged to the elect and who did not, it was believed that one might gain reasonably conclusive evidence by examining one's life and behavior for signs of a conscious willingness to serve as an instrument for the realization of divine purposes. The agony of mind and spirit which was endured by persons who were desperately eager to believe that they were among those predestined to be saved was capable of producing an intense, driving activism in the affairs of everyday life. It was logical to believe that people who had been singled out by God to be special recipients of His grace also had a mandate to govern the affairs of men, and this attitude was therefore capable of producing a distinctively paternalistic reform impulse.

Yet to see only the authoritarian aspects of Puritanism in its bearing upon social reform would be to oversimplify and distort the past. One must also acknowledge that many elements of Calvinist thought in early New England, such as individualism, an emphasis upon a higher law superior to the claims of earthly powers and institutions, and a belief that divine grace was visited upon persons irrespective of social class or

---

[9]Ernst Troeltsch, *The Social Teaching of the Christian Churches*, Olive Wyon, trans. (2 vols.: New York, 1931), *passim.*

station, were of a liberalizing and democratic tendency. Similarly, the idea that education must be available to all citizens in a Bible-reading commonwealth was a characteristic tenet of Puritan leaders. Nor should it be forgotten that, although many aspects of Puritanism may seem harsh by modern standards, it possessed a "moral vigor," to use Clinton Rossiter's words, which contributed a healthy sense of communal responsibility to the development of American democracy.[10]

Although the moral earnestness characteristic of Calvinism was manifested in the middle Atlantic and southern colonies by Scotch-Irish Presbyterians and other groups, these never brought about a church-state alliance, in part because of the prior arrival of other settlers and the fact that Anglicanism was already established in many colonies. The case was different in New England, however, where Puritan Congregationalists were first on the scene and able to implement their plans for a model Biblical commonwealth in the American wilderness.

In such colonies as Connecticut and Massachusetts, church and state were tightly connected. Political power was reserved for those who possessed membership in a congregation, and this was in turn extended only to "visible saints" who could give satisfactory evidence of having experienced saving grace.[11] The connection between religion and the secular order was rationalized at every level in terms of a complicated "federal theology" involving a series of covenants between believers and God on an individual plane, between congregations and God on a group basis, and between the entire commonwealth and God on a still broader plane.[12] It was believed that God had chosen the New England settlements for the realization of special purposes just as He had once set apart the Hebrew nation; and the faithful were urged constantly to examine not only their own lives, but also those of their neighbors, in an effort to ensure that the conduct of the community would conform as closely as possible to Scriptural teaching.

Despite the tightly-knit character of the theocracy which had thus been established, it proved difficult to maintain indefinitely the type of piety which Puritan leaders desired. This was particularly true after the first generation of settlement, in which common recollections of persecution in the mother country and the shared hardships of emigration promoted a degree of group cohesion which was never fully recaptured. Anxiety about sinful behavior among the inhabitants mounted as worldliness became more widespread and fewer persons

[10]Clinton Rossiter, *The First American Revolution* (New York, 1956), p. 94.

[11]For an illuminating discussion of this particular aspect of Puritan thought, see Edmund Morgan, *Visible Saints: The History of A Puritan Idea* (New York, 1963).

[12]The covenant theology is analyzed at length in Perry Miller, *The New England Mind: The Seventeenth Century* (New York, 1939), pp. 365–462.

sought congregational membership; in turn, worried ministers developed a distinctive type of sermon known as the "jeremiad," which warned that a chosen people who became guilty of backsliding could expect visitations of divine wrath. In addition, some clergymen, like Solomon Stoddard, deliberately relaxed standards of admission to the church, reasoning that if people were to be spiritually awakened it was necessary to keep as many of them as possible fully affiliated and thus potentially susceptible to religious teaching.[13]

With the spreading of special efforts to induce repentance and public rededication, a pattern of American revivalism gradually took shape, appearing sporadically from the late seventeenth century onward and bursting into flame during the celebrated "Great Awakening" that began in the 1730's. Seasons of mass anxiety and conversion heartened many religious leaders, but caused others to recoil when it was observed that excesses of enthusiasm posed no less of a danger to established institutions than had the indifference of an earlier day. Some groups of "awakened" persons split away from their previous congregations to join sectarian denominations or set up schismatic bodies of their own, often emphasizing the direct operation of divine grace to the point of denying the need for an educated clergy. The sermons of certain incendiary preachers, notably James Davenport, led to such outbursts of mob action as a book burning episode in Connecticut that seemed to presage assaults by the rabble upon existing social and economic arrangements. Endeavoring to shut what had proved to be a Pandora's box, various ministers wrote antirevival treatises and succeeded in dampening the fires of excitement at least temporarily.[14] In the future, the standing clergy would have to learn how to arouse spiritual renewal without endangering the security of the established order.

This dilemma, which is important for an understanding of the conservative reform efforts of the early national period, became ever more critical throughout the remainder of the eighteenth century, for spiritual indifference and ungodly behavior increased while the church became less and less capable of preserving its traditional role in society. Attendance at divine worship fell off in the late colonial era, and

[13]These and other developments are discussed in Perry Miller, *The New England Mind from Colony to Province* (Cambridge, Mass., 1953). For a newer work challenging the traditional interpretation of declension in New England churches and discussing more fully the innovations in church membership made in the second half of the seventeenth century, see Robert G. Pope, *The Half-Way Covenant: Church Membership in Puritan New England* (Princeton, N. J., 1969), which appeared after this essay was completed.

[14]See especially Edwin S. Gaustad, *The Great Awakening in New England* (New York, 1957), and C. C. Goen, *Revivalism and Separatism in New England, 1740–1800: Strict Congregationalists and Separate Baptists in the Great Awakening* (New Haven, Conn., 1962), *passim*.

ministers worried about the growing influence of Deism in popular thought. Then came the Revolutionary years, accompanied by governmental instability, economic confusion, and complaints of excessive gambling, drinking, cursing, and lewdness amid the unsettling conditions which inevitably followed the movements of armed forces about the countryside. Next appeared the troubled postwar period, with depression stimulating discontent among lower-class and debtor elements, while further evidence of declining public morality aroused bitter complaints among clergymen like Timothy Dwight of Connecticut and Jedediah Morse of Massachusetts. The outbreak of the French Revolution intensified such anxieties, for it was now feared that subversive groups influenced by Jacobinism and other alien doctrines were plotting the overthrow of American institutions and poisoning the country with insidious propaganda. The growing strength of the Republican party under Thomas Jefferson also contributed to clerical concern, especially in New England. Considered a vehicle for atheism and French ideas, its presidential victory in 1800 seemed to many pious citizens to indicate that a veritable day of doom was at hand.[15]

Imbued with ever mounting apprehensions, various Protestant leaders in New England and elsewhere began, during the closing years of the eighteenth century, to organize a powerful reform movement to counter the undesirable influences which they detected in American life. The task was not easy, for in some parts of the country certain denominations were engaged in a difficult process of reorganization following the breaking of former administrative ties with parent European bodies as a result of national independence. Anglicanism, though established by law in a number of colonies, had become increasingly enfeebled in the pre-Revolutionary years, and the Protestant Episcopal Church which succeeded it after independence struggled both with organizational problems and with popular prejudice in areas where Tories had been especially prominent among its members. Furthermore, not all denominations were strongly imbued with a sense of need for involvement in secular affairs, nor identified with classes having most to lose from the weakening of established institutions. It is therefore not surprising that

---

[15]Among older sources on the growth of ministerial fears during the Revolutionary and post-Revolutionary periods, see especially Charles E. Cuningham, *Timothy Dwight, 1752–1817* (New York, 1942), pp. 294–300, and Vernon Stauffer, *New England and the Bavarian Illuminati* (New York, 1918), pp. 13–141. For a more recent analysis, see Gary B. Nash, "The American Clergy and the French Revolution," *William and Mary Quarterly*, 3rd Ser., XXII, 3 (July, 1965), pp. 392–412. Nash argues cogently that vehement clerical attacks upon the French Revolution did not appear in the United States until 1794–1795, and were then prompted by rising tides of irreligion, social disorder, and Jeffersonian political activity in America itself rather than by the actual situation prevailing in Europe.

although the Protestant counteroffensive found support among prominent citizens in various parts of the country, it derived its main thrust
from New England, where the tradition of an established church still
survived, and where the clergy still enjoyed considerable power and
prestige in the sphere of secular, as well as sacred, concerns.

By the late eighteenth century, the religious tenets characteristic of
New England in the period preceding the Great Awakening had been
modified in various ways.   Some clerical leaders de-emphasized strict
predestinarian doctrines and were approaching a belief that God's grace
was available to all who would earnestly seek it.   Others, however,
followed the preaching of Samuel Hopkins in stressing God's total
sovereignty so much as to postulate that one must love Him to the point
of glorying in one's own damnation if this proved to be His will.   This
concept of "disinterested benevolence" had an important bearing upon
later reform movements, arousing an almost pathological self-abnegation
among some converts.   As Whitney Cross had pointed out, revivalists
were to draw on both of these new tendencies and breed of them "an
illogical, but effective, doctrine."[16]   To men like Dwight, it made tactical
sense to overlook "fine theological distinctions and subtleties" if this
would enable conservatives to unite more effectively against such menac-
ing forces as Jacobinism and infidelity.[17]   Nevertheless, doctrinal differences, though submerged, remained latent among defenders of the standing order and would return to plague the conservatives in the future.

Though clinging to an official church-state connection in New England, leaders of the Protestant reform movement had no thought of
attempting to secure such an arrangement in other parts of the country,
which would have been impossible anyway in view of adverse popular
sentiment and the existence of various constitutional safeguards.   This
did not mean, however, that there might not be achieved a strong
unofficial alliance between organized religion and the several levels of
government, particularly if political leaders who sympathized with the
objectives of Protestant spokesmen could be maintained in power.   Indeed, such an alliance seemed almost imperative to some clerical leaders
whose dislike of certain trends which were taking place in America did
not prevent them from sharing a good deal of the nationalism that was
emerging throughout the country at the time.   From the venerable ideas
of the federal covenant theology it was but a short step to the conviction
that the United States had been chosen by God for the achievement of
special purposes; but this meant also that it would feel the full force of

---

16Whitney Cross, *The Burned-over District: The Social and Intellectual History
of Enthusiastic Religion in Western New York, 1800–1850* (Ithaca, N. Y., 1950), pp.
27–28.
17Mead, *Nathaniel William Taylor*, p. 48.

His displeasure if it failed to live up to its divine commission. To minds influenced by such beliefs, it was inconceivable that organized religion should not have an important part to play in guiding the secular development of the young republic.[18]

Though confident that they were in league with the Almighty, Protestant reform leaders were under no illusions about the difficulties that lay in their path. For the better part of a generation, until the final downfall of Napoleon in 1815, they were acutely conscious of a grave international threat to the principles in which they believed. Even during this period, however, and for some time afterward, they were also intensely aware of the growth of egalitarian democracy at home, unrestrained by many of the barriers that existed in older, more aristocratic cultures. If this force could not be arrested—and it became increasingly clear that it could not—every effort would have to be made to inculcate within Americans a respect for order and propriety. This type of reform activity, if successful, would produce "inner controls" that might compensate for the wide external freedoms enjoyed by citizens of the United States. Otherwise, the result of unbridled popular rule could well be catastrophic.

These issues were portentous even in the well-established and long-civilized areas along the Atlantic Seaboard; but they were even more pressing in western regions to which increasing numbers of persons were migrating during the late eighteenth and early nineteenth centuries. New England was experiencing such an outpouring as early as the 1780's, and the exodus accelerated in the years that followed. Protestant leaders recognized that life in the newly opened areas lacked the restraining influence of many institutions that were taken for granted in the better-settled parts of the country, and feared a complete breakdown of established morals and amenities on the frontier unless immediate attempts were made to forestall it. A conviction that the fate of American democracy might well be decided by the outcome lent additional urgency to the struggle, accounting in large measure for the intensity with which western missionary ventures were organized and propagated by eastern congregations. Being adjacent to New England, upstate New York was a particularly favored target for such endeavors, and became the scene of so many enthusiasms and revivals that it earned the name of the "burned-over district."[19]

---

[18]A useful book on ministerial attitudes toward social problems during this period is John R. Bodo, *The Protestant Clergy and Public Issues, 1812–1848* (Princeton, N. J., 1954), on which I have drawn at a number of points. See also Charles C. Cole, Jr., *The Social Ideas of the Northern Evangelists, 1826–1860* (New York, 1954).

[19]Cross, *Burned-over District, passim.* Chapters I–VII, pp. 3–137, are particularly relevant to the concerns and activities here described.

The task of promoting civilization on the frontier, however, could hardly be performed if there was a further deterioration of manners and morals in the very citadels of organized Protestantism. To insure that this would not happen, religious leaders along the east coast launched a revival movement reminiscent of the earlier "Great Awakening." In Connecticut, for example, Congregationalist ministers turned to the tactics of their Puritan predecessors and preached somber jeremiads about prevailing wickedness, resulting in an early wave of revivals that reached its peak in the years 1797–1801. The desire to enkindle a moral renewal, however, was tempered by a remembrance of dangers that had appeared in the past. Mindful of the excesses which had taken place under such men as James Davenport, Connecticut clergymen made every effort to see that a desirable spiritual reinvigoration did not get out of bounds, to guard against the splintering of congregations, and to discourage violent outbursts of emotion. Whenever possible, revivals were conducted by resident pastors among their own flocks; when itinerant evangelists were needed, the choice fell upon soberly dignified men like Nathaniel Emmons and Asahel Nettleton. Under this careful type of approach, seasons of repentance and conversion took place regularly throughout the first three decades of the nineteenth century.[20]

Because of their realization that theological bickering would only weaken them in their fight against evil and subversive influences, Protestant reformers made a variety of moves to end unnecessary divisions and coordinate the activities of like-minded men on a national basis. The most significant step to be taken in this direction was the adoption of the widely hailed Plan of Union by New England Congregationalists and Presbyterians in other parts of the country, beginning in 1801. Negotiated by two groups which differed over organizational methods but shared a common Calvinist heritage, this arrangement applied to western areas into which Congregationalists and Presbyterians migrated, thus preventing wasteful duplication of effort. Another unity move took place in New England itself, where schisms within Calvinist ranks had facilitated the spread of Unitarianism. Bitterly hostile toward the latter, conservative leaders like Jedediah Morse were deeply chagrined when a lack of effective cooperation between Hopkinsians and "Old Calvinists" enabled the Unitarians to win the coveted Hollis professorship of divinity at Harvard in 1805. Partly as a result of this lesson, the two traditionalist groups joined forces by 1808 in the establishment of Andover Semi-

[20]For a detailed account of revivalism in Connecticut during this period, see Charles R. Keller, *The Second Great Awakening in Connecticut* (New Haven, Conn., 1942), pp. 36–69. On the consciously conservative nature of the tactics used, see also Bernard Weisberger, *They Gathered at the River: The Story of the Great Revivalists and Their Impact Upon Religion in America* (Boston, 1958), pp. 53–86.

nary in Massachusetts, which quickly became a leading center of conservative reform activity.[21] Princeton Seminary, founded shortly thereafter in New Jersey, and Auburn Theological Seminary, located in upstate New York, were similarly oriented.

The trend toward cooperation among Protestant groups, especially those of a conservative variety, was also exemplified in the formation of interdenominational societies patterned after English counterparts which had been organized to combat the spread of French Revolutionary ideas. Centered in the Anglican church, but maintaining a cooperative attitude toward various nonconformist denominations, a strong counter-subversionist movement had emerged in Britain during the late eighteenth century, attacking radical influences through the medium of such organizations as the Religious Tract Society, which issued inexpensive devotional literature to the masses; the British and Foreign Bible Society, which distributed copies of the Scriptures; the London Sunday-School Union, which helped overcome illiteracy and thus promoted the reading of religious materials; and the London Missionary Society, which spread the Gospel abroad and gave supporters the invigorating feeling of participating in a worldwide crusade. The example of these societies was quickly emulated in the New World by Protestant organizations which first appeared on the state and local level and were ultimately transformed into such large national ventures as the American Tract Society, the American Sunday School Union, the American Bible Society, and the American Home Missionary Society.[22]

Although these organizations welcomed members from various denominations, they were dominated by conservative leadership as represented by the Congregational, Presbyterian, Dutch Reformed, and Associated Reformed churches. In most of them, the bulk of official duties were performed by laymen, especially prominent politicians like Theodore Frelinghuysen of New Jersey and wealthy merchants like Robert Ralston of Philadelphia or Arthur and Lewis Tappan of New York. In some cases, the piety of Protestant businessmen was buttressed by a realization of the need for inculcating such virtues as sobriety, frugality, and diligence among the citizens of a country which was in the beginning stages of industrialization and which needed a dependable labor force as well as a maximum of saving in order to release capital for purposes of economic expansion. It is evident, too, that participation in the work of interdenominational societies and the reform organizations

---

21William W. Sweet, *Religion in the Development of American Culture, 1765–1840* (New York, 1952), pp. 99–102; Mead, *Nathaniel William Taylor*, pp. 129–30.

22Foster, *An Errand of Mercy*, previously cited, is particularly informing and detailed on the British counter-subversive movement and its influence upon similar developments in America.

that came to be associated with them provided an outlet for the energies of people who yearned to accomplish something of transcendent worth but found this impulse difficult to satisfy in an increasingly secularized social order. The growth of egalitarianism and the erosion of traditional class lines though feared by conservatives, also stimulated the development of benevolent and religious societies, for membership in these groups and collaboration with like-minded persons in a common cause created a sense of belonging that appealed strongly to individuals who felt uncertain about their status in the community at large. For various reasons, therefore, the Protestant campaign attracted widespread support among different types of people and quickly became a force of considerable power.[23]

The rise of tract, Bible, Sunday School, and missionary societies afforded means by which conservative reformers could inculcate piety among Americans in a general way. To such men, however, it was not sufficient merely to disseminate the Gospel, important as that objective might be; it was also necessary to apply Christian teachings to specific social evils and problems in an organized, effective manner. Accordingly, the Protestant offensive soon branched out into a variety of reform activities. These were promoted through the use of various techniques, ranging from subtle persuasion to outright coercion, but the end remained constant. If the United States were to achieve its God-given mission, if order and stability were to be preserved in a democratic nation, action was needed to bring social behavior into line with proper standards and values.

The implications of this attitude were quickly borne out in various aspects of American life, minor as well as major. Card playing, dancing, the use of tobacco, horse racing, and other practices which had earlier been regarded as harmless diversions were now branded as frivolous or hurtful forms of self-indulgence which had no place in a God-fearing nation.[24] The social effects of such beliefs were pervasive in many sections of the country for generations, especially in villages and small towns where the strictures of Protestant conservatism retained force long after their influence had been weakened in urban centers. These stand-

[23]The fullest account of the development and activities of American tract, Bible, Sunday School, and missionary societies is provided by Griffin, *Their Brothers' Keepers*, already mentioned. See also Cross, *Burned-over District*, pp. 126–30; Foster, *An Errand of Mercy*, *passim*; Colin B. Goodykoontz, *Home Missions on the American Frontier* (Caldwell, Idaho, 1939), *passim*; Keller, *Second Great Awakening*, pp. 94–130; and George M. Stephenson, *The Puritan Heritage* (New York, 1952), pp. 141–80.

[24]See particularly Dixon Ryan Fox, "The Protestant Counter-Reformation in America," *New York History*, XVI, 1 (January, 1935), p. 31. This short, well-written article anticipates some of the themes which were later to be developed systematically by Foster, Griffin, and other historians.

ards of behavior became badges of middle class respectability for many people and were accepted, not only by believers with a Calvinist heritage, but also by members of various sectarian groups whose growth in numbers was accompanied by desires to escape previous lower-class associations. They were also vigorously inculcated among aspiring young businessmen who could keep their eyes more firmly fixed upon the goal of financial success if their attention was not diverted by various forms of extravagance and dissipation.[25]

Many of the pressures exerted in behalf of social order and decorum were applied in an undramatic, but nevertheless effective, manner through the means of everyday discourse, the exhortations of teachers and preachers, and the admonitions and disciplinary tactics of parents imbued with the strict standards of conduct propagated by conservative reformers. In other cases, however, well-organized societies were created to reinforce conventional methods of securing conformity with the power of systematic group effort, leading, if necessary, to the enactment of legislation aimed at specific evils. Such action was frequently manifested at the town or village level in the form of blue laws prohibiting certain minor practices deemed objectionable by local religious leaders, but it was also exemplified on a state or national basis by the appearance of concerted drives against forms of behavior about which conservative spokesmen were particularly concerned, such as dueling, Sabbath-breaking, intemperance, and outright crime. Although the societies which were formed to combat such evils enlisted members from various religious groups, the influence of New England was again pronounced, especially during the early stages of the attack.

One of the most noteworthy leaders in the Protestant reform efforts of the early nineteenth century as Lyman Beecher, a native of Connecticut who during his college years at Yale in the mid-1790's came under the influence of Timothy Dwight, who had launched a revival movement among the students after assuming the presidency of that institution in 1795. After graduation, Beecher entered the Congregational ministry and held a pastorate on nearby Long Island, returning after a few years to his home state to take charge of the church at Litchfield. Here in 1806 he launched an attack upon the practice of dueling in a New Year's Day sermon cast in the best traditions of the New England jeremiad. Terming the custom which had recently taken the life of conservative idol Alexander Hamilton "a great national sin," he warned that God's judgment would surely be visited upon a country which tolerated its continuance. The sermon was published widely, and at a subsequent

---

[25]On the place of such ideas in the nineteenth-century American business tradition, see especially Irvin G. Wyllie, *The Self-Made Man in America* (New Brunswick, N. J., 1954), *passim.*

ecclesiastical meeting in New Jersey, Beecher urged the formation of antidueling societies, which were soon flourishing in a number of states. By 1818 Connecticut had become the first state to take legal action against the practice when its new constitution disqualified from voting any person convicted of participating in a duel. From this time onward, other states passed various types of laws against the custom, leading to its ultimate disappearance from the American scene.[26]

Not all of the practices against which conservative reformers directed their fire, however, seemed as pernicious to their fellow citizens as that of dueling. Taking part in various light diversions on Sundays, for example, did not appear especially heinous to many persons who worked long and gruelling hours on the other six days of the week. Nevertheless, to many ministers and laymen a strict observance of the Sabbath was a matter of vital concern if the United States was to set a proper example as a truly Christian nation. Laws demanding the cessation of many ordinary weekday activities on Sunday had existed in New England from colonial days, and were also on the books in other parts of the Union. In this respect, a proper discharge of Protestant duty seemed in some degree to lie upon the mere enforcement of statutes already in being rather than the enactment of new coercive measures; but Sabbatarians also seized upon new issues to dramatize their case.

At the local level, the fight for a strict observance of the Sabbath consisted, for the most part, of using various social pressures to see that citizens observed Sunday in a quiet and decorous manner, encouraging attendance at public worship, and employing legal or other means to prevent business transactions or other activities—especially recreations and amusements. One aspect of the movement, however, was national in scope and drew much attention to the cause. Sunday mail deliveries by Federal post offices had stirred controversy in Massachusetts as early as the 1790's, and when Congress passed a law in 1810 requiring postal employees to process mail on every day of the week, a number of Protestant groups began to remonstrate vigorously. Beginning in 1814, Lyman Beecher organized a campaign of petitions to Washington on the issue; this movement spread rapidly and culminated in 1828 with the formation, at a large meeting in New York City, of the General Union for Promoting the Observance of the Christian Sabbath. Petitions bearing thousands of signatures were dispatched to the national capital from such places as New York, Boston, Albany, and Charleston, demanding the repeal of laws requiring post offices to stay open on Sundays, while in upstate New York boycotts were organized against transportation enterprises which ran on the sacred day. The crusade backfired, however, by

[26]Anson P. Stokes, *Church and State in the United States* (3 vols.: New York, 1950), II, pp. 5–12.

arousing determined opposition from citizens who prized Sunday as a time of diversion from the grinding routine of weekday labor and resented what they regarded as theocratic attempts to dictate how it should be spent. In addition, liberal groups, and such religious denominations as the Baptists, assailed the effort to halt Sunday mail delivery as a blatant attempt to violate the separation of church and state. The controversy finally resulted in the submission of a report to Congress by Senator Richard M. Johnson of Kentucky roundly condemning religious interference with civil institutions. This document secured widespread endorsement throughout the country by state legislatures and private citizens alike. Thus one conservative reform effort encountered a humiliating defeat.[27]

By all odds the most intensive campaign to impose rigid new standards of behavior upon American society was the drive that began late in the eighteenth century to diminish, and ultimately to abolish, the use of alcoholic beverages.[28] During the colonial period, such drinks had been widely regarded as products of God's bounty, though subject to possible abuse. Nevertheless, a number of religious leaders like Increase and Cotton Mather, Jonathan Edwards, Anthony Benezet, and John Woolman had become greatly concerned about the sinfulness of imbibing to excess, while during the Revolution the physician-general of the Continental forces in the Middle Atlantic area, Benjamin Rush, had become convinced that many camp illnesses were aggravated by the use of liquor. After the war, Rush came to the conclusion that even the moderate use of ardent spirits was harmful, and he wrote a widely circulated treatise urging Americans to substitute malt drinks like beer and ale for distilled beverages. As the incidence of hard drinking continued to climb throughout the country, despite such warnings, an organized campaign eventually got underway to combat it. The first temperance society in the United States was founded in 1808 by residents of the small community of Moreau in eastern New York under the leadership of a Congregationalist minister and a physician who had read Rush's writings. From this beginning there quickly flowered a movement which became a key element in the Protestant drive for a stable and virtuous America.

Throughout the growth of the temperance movement, there was much evidence of the fear that political democracy would degenerate

---

27 *Ibid.*, II, pp. 12–30; Bodo, *Protestant Clergy and Public Issues*, pp. 39–43; Cross, *Burned-over District*, pp. 131–34.

28The following account of the temperance movement is based chiefly upon John A. Krout, *The Origins of Prohibition* (New York, 1925). Despite the continuing usefulness of Krout's book, an up-to-date historical analysis of the antebellum temperance movement would, I believe, be a worthwhile undertaking. Andrew Sinclair's excellent *Era of Excess: A Social History of the Prohibition Movement*, Colophon ed. (New York, 1964) deals chiefly with the post-Civil War era. For a commendable work on one particular antebellum temperance reformer, see Frank L. Byrne, *Prophet of Prohibition: Neal Dow and His Crusade* (Madison, Wis., 1961).

into chaos unless means were taken to control the baser instincts of classes which were gaining powers once reserved for the privileged few. Drunkenness served to accentuate those aspects of irresponsible behavior which conservative reformers dreaded among elements of the population referred to by Lyman Beecher as the "ruff-scuff." As Joseph R. Gusfield has pointed out, the espousal of temperance also enabled upper-class elements to sharpen their feelings of difference from groups lower in society, serving to buttress a sense of status which was, in reality, already being eroded by the social changes that men like Beecher feared.[29] The Connecticut Society for the Promotion of Good Morals, founded by Beecher and others in 1813, was primarily devoted to temperance. The Massachusetts Society for the Suppression of Intemperance, organized during the same period, performed similar work under the direction of prominent clergymen and wealthy merchants. Beecher gave the cause great impetus in a series of six sermons preached at Litchfield in 1825 and subsequently published throughout the country. Defining intemperance as any use—however moderate—of distilled liquors, and rejecting the idea of gradual withdrawal from the drinking habit through the use of such substitutes as wine, he called for "the banishment of ardent spirits from the list of lawful articles of commerce, by a correct and efficient public sentiment." The following year witnessed the formation of the American Society for the Promotion of Temperance, and by 1833 it was estimated that there were over four thousand societies devoted to the cause throughout the nation, with more than one half million members. The heart of the movement, however, remained in New England and upstate New York, while other centers of strength were particularly evident in areas to which Yankee settlers had migrated.

Space does not permit a detailed treatment of the later evolution of the temperance crusade, which ultimately became more strongly associated with such denominations as the Methodists than with the religious denominations that had originally been its strongest champions. This suggests a pronounced urge for middle-class status on the part of sectarian groups which had at first drawn most of their membership from the humbler elements of society. As Samuel P. Hays has shown, opposition to the sale of alcoholic beverages also became part of a rural attack upon the values of an increasingly urban society in the late nineteenth and early twentieth centuries.[30] If the movement derived its strength from a

---

[29]Joseph R. Gusfield, *Symbolic Crusade: Status Politics and the American Temperance Movement* (Urbana, Ill., 1963), pp. 36–44 and *passim*. This is a valuable book which, among other things, comments perceptively on many of the new elements and motives that appeared in the temperance movement during the 1830's and 1840's. However, it is essentially a sociological treatise based upon historical evidence which, through no fault of Gusfield, is in some spots relatively thin, underscoring once more the need for some fresh spadework in the field.

[30]Samuel P. Hays, *The Response to Industrialism, 1885–1914* (Chicago, 1957), pp. 114–15.

variety of impulses, however, it is important to note that even in its early stages, as Beecher's sermons indicate, it began to manifest strongly coercive strains which had been latent from the beginning in the attitudes of many conservative reformers.   Initially confining themselves to the use of moral suasion, proponents of the cause eventually campaigned for laws banning the sale of all alcoholic beverages, resulting in prohibition statutes at the state, and ultimately the national, level.   If people would not willingly listen to the advice of those who knew what was best for them, self-appointed custodians of their moral welfare were prepared to resort to naked force.

This spirit, which was implemented in the temperance drive only after considerable hesitation on the part of reformers who recognized the extent to which it conflicted with individual liberty, was manifested somewhat earlier in another variety of meliorative activity, involving the care and treatment of criminals.[31]   America had been the scene of important correctional developments during the Revolutionary era, with Quakers playing an especially prominent role in securing the establishment of penitentiaries in which felons were confined over protracted periods of time instead of being subjected to the brutal methods of lashing, branding, ear-cropping, and pillorying that had formerly been used. In the new institutions, disciplinary methods were generally mild, and the professed aim of treatment was to produce repentance and amendment of life.

These changes, however, did not fulfill the sometimes extravagant hopes of reformers who had expected the penitentiary to lessen the incidence of crime to a significant degree.   Furthermore, a number of the prisons which were constructed in the first flush of enthusiasm for the new correctional techniques proved seriously defective in design.   During the early nineteenth century, mounting crime rates in various parts of the country, coupled with lax discipline and internal disorder prevailing in many penitentiaries, led to increasing exasperation among private citizens and public officials alike.   These conditions also contributed to the alarms of conservative reformers, who, not surprisingly, viewed lawbreaking and prison disturbances as further indications of the social unrest which they so greatly feared.

Thus the stage was set for a new type of prison reform which contrasted sharply with the humanitarian efforts that had characterized the Revolutionary era.   Vividly demonstrating the impact of impulses far different from those which had animated earlier penal experiments, the approach that now prevailed was best characterized at Auburn, a community located in the heart of the "burned-over district."   Here, under a

---

[31]For a more extended discussion of the developments that follow, see Lewis, *From Newgate to Dannemora*, Chapters I–IV, pp. 1–110.

harsh, repressive despotism, convicts were kept in solitary confinement at night and forced to work together in absolute silence by day. Their lives were regulated to the tiniest detail, and any breach of discipline was immediately punished by flogging. Some officials at Auburn went so far as to ridicule the very idea of rehabilitation and based their practices exclusively upon a philosophy of deterrence; but others, like Gershom Powers, a native of New Hampshire who became warden in 1827, held that convicts could be reformed through hard work and religious influences after they had been thoroughly humbled and subdued by an initial "breaking" process. However it was justified in theory, the Auburn system spread rapidly throughout the United States and soon became the country's most widely used method of penal discipline.

The popularity of the Auburn system resulted partly from its relatively low cost of administration, but was also enhanced by the support given by conservative reformers who saw in it an ideal vehicle for the implementation of their beliefs. Chief among these spokesmen was Louis Dwight, a zealous New England Congregationalist who founded the Boston Prison Discipline Society and made it a powerful agent for disseminating propaganda concerning the new correctional methods developed in New York. An ardent exponent of temperance and Sabbatarianism, Dwight was attracted by the various features of a system which produced the tightest form of order and literally compelled men to be abstemious and industrious. Indeed, he was so impressed that he wanted to see the Auburn techniques applied not only in the treatment of convicts but also in the management of schools, orphanages, workshops, factories, and even private homes, where he believed such methods would promote "order, seriousness, and purity." Although the extent to which this advice was taken would be impossible to determine, it provides an excellent illustration of the lengths to which some conservative leaders were willing to go in imposing regimentation upon their fellow citizens.

Men like Louis Dwight were also concerned about another social evil, slavery, but seldom could bring themselves to propose its outright abolition. Although some persons like Arthur and Lewis Tappan became abolitionists, most leaders of Protestant counter-subversion devoted themselves to the colonization movement, which aimed to solve the problem by removing Negroes, both slave and free, from America and transporting them back to Africa. This approach was particularly attractive to some Protestant reformers because it was assumed that the blacks, having been converted to Christianity in the United States, would form a powerful missionary spearhead when returned to their native continent. In addition, the colonization idea was easily reconciled with a belief in the slaveowner's property right in his human chattels until he had voluntarily emancipated them, and it skirted the difficult question of how American society could absorb large numbers of free Negroes in the event of widespread manumission. For such reasons, the deportation approach retained considerable support among conservative leaders long after its impracticability had been demonstrated and its tenets rejected by slaveholders and abolitionists alike.[32]

In view of the circumstances which had inspired the Protestant offensive against unsettling influences in American society and the anti-subversive attitudes of many of its proponents, it is not surprising that movements to protect the United States from allegedly dangerous foreign ideologies and other alien influences found willing recruits within the ranks of conservative reformers. The antimasonic crusade which began in upstate New York in 1826, after the abduction of William Morgan, drew much of its strength from the same denominations which supported other Protestant reform causes during the same period. During the late eighteenth century, Masonry had been popularly associated with the doctrines of the French Revolution, and one offshoot, the Order of the Bavarian Illuminati, had been particularly feared by the New England clergy. The antimasonic impulse was present in many Protestant groups, but, as Whitney Cross has shown in his pioneering study of religious enthusiasm in western New York, emigrant Yankees were among those most susceptible to its influence. The rhetoric of the cause was trenchantly exemplified in the writings of Lebbeus Armstrong, a minister whose treatise, *Masonry Proved to be a Work of Darkness*, was widely circulated throughout the country. The frequency with which devotees of Sabbatarianism and other conservative reform efforts were found among antimasons gave the movement a semireligious aura and led opponents to claim that it sought to reestablish a strong connection between church and state in America.[33]

---

[32]P. J. Staudenraus, *The African Colonization Movement, 1816–1865* (New York, 1961), is the standard general work on this subject, superseding previous accounts. See also Bodo, *Protestant Clergy and Public Issues*, pp. 112–51, for helpful supplementary information on ministerial attitudes.

[33]Stokes, *Church and State*, II, pp. 20–25; Lorman A. Ratner, "Antimasonry in New York State: A Study in Pre-Civil War Reform" (unpublished M. A. thesis, Cornell University, 1958), *passim*; Cross, *Burned-over District*, pp. 74, 113–25, 135. On the "quasi-religious" nature of Antimasonry, its church-and-state orientation, and its identification with such causes as Sabbatarianism, see also Lee Benson, *The Concept of Jacksonian Democracy: New York as a Test Case* (Princeton, N. J., 1961), p. 35. I am, however, skeptical about some of Benson's theories on the "leveling" characteristics which he attributes to the Antimasonic impulse. For a lucid discussion about the place of Antimasonry among the counter-subversionist movements of the antebellum era, see David B. Davis, "Some Themes of Counter-Subversion: An Analysis of Anti-Masonic, Anti-Catholic, and Anti-Mormon Literature," *Mississippi Valley Historical Review*, XLVII, 2 (September, 1960), pp. 205–24. Professor Ratner's *Antimasonry: The Crusade and the Party* (New York, 1969), based in part upon his unpublished M.A. thesis mentioned above, appeared after the present essay had been

The same fears which contributed to the spread of antimasonry were also evident in the progress of hostility toward Roman Catholicism in the United States during the early nineteenth century. As the country experienced a rapid rise in immigration from Catholic sections of Europe after 1815, many Protestant leaders became convinced that a Papist conspiracy was endangering the security of American institutions. The "trusteeship controversy" of the 1820's, in which a number of Catholic laymen attempted unsuccessfully to wrest control of church property from the hierarchy, highlighted differences between Romanists and Protestants, and animosities were intensified by public debates and journalistic controversies which became increasingly common between spokesmen for the two groups. Leaders of conservative Protestant reform activity willingly enlisted in such hostilities; Lyman Beecher, for example, preached a series of bitterly anti-Catholic sermons in Boston in 1830, and returned in 1834 to deliver another set of addresses which helped fan the type of public animosity that led to the burning of the Ursuline convent in Charlestown later in the same year. Some Protestant spokesmen were also greatly alarmed about a supposed plot on the part of Catholicism to gain control of the Mississippi Valley through the activities of such European missionary societies as the Association for the Propagation of the Faith, prompting Beecher to write an inflammatory *Plea for the West* in 1835. To combat the alleged Papist menace, the interdenominational American Protestant Association was ultimately formed in 1842, paralleling the earlier establishment of similar joint efforts in other spheres of concern.[34]

In assaying the impulses which underlay the Protestant reform activities of the early nineteenth century, it is instructive to examine not only the causes to which many clergymen and lay leaders gave vigorous support, but also the movements in which their energies were enlisted only weakly or not at all. In view of the fact that criticism of the War of 1812 had been widespread throughout New England, it is not surprising that some Congregationalists were temporarily active in the peace crusade that appeared in America shortly after the second conflict with Britain came to an end in 1815. Although a number of peace societies were

---

completed, but should be consulted by students interested in the movement. It contains valuable primary sources as well as an able introduction discussing the antimasonic crusade generally.

[34]This summary treatment is based chiefly upon Ray A. Billington, *The Protestant Crusade: A Study in the Origins of American Nativism* (New York, 1938), *passim*. See also Bodo, *Protestant Clergy and Public Issues*, pp. 61–84. Although nativist anti-Catholicism enlisted the support of persons whose reform impulses were of a conservative nature, it also drew upon a radical anti-clerical tradition whose influence has, I believe, been underplayed in scholarly treatments of the subject. A fresh study of the extent to which this motivation was present, particularly in the latter decades of the ante-bellum period, would in my opinion be a worthwhile project.

formed throughout the country, however, apathy quickly set in and the movement would have collapsed but for the efforts of a handful of zealots who barely managed to keep it alive. Conservative religious leaders were especially quick to defect; in general, they were too heavily influenced by Old Testament concepts to endorse pacifism, and ultimately came to feel that military conquest might provide one means of spreading the Gospel into unconverted regions. Thus, while the peace movement was strong for a time in Connecticut and a society was even formed at Andover Seminary, the cause never commanded the support given to tract, Bible, missionary, Sabbatarian, and temperance efforts.[35]

Even less popular among many conservative reformers were movements devoted to female rights, abolitionism, the elimination of capital punishment, and the rights of the working classes. Although such causes as temperance unquestionably provided outlets for female activity, it was impossible for counter-subversionist spokesmen to endorse the radical ideas of such persons as Mary Wollstonecraft and Frances Wright, who argued for basic changes in the status of women and even for a modified approach to such institutions as marriage.[36] Similarly, abolitionism challenged deeply ingrained concepts of private property and threatened to split the Union itself, thus endangering the national destiny envisioned by many Protestant leaders. The use of capital punishment appealed to most conservatives as an excellent means of social control for intimidating would-be lawbreakers.[37] So far as the workingmen's movement was concerned, persons like Beecher and his associates were too firmly committed to an aristocratic conception of society and too fearful of class struggle to countenance the activities of most labor leaders, and found it easy instead to attribute the troubles of craftsmen and artisans to such causes as laziness, intemperance, and lack of thrift.[38]

However selective in its approach to social reform, the drive for an

[35]Merle Curti, *The American Peace Crusade, 1815–1860* (Durham, N. C., 1929), pp. 3–66; Bodo, *Protestant Clergy and Public Issues*, pp. 226–32.

[36]For perceptive insights on the ambivalence felt by many Protestant ministers toward the participation of women in charitable and reform activities at this time, see Keith Melder, "Ladies Bountiful: Organized Women's Benevolence in Early 19th Century America," *New York History*, XLVIII, 3 (July, 1967), pp. 240–42.

[37]Opposition by the conservative clergy to the abolition of capital punishment was particularly intense during the 1840's, when the anti-gallows movement was reaching its crest on waves of romanticism and humanitarianism that had been unleashed in the United States by that time. See David B. Davis, "The Movement to Abolish Capital Punishment in America, 1787–1861," *American Historical Review*, LXIII, 1 (October, 1957), pp. 23–46. Like some other types of conservative activity stemming from social control motivations that persisted in the late ante-bellum period, this ministerial effort in my opinion has something of a "rear guard" character in an age when the dominant reform impulses were considerably different from those which had prevailed during the earlier heyday of the Protestant counter-offensive.

[38]Bodo, *Protestant Clergy and Public Issues*. pp. 175–76.

orderly and God-fearing nation was clearly a force of great significance in the development of American culture during the early nineteenth century. Representing what was left of a once powerful theocratic tradition, and exemplifying the conviction that the church still had a vital part to play in the conduct of secular affairs, a conservative reform coalition attempted through the use of voluntary associations and other means to protect social order and play the traditional role of an ecclesiastical establishment in a country which was rapidly abandoning all vestiges of the time-honored connection between church and state.

Despite the vigor with which this movement was prosecuted, however, and even though church membership in the United States increased greatly during the early nineteenth century, it was clear by the 1830's that the course of developments in America had shattered many of the ideas most deeply cherished by the champions of conservative reformism. Instead of providing an environment in which a traditionalist church could guide the destinies of an orderly commonwealth, conditions in the young republic had nourished ever greater tendencies toward competitive denominationalism in a society characterized by ceaseless and often bewildering change. Conservative teachings still tinged to some extent with a predestinarian heritage were proving less and less attractive to the citizens of a democratic nation, who preferred instead to identify themselves with religious groups preaching that grace was freely available to all. Voluntary societies, employed with great effect by orthodox spokesmen, were also organized by reformers who operated on different premises and often turned bitterly on church leaders for their unwillingness to endorse radical solutions to such problems as slavery. Class distinctions which had once seemed fundamental were overwhelmed in a rising tide of egalitarianism, and the maintenance of traditional ethical standards was complicated by the emergence of a highly speculative economy toward which the government took an increasingly *laissez-faire* attitude. Despite a generation of concerted effort by various Protestant reformers, events were still moving in a direction calculated to arouse alarm among conservatives.

Although space will not permit a detailed examination of these trends, some aspects deserve brief attention. One of these was the final collapse in New England of the church-state connection that had survived there despite being swept away elsewhere in the Revolutionary era. In Connecticut, a mounting campaign against the Congregational establishment by Methodists, Baptists, Episcopalians, and other dissenting groups culminated in the adoption by 1818 of a new state constitution making the support of religion a voluntary matter. In 1819, legislation was enacted in New Hampshire making it impossible to coerce dissenters to pay for the support of a standing clergy, which had previously been done in some localities. In Massachusetts, the struggle between Unitarians and more theologically conservative elements so weakened what was left of the church-state connection that a constitutional amendment was overwhelmingly passed in 1833 ending the establishment and leaving a voluntary system in its place. Along with the final demise of the Federalist party in the 1820's, these events terminated any hope for an effective coalition between conservative religious leaders and political authorities in the supervision of public affairs at the state level.[39]

If the church of the Puritan fathers was now only one of many competing denominations in New England, divided within itself and forming a minority caught between growing Protestant sects on the one hand and a rapidly increasing Roman Catholic population on the other, its position was certainly no better elsewhere in the country. Despite the Plan of Union and other tactical measures, the Congregational and Presbyterian churches lacked the growth potential of other varieties of Protestantism in a nation in which power was ever more closely associated with numbers. The chief beneficiaries of the religious harvest in the west, and in other parts of the country as well, were the Methodists and Baptists, who had no fear of the common masses, did not emphasize an educated clergy, and welcomed excesses of emotionalism in revivals which repelled many traditionalists.[40]

Furthermore, by the 1830's it was clear that many who still remained within the organizational confines of the Calvinist churches were badly infected with unorthodox ideas. This was especially true in upstate New York, where Charles G. Finney had enjoyed spectacular success conducting revivals far different from those presided over by persons like Asahel Nettleton and Nathaniel Emmons. Finney's "New Measures," as they came to be called, included the use of protracted and spiritually agonizing prayer meetings, the singling out of unconverted sinners by name, the use of an "anxious bench" where persons in a state of near-conversion could obtain special assistance from the preacher and his helpers, the encouragement of speaking by women, and the employment of other techniques for the production of emotional conversion. Although theoretically within the fold of the Congregationalist-Presbyterian alliance established by the Plan of Union, Finney openly flouted various Calvinist tenets, repudiating the doctrine of predestination altogether and

---

[39]Keller, *Second Great Awakening*, pp. 188–89; Charles B. Kimmey, Jr., *Church and State: The Struggle for Separation in New Hampshire* (New York, 1955), pp. 107–18; Jacob C. Meyer, *Church and State in Massachusetts from 1740 to 1833* (Cleveland, 1930), pp. 201–20.

[40]See Winthrop S. Hudson, *American Protestantism* (Chicago, 1961), pp. 97 ff. Calvinist doctrines were still widespread among Baptists in 1830, but became steadily less so. As Hudson comments, "by 1850 Evangelical Protestantism had become defined almost wholly in Methodist terms." *Ibid.*, p. 99.

declaring that any man could lay hold of salvation if he were willing to accept the redemption which God freely offered him.[41]

Despite the controversy which they aroused, Finney's practices and ideas were not really as revolutionary as they seemed.[42] In areas like western New York, as Whitney Cross had pointed out, some of the "New Measures" had already appeared before Finney started conducting his revivals. And in New England, the disciples of Timothy Dwight had fallen increasingly under the influence of ideas which Finney merely preached in unequivocal form and with greater dramatic flair. In the conservative Connecticut bastion of New Haven, Nathaniel W. Taylor, a Congregationalist minister who had at one time been Dwight's personal secretary, developed a theology which was ostensibly Calvinist but nevertheless conceded a degree of human ability to lay hold of divine grace which ill comported with rigid predestinarianism. Lyman Beecher, a close friend of Taylor's, was in sympathy with his ideas. But other conservative clerical leaders in the Nutmeg State were not, and began a revolt which exposed some of the theological differences that Timothy Dwight had tried to de-emphasize. The news of Finney's revivals helped to trigger this important development, with divisive consequences for the Protestant reform front.

Lyman Beecher himself was somewhat disturbed by reports of the sensationalism and emotional upheaval which accompanied Finney's revivals, but men like Asahel Nettleton were horrified by them, and demanded some form of action by New England clergymen against the spread of the "New Measures." Finney's methods seemed reminiscent of those adopted by such preachers as James Davenport at the time of the Great Awakening, and furthermore smacked of the rising turbulence of Jacksonian democracy. The fact that Finney was neither a college graduate nor a trained theologian was an additional source of alarm to settled clergymen who clung to traditional ways.[43] Beecher was sensitive

[41]Among various treatments of Finney and his "New Measures," see especially Cross, *Burned-over District*, pp. 151–84; William G. McLoughlin, Jr., *Modern Revivalism: Charles Grandison Finney to Billy Graham* (New York, 1959), pp. 11–121; and Weisberger, *They Gathered at the River*, pp. 87–126.

[42]The analysis that follows is drawn principally from Cross, *Burned-over District*, *passim*, and Mead, *Nathaniel William Taylor*, pp. 200–21.

[43]On the congruence between Finney's outlook and various currents of popular thought and ideology which were beginning to appear strongly in America at this time, including those associated with the rise of Andrew Jackson, see especially the portions of McLoughlin's introduction to Finney's *Lectures on Revivals of Religion* (Cambridge, Mass., 1960), reprinted in Davis, *Ante-Bellum Reform*, pp. 97–107. As Davis notes, this congruence does not indicate that Finney himself was one of Jackson's followers or was any less conservative in many of his social and economic beliefs than the New Englanders who responded to his sudden rise to prominence with a

to these fears but found himself in a tight spot. He was trying to keep the conservative coalition alive, particularly against the spread of such dangers as Unitarianism, which had been making alarming strides in New England, and he badly needed the support of Nettleton and his associates. On the other hand, he felt that he could not support drastic action against Finney without giving aid and comfort to the enemies of revivalism and impugning some of his own theological beliefs in the process.

It was not surprising, therefore, that when a face-to-face encounter with Finney and a delegation of his followers was arranged in 1827 at New Lebanon in eastern New York at Nettleton's behest, Beecher and his New England supporters disappointed Nettleton by temporizing with the upstart revivalist and settling for a truce rather than risking an open break with him. Finney's behavior did become somewhat more moderate over the course of the next few years, but many western preachers who followed his leadership were even more quick than he had once been to resort to new techniques for stimulating mass conversions; during the 1830's the worst fears of people like Nettleton were realized when such areas as upstate New York became hotbeds of "ultraist" beliefs among those whom Finney had helped to evangelize. Within a decade of the New Lebanon meeting, differences between Finneyite "New Lights" and more traditionalist Presbyterian-Congregational elements became so pronounced as to undo the Plan of Union and create factions which were to struggle bitterly with one another until after the Civil War. Meanwhile, Finney's beliefs led him into a type of Christian perfectionism which proved far more amenable to such radical causes as abolitionism than the ideas of the conservative reformers had ever been, and which was in time drawn upon as a source of inspiration by American labor leaders in the late nineteenth century.[44]

In brief, although some continuities can be observed between the antisubversive crusades of the post-Revolutionary period and developments transpiring after the dawn of the Jacksonian age, it is clear that by the 1830's the crest of conservative Protestant reform activity had been reached.[45] The work of interdenominational, Bible, and missionary societ-

---

measure of alarm; rather, it helps us to see how Finney's thought "could inspire far more radical reformers than himself." *Ibid.*, p. 97. For another assessment of the differences between Finney and his predecessors, and of the reasons why his tactics aroused fear in some quarters, see Perry Miller, *The Life of the Mind in America from the Revolution to the Civil War* (New York, 1965), pp. 22–35.

44See especially Herbert G. Gutman, "Protestantism and the American Labor Movement: The Christian Spirit in the Gilded Age," *American Historical Review*, LXXII, No. 1 (October, 1966), p. 83.

45Since the substantial completion of this essay, there has appeared Clifford S. Griffin's brief interpretive study, *The Ferment of Reform, 1830–1860* (New York,

ies went on, but money was increasingly drained off into strictly sectarian, competitive enterprises, and the Panic of 1837 also dried up some sources of funds upon which previous conservative efforts had depended. The temperance movement enjoyed a growing influence, but the failure of the attempt to halt Sunday mail delivery had already dealt Sabbatarianism a heavy blow. In the field of penal reform, the heyday of the Auburn system was past by the mid-1830's, and developments in New York and elsewhere entered a new phase marked by the emergence of environmental concepts of criminality which alarmed traditionalists because they threatend long-accepted ideas about human guilt and freedom of the will. The colonization movement had entered a moribund state and was rapidly giving way to abolitionism, which most conservative religious leaders could not endorse. Above all, the development of a democratic society in an age of emergent laissez-faire capitalism had destroyed whatever hope had once existed for a stable commonwealth evolving in an orderly manner under the restraining hands of a paternalist government in open alliance with established religious institutions. In such respects as these, American life continued to produce a distinctively pluralistic culture which, however extensive its borrowings from other sources, possessed a vitality uniquely its own.

1967). This work contains the best summary in print of the historiography of antebellum social reform movements, and presents a number of acute and cogent insights about the varieties and consequences of reform activity. Despite its very considerable merits, however, it fails in my opinion to perceive the crucial differences between the dominant reform impulses of the late ante-bellum era, which usually manifested a receptive attitude toward fundamental social change, and the conservative impulses which characterized the period from c. 1795 to c. 1830.

CARL DEGLER
Stanford University

the
two cultures
and the
cívíl war

The United States is the only country that required a civil war to eradicate slavery. It is true that the slaves emancipated by the European nations were to be found only in the colonies, a fact that certainly made emancipation politically and socially easier than it would otherwise have been. Yet imperial Russia managed to emancipate the serfs in 1861 without civil war even though great economic and social interests were at stake. More pertinent still are the examples of abolition in Latin America, where the social and racial circumstances were analogous to those in the United States. Of all the comparisons with the experience of the United States with slavery, that of Brazil is probably the closest. Brazilian slavery, like that in the Southern states of the United States, was an integral and important part of the economy, providing the principal labor supply for the production of the chief exports of the country. Also, in Brazil, as in the United States, there was an agressive abolitionist movement that carried on its campaign for years. In fact, abolition in Brazil was not finally achieved until 1888, some two decades after emancipation in the United States. Yet, unlike the United States, Brazil managed to rid itself of slavery without civil war.

There are at least two inferences that might be drawn from the uniquely violent conclusion to slavery in the United States. One is that slavery was more deeply and firmly established in the United States than anywhere else and hence required more strenuous efforts to remove it. The other is that the necessity for civil violence was a measure of the weakness of American nationalism. For no matter how else one might view the Civil War in the United States, it was at least a failure in the building of a nation.

The first inference can be disposed of rather quickly. It is not really possible, of course, to measure precisely the relative firmness with which slavery was embedded in American and Brazilian society. But the general measures that might be used suggest that, if anything, slavery was more firmly established in Brazil than in the United States. Slaves made up a larger proportion of the laboring force in Brazil, slavery lasted longer there, and the importance of slave labor in the total economy was at least as great as in the United States. The ending of slavery, moreover, was one of the principal causes for the bloodless fall of the monarchy and the establishment of the republic the following year.

Why then was a civil war necessary only in the United States? Certainly it was not that slavery was shored up by public opinion at home or abroad. Indeed, by the middle of the nineteenth century all European nations had not only abolished the institution, but looked upon it as outmoded and cruel. In the United States and wherever else it existed, it was under attack from every angle, being denounced as un-Christian, inefficient, undemocratic, and contrary to natural law. Why, we ask again, was American nationalism so fragile that it could not accommodate a social change that all the civilized world supported and peacefully carried out? The answer to the question goes to the heart of American cultural development in the generation prior to 1860.

The explanation must begin with the size of the country and the rapidity with which it was settled. For half a century or more prior to 1860, Americans were a people in motion. As they moved west of the Appalachians they created, in less than a man's lifetime, not only several countries, as measured by European standards, but several cultures as well. As early as the 1820's Americans recognized that their sprawling country was divided into three quite distinct regions—East, West, and South. The nationalism aroused by the war of 1812 soon proved to be premature; the era of good feelings dissolved in the face of Eastern demands for a protective tariff, Western demands for internal improvements, and Southern objections to both. The three sections did not quite follow Thomas Cooper's cynical advice to "calculate the value of the Union," but each clearly consulted its own interests and rejected any others that seemed to limit its freedom of development. Moreover, the traditional forces of national cohesion so evident in Europe were few in the United States. In fact there were no really national organizations of any strength to knit together a country spread across great distances in an age of slow, uncertain travel and overland communication. There was no national bench or bar; no established church; no labor organization or business group of national extent. Even the major Protestant churches split apart in the 1840's.

But the customary emphasis upon a tripartite division obscures a deeper social cleavage in American culture. Southerners and Westerners, it is true, in the 1830's and 1840's spoke of their common agricultural interest as distinguished from the growing commercial and industrial interest of the East. Hindsight, however, now allows us to see that the West was not essentially different from the East. In the years between 1820 and 1860 the social and economic differences between the East and West gradually, yet significantly, lessened. Part of the weakening of differences is attributable to improved communications, like the Erie and other canals in the 1820's and 1830's and the extensive east-west railroad construction in the 1850's. But the most important reason was less measurable. It was that the two regions were divided by little except time. Give the West a generation and it would reproduce the social and cultural forms and values of the East, as in fact it did. Its small towns became cities, its shops factories, its river and lake ports bustling centers of commerce, and its agriculture increasingly commercial and scientific. The West's cultural values and economy were modeled after those of the East. By the 1850's, there were only two sections, culturally speaking, the North and the South. And the most obvious difference between them was that in one slavery and the plantation flourished while in the other the plantation was absent and slavery was almost gone.

The slave plantation originated in the tobacco areas of seventeenth-century Virginia and Maryland and in the eighteenth-century rice and indigo regions of South Carolina and Georgia. When the plantation with its slave labor force was adapted to cotton culture in the early nineteenth century it spread westward, for climate prevented cotton from being grown in the northwest. Thus new Southern states like Alabama, Mississippi and Tennessee drew their values, not from the commercializing and industrializing East, but from the rural, slave society of the Southern seaboard states.

It is debatable when Southerners first began to be viewed as different from other Americans, but certainly differences were already being noticed and commented upon early in the nineteenth century. At the time of the Missouri Compromise debates in 1820, for instance, both Northerners and Southerners recognized that slavery set the South apart. It is possible, of course, to exaggerate the cultural differences between the North and the South before the Civil War, as some historians have warned. For even at the height of the sectional conflicts of the 1850's, Southerners and Northerners still spoke the same tongue, read the same literature, looked back upon a common past, worshipped in the same Protestant manner, and praised the same Constitution. But these shared interests are broad categories; within virtually all of them, as we shall see, there were differences between Northerners and Southerners that in truth resulted in two cultures.

The mere fact that slavery and the plantation flourished in one region and not in the other was only the beginning of the divergence. For, as we shall see, the differences in labor system (slavery) and agricultural organization (plantation) produced still other, and more enduring, cultural differences. Even after slavery was gone those cultural values and traits would remain, much as the waves of a pond lap the shore long after the stone that produced them has sunk below the surface. The ways of life that a society evolves may begin with one set of circumstances, but they find justification and perpetuation through long familiarity, usefulness and sheer habit. And so it was with the Southern tradition that grew up around the slave plantation.

Let us look now at some of the immediate ways in which slavery set off the South from the North; later, we will examine some of the more remote cultural effects of the South's "peculiar institution." Whether slavery existed or not, Southerners would probably have grown their distinctive crops of cotton and tobacco, though probably not sugar and rice, since the latter two required large work forces. The importance of slavery is that it wedded the South to the extensive cultivation of these staples. Slavery provided an agricultural labor supply that was otherwise difficult, if not impossible to secure in a new country, where land was plentiful and cheap, and labor was scarce and expensive. By providing a ready labor supply, slavery made the plantation possible, thereby providing a source of quick wealth and perpetuating a rural society.

There were other ways in which the peculiar agriculture of the South set the region apart from the North. The very crops which the slaves produced were uniquely Southern, for cotton, sugar, and rice could be grown only in the South and tobacco and hemp found their best localities there. Moreover, cotton was almost entirely sold abroad; indeed, southern crops as a whole constituted about two-thirds of the total exports of the United States in the antebellum years. The market for western wheat and pork, on the other hand, was primarily domestic. Thus the facts of trade compelled the South to look outside the country, while the same facts of trade brought the East and West together.

Furthermore, the very concentration of slaves in one section, which was largely the accident of geography and the world demand for cotton, made it inescapable that once slavery became a social and political issue, it would also be a sectional bone of contention. As such it could not help but threaten the unity of the nation as it would not if it had been spread throughout the country. In Brazil, for example, where slavery was legal in all states until within four years of final emancipation in 1888, sectional conflict over abolition was late in developing and therefore constituted no threat to national unity.

But slavery did more than polarize political and moral opinion; it encouraged Southerners to build a system of values and a society that were different from those of the North. What began often as defenses of slavery ended as cherished parts of a Southern tradition that came to be defended for their own sake, regardless of origins.

As an anachronism in the middle of the nineteenth century, slavery naturally provoked attacks from many quarters. Just as naturally, such criticism evoked defensive measures by Southerners to protect their "peculiar institution," as they aptly referred to slavery. Sometimes it is argued that Southerners defended slavery only because it was attacked by outsiders, that if left alone Southerners would have found the institution unworthy of defense. Undoubtedly much of the animus and bitterness evident in the developed proslavery argument of Southerners stemmed from those alien criticisms. But the roots of the Southern defense of slavery go deeper than simple resentment of criticism. For one thing, slavery was economically important to the prosperity of the region, a fact that in itself generated a strong defense. Perhaps as much as 75 per cent of the Southern cotton crop was produced by slave labor; virtually all of the sugar, rice, and hemp crops and most of the tobacco came from the labor of slaves. In short, despite the fact that about three-quarters of Southern families did not own a single slave and that plantations made up less than 20 per cent of the agricultural units of the region in 1860, slavery was central to the production of Southern wealth. The rising price curve for slaves during the last antebellum decade further attests to the economic value that Southerners placed upon slavery.

The peculiar institution provided more than wealth for the South; it also helped to preserve the supremacy of the white man. Southerners did not need slavery to make them believe that Negroes were inferior to white men. That prejudice antedated slavery. But slavery certainly reinforced the Southerner's sense of superiority by making the typical black man a legal chattel. It served the additional end of providing the means for keeping the white man on top. Whether slaveholder or not, most Southern whites defended slavery because it controlled and subordinated Negroes. Even Southern white men who opposed slavery could not really imagine what to do with the Negroes if they were not slaves. As one back-country Southerner confessed to Frederick Olmsted, the northern traveler in the South during the 1850's: "I wouldn't like to hev 'em free, if they gwine to hang around...because they is so monstrous lazy." Besides, he continued, "How'd you like to hev a nigger steppin' up to your darter? Of course you wouldn't; and that's the reason that I wouldn't like to hev 'em free; but I tell you, I don't think it's right to hev 'em slaves so; that's the fac—taant right to keep 'em as they is."[1]

As will be evident a little later, a belief in Negro inferiority was not peculiar to Southerners; Northerners held similar views. What made the South distinctive was its defense of slavery as the proper status for the Negro. In advancing that defense against the criticisms, not only of Northern antislavery people, but of the modern world as well, the South differentiated itself from the rest of the western world. In fact, by defending slavery as a desirable thing, Southerners sacrificed cultural values they had once shared with the rest of the country, like freedom of speech, the right to dissent in politics and religion, and toleration of the opinions of outsiders. In North Carolina, for example, a Southern professor at the University who dared to say he intended to vote Republican in 1856 was dismissed and forced to leave the state; in Kentucky, a Southern newspaper editor who publicly opposed slavery saw his press destroyed. Farther south, in South Carolina, where there was no local dissent, postmasters destroyed any abolitionist literature that came through the mails. In Congress in the 1830's Southern representatives insisted that all Northern abolitionist petitions be barred because of their hostility toward a cherished Southern institution. Freedom of inquiry and dissent stopped in the antebellum South where the security of slavery began. Moreover, the beatings and mob action that accompanied this search for security bequeathed to the region, even down to our own time, a tradition of violence and extralegal action that has been a burden and a characteristic of the South.

In the early years of the nineteenth century, it was New England that was the conservative region while the South was the home of free-thinking Thomas Jefferson and social progress. (Before 1820, for example, most antislavery societies were in the South.) But in the middle of the nineteenth century a society organized around slavery and the plantation could not be progressive and flexible; its ways were too much at odds with those of the rest of the world. Reform and change, which had been cherished words for Jefferson, became dangerous ones in the South of John C. Calhoun. During the 1830's and 1840's all kinds of reforms, from women's rights to phrenology, engaged the restless minds of Northerners, but in the South reform was shunned, for it might endanger slavery. Some Southerners even took public pride, as one North Carolina editor wrote, in being free from "the isms which infest Europe

[1]Frederick Law Olmsted, *The Cotton Kingdom* (Arthur M. Schlesinger, ed., New York, 1953), p. 225.

and the Eastern and Western states of the country." In this connection, it is significant that only two of the one hundred or more utopian communities that were established as a result of the reform outburst of the early nineteenth century were located in the South. Utopias were not for down-to-earth, realistic Southerners.

Southerners may have been Protestants like most other Americans, but as the need to defend slavery mounted in the 1830's and 1840's, southern Protestantism became increasingly conservative. At one time, Jefferson had supported and urged upon his fellow Southerners the widespread acceptance of the radical Unitarian church. But by 1860 that church was no longer to be found in the conservative South, though it flourished in New England. Instead, Southerners turned to a narrow and literal interpretation of the Bible, just as in politics they turned to a literal interpretation of the Constitution. In 1817, when he was still a nationalist, John C. Calhoun told Congress, "I am no advocate for refined arguments on the Constitution. The instrument was not intended as a thesis for the logician to exercise his ingenuity on. It ought to be construed with plain, good sense. . . ."[2] But, as is well-known, by the 1840's and 1850's Southerners were construing the Constitution narrowly and literally.

A literal interpretation of a traditional document, whether the Constitution or the Bible, is typical of a conservative cast of mind, for insistence upon the letter of the law discourages innovations that might be introduced by interpretation. The narrow interpretation of the Constitution that Calhoun used to defend slavery, other Southerners used later to frustrate reform in other areas. Southern religious leaders followed the same path, first looking to a literal interpretation of the Bible to defend slavery and then moving on to a fundamentalist position on questions of theology as well. Ever since, the South has been the principal locale of religious fundamentalism in the United States.

Earlier it was suggested that the South differed from the rest of the United States in its predominately rural character. Let us look more closely now at the causal connection between that fact and the slave-plantation system. In the 1850's the South was the least urbanized of any section of the country, its only large cities being ports around its periphery, like Baltimore, New Orleans, St. Louis, and Louisville. Even when the region was compared with the agricultural West it was conspicuously rural. In 1860, only 7 per cent of all Southerners lived in cities as compared with twice that proportion in the West. In 1850 there were more cities over 3000 population in Indiana and Illinois alone than there were in the nine states south of Kentucky and Virginia. Arkansas counted not a single city of 2500 or more and Mississippi contained only two, each of which was less than 5000.

[2]John C. Calhoun, *Works* (Richard K. Crallé, ed., New York, 1883), II, 192.

One of the direct consequences of the rural character of the South was that the proportion of illiteracy among Southern white people was the highest of the three sections. The concentration of population necessary for a good school system was simply lacking. In 1850 one out of every five white Southerners was unable to read as compared with one out of ten in the western states and one out of thirty-five in the middle Atlantic states. (That these proportions were more a function of the rural character of the region than of hostility toward education was shown by the greater proportion of college students in the South than in either of the other two sections.)

The lack of cities in the South was largely the result of the failure to develop manufacturing in the region. There was some cotton textile manufacturing in Georgia, as well as the impressive Tredegar Iron Works and extensive tobacco manufacturing in Richmond which were well-known, but the region as a whole lagged behind even the new West in manufacturing. Again, the two western states of Illinois and Indiana in 1860 counted more capital invested in manufacturing than all the seven states of the deep South combined. Basically, Southerners found staple agriculture a more profitable and a more socially rewarding field of activity than manufacturing or trade. The reason they did can be explained by slavery and the plantation. One of the necessary bases for the growth of manufactures is an adequate market. A society in which a quarter of the producing population is slaves does not provide a wide market since the slaves consume only the barest necessities. It is not surprising, for example, that Southern states with few slaves, like Kentucky and Missouri, and western Virginia, were the largest producers of manufactures in the South.

The narrowness of the Southern market also helps to account for the inability of Southern ports to maintain direct trade with Europe. Most foreign imports to the South came through New York and other Northern ports. Southerners resented the fact that few ships came to Charleston or New Orleans directly from Europe though Southern cotton paid for half of all United States imports. Southern importers had to pay for extra handling in New York as well as higher shipping charges because of the circuitous routing. This dependence on the North aroused Southern resentment; complaints about it appeared in all Southern demands for political independence. The lack of direct trade with Europe, however, was not the result of Northern conspiracy as many Southerners contended; it was simply the economics of trade. It was unprofitable to run shipping lines to Southern ports when the markets there, because of slavery, were so meager.

The South's failure to develop manufacturing, however, was not only a question of economics. As Southern society perpetuated its rural character through its commitment to slavery and the plantation it also perpetuated and elaborated rural hostility toward industrial and commercial pursuits. As Southerners at the time pridefully said, the Southern gentleman was a landed man with slaves. Even a Southerner like William Gregg, the South Carolina cotton mill owner, who wanted the South to do more manufacturing, feared the social changes industry would introduce. He advised, for example, that cotton mills be located in the country rather than in the cities, for Southern workers, he warned, would be corrupted by urban life.[3]

By retarding the growth of cities and manufacturing, the slave-plantation system shaped still further a distinctively Southern culture. The 1840's and 1850's witnessed a flood of German and Irish immigration into the United States, but the South saw few of the newcomers. There simply was little need for them on the plantations and there were few cities to provide work for them. In 1860 less than 7 per cent of the South's population was foreign-born at a time when 12 per cent of Ohio's and 33 per cent of Wisconsin's were. No Southern state in 1860 counted as high a proportion as Ohio and most were considerably below that figure. Thus, during the 1850's the South avoided both the negative and the positive effects of immigration that were then transforming the North. Socially, the South was fortunate in avoiding the nativist violence born of fear of the immigrant that erupted in Northern cities. But, more important, its economy *lacked* the skills and labor of the new arrivals, which gave an impetus to Northern economic growth in these same years.

The absence of immigrants in the South, except in a few seaports like New Orleans and Baltimore, helped to make the already rural region still more provincial and isolated from world intellectual currents. That provinciality was further enhanced by the South's need to draw away from any outside contacts that might endanger the security of the slave system. Increasingly, connections with the North aroused suspicion, and opinion from abroad was stigmatized as irrelevant if it entailed adverse criticisms of Southern institutions. William Gilmore Simms, the South Carolina novelist, complained in 1846 that he was in danger of being defeated for public office in the coming election because of his frequent visits to the North. "The cry is that I am a Northern man," he despairingly wrote a friend, "that my affinities are with the North etc...."[4] And defeated he was, even though the period of intense suspicion of Northern ties had not yet begun. By the late fifties a defender of the proposal to reopen the slave trade argued that the opinion "of the outside world on slavery is entitled to less weight than upon almost any other subject, being destitute of every foundation which renders opinion

[3]Quoted in Clement Eaton, *The Growth of Southern Civilization, 1790–1860* (New York, 1961), p. 229.
[4]*Ibid.*, p. 297.

respectable."[5] His point was that no one was entitled to comment on the merits of slavery unless he lived under the system. To many Southerners by the close of the antebellum period, the world was out of step with the South.

Around slavery and the plantation, Southerners erected a distinctive way of life that reached its height in the Southern gentleman, whose charming manner, genteel and gracious style of living and conservative leadership of the community became the ideal of the region. It is true that the so-called aristocrats of new states like Mississippi and Alabama were more often first generation nabobs rather than the descendants of cavaliers, as the myths of the region asserted. But new and even crude as the society as a whole may have been—much of the Southwest was still frontier in the 1850's—the Southern planter was the social ideal. For despite the lowly origins of many of the great planters, the fact was that as owners of land and slaves they affected a way of life that fitted the classic ideal of the country gentleman and man of affairs. The semi-literate overseer who hoped one day to own a farm and slaves, the small commercial farmer who was saving for his second or third slave, or the village merchant who worked long hours to gain a competence for his old age, all looked to life on a plantation with a great house as the measure of ultimate success. Being a manufacturer, a cotton factor, or a storekeeper, all of whom were a part of Southern society, may have been a way of making money, but the end of life was not simply wealth but style of life. Money making as such was for Yankees. The Southern planter's ideal and its connection with slavery was spelled out clearly by Samuel Walker, a Louisiana sugar planter in 1856: "Slavery is from its very nature eminently patriarchal and altogether agricultural. It does not thrive with master or slave when transported to cities. . . . I do not care for the general introduction of manufacturing into the South as a system. The assemblage of negroes and whites, or even negroes alone in large bodies in sedentary pursuits deteriorates the animal and unfits them for labor in the field. . . ."[6]

The very management of the plantation revealed the predominance of style over profit. Southern planters' account books were notoriously poorly kept, and the constant interference of the planter in the overseer's management, about which there was much grumbling among the overseers, attests to the fact that planter attitudes were only secondarily directed to efficiency or money making. The large number of poorly paid, poorly trained overseers that planters hired, shows that many planters were thinking more of slave discipline than they were of agricultural

[5]*Ibid.*, p. 323.

[6]Quoted in Eugene D. Genovese, *The Political Economy of Slavery* (New York, 1965), p. 182.

efficiency. Indeed, as one overseer wrote in 1844, "our farmers pride themselves upon being Captains, Colonels, Majors and Judges, far above the honor of being the President of an agricultural society."[7] On the other hand, it was not uncommon for planters to interfere with the overseer's disciplining of slaves because in the planter's mind the Negroes were more than simple chattels; they were his "people." Overseers particularly objected to the practice, common among planters, of checking up on their overseers by asking the opinions of the Negroes. Those planters who did push their slaves hard and emphasized money making were stigmatized as "Southern Yankees."[8]

Considering the emphasis upon a gracious style of living and a disdain for mere money making, it is not surprising that Northerners were strikingly prominent in some of the commercial enterprises in the South. Southerners simply did not care to enter such professions, or they did not have the necessary attitudes and skills for success. A disproportionately large number of native Northerners, for example, were to be found among the merchants and cotton factors in Southern ports. The managers of the most fashionable and financially successful hotels in the South were also displaced Yankees. Indicative of the extra-Southern origins of Southern merchants as well as the high social value accorded the planter class are the careers of Maunsel White and John Burnside of New Orleans. Both were immigrants, both made fortunes as businessmen, yet both ended their lives as great sugar planters.

The planter ideal stressed values and practices that were frankly old world and sometimes even feudal in origin and tone. Reenactments of medieval joustings, in full knightly regalia, were not unknown in the Old South, for Sir Walter Scott and his medieval romances were highly thought of since they extolled a hierarchical, rural society, which Southerners liked to think was similar to their own slave society. The chivalric ideal also carried over into Southern attitudes toward women, who were accorded an exaggerated deference for their delicacy and innocence, despite the undeniably hard labor that was the daily routine of the wife of the average planter. Not surprisingly, the women's rights movement which gained attention in the North in the 1850's found no echo in the South. Or if it did, as in the example of the Grimké sisters of South

[7]Quoted in William K. Scarborough, *The Overseer* (Baton Rouge, La., 1966), p. 122.

[8]An antebellum Southerner, writing on social classes in the South described the "Southern Yankee" as "bent on the accumulation of the sordid pelf; and the crack of his whip is heard early, and the crack of the same is heard late, and the weary backs of his bondsmen and his bondswomen are bowed to the ground with overtasking and over-toil; and yet his heart is still unsatisfied; for he grasps after more and more, and cries to the panting slave: 'Another pound of money, dog, or I take a pound of flesh.' And the lash is never staid, save by one single consideration only—*will it pay?*" D. R. Hundley, *Social Relations in Our Southern States* (New York, 1860), p. 132.

Carolina, the proponents felt compelled to leave the region for the more congenial North.

If women were expected to remain in the home, the men were expected to be forthright and even aggressive leaders in politics and war. Southern interest in military education and the military life was well recognized. (There were more military academies in the South than in any other section, and in 1850 Southerners made up 47 per cent of the members of the West Point graduating class that year, but only 35 per cent of the population of the country.) The prevalence of military titles in the South was both a reflection of their military interests and the romantic outlook of Southerners. "Almost every person of the better class is at least a Colonel, and every tavern-keeper is at least a Major," reported one astonished English visitor to the South in 1834.[9] The addiction of Southerners to dueling was widely acknowledged as a regional characteristic. Dueling occurred at times in the North, to be sure, but it was illegal and carried out in secret. In the South, legal prohibitions, where there were any, were openly flouted and the niceties of the *code duello* both adhered to and appreciated. When Congressman Preston Brooks decided in 1856 to punish Senator Charles Sumner for his public insult to a relative, he carefully chose a cane rather than a whip or a challenge with pistols, for a cane conveyed precisely his low opinion of Sumner while acknowledging Sumner's high station.

Southern social values were at once individualistic and communal. The justification for dueling, for example, was that a man did not expect society to give him satisfaction for an insult; that was a personal matter to be settled by individuals. David Donald has been so impressed by the Southern lack of social obligation and discipline that he named it a significant contributory cause for the defeat of the Confederacy.[10] The world of the Southerner was bounded by the family and his immediate locality; it did not extend to society at large. To that closer and smaller society he owed his primary obligation and from the more detached and larger society he expected little.

By the 1850's Southerners and Northerners alike recognized that they were different, that two civilizations now existed within the United States. (In June, 1860 the *Southern Literary Messenger*, published in Richmond, carried an article entitled, "The Difference of Race Between the Northern People and the Southern People.") But these differences in themselves cannot account for the failure of nationalism that took place in 1861. In fact there is some reason to believe, as David Potter has written, that

---

[9]Quoted in Rollin G. Osterweis, *Romanticism and Nationalism in the Old South* (New Haven, Conn., 1949), p. 105.

[10]See the essay "An Excess of Democracy: The American Civil War and the Social Process," in David Donald, *Lincoln Reconsidered* (2nd ed., enlarged, New York, 1961), pp. 209–35.

today Southerners and Northerners are as different as they were in 1860; yet separation is not likely.[11] Moreover, other societies have developed divergent cultural patterns without splitting apart. One can think of Switzerland in the nineteenth century along with northern and southern Italy, and French and English Canada in the twentieth century. Countries can often survive deep differences in cultural patterns and even different sectional rates of economic growth, if the political ties are sufficiently strong. In the case of the United States, however, strong political ties were not only absent, but as the cultural differences developed, political ties weakened.

One reason they weakened was that almost from the beginning of the Union the doctrine of states rights was ready for use. The significance of this doctrine is not that a Southerner, Thomas Jefferson, introduced it with his Kentucky resolutions, or that another Southerner, John C. Calhoun, raised it to a sectional principle; New Englanders in 1804 and 1814, after all, also had recourse to it. Its importance lies in the fact that states rights provided a *constitutional* or legal basis for the disruption of the Union. For a region as traditional and conservative as the South such a means of protest was necessary as well as congenial. As the rhetoric and facts of Southern secession now make clear, an appeal to revolution would not have carried the South out of the Union in 1860–61. Even in the heated atmosphere of 1860 the average Southerner, who was also conservative, required a legal, constitutional justification for his strike for independence.

But the formal argument of states rights and constitutional secession was not as important in accounting for the breakdown of American nationalism as the conception of the Union that Southerners and many other Americans had come to accept by the 1850's. In part, to be sure, this conception of the Union was an outgrowth of the increasing Southern emphasis upon states rights in the 1830's and 1840's. But to a much greater extent it was the result of American social and cultural development over the preceding half century. The very looseness and mobility of American society, its individualism and lack of traditional institutions like a national church, a national aristocracy, or a dominating national capital predisposed Americans to define the Union in similarly loose and individualistic terms. It was to them a Union freely entered into and freely adhered to. Unlike other countries, Americans believed, the Union was composed of states which linked their fates out of the self-interest of their citizens, not out of military force or fear. Americans regarded their country as the freest in the world simply because its continued existence rested upon the free choice of its inhabitants. Conversely, to

[11]David M. Potter, "The Historian's Use of Nationalism and Vice Versa," *American Historical Review*, LXVII (July, 1962), 924–50.

maintain the Union through force was to destroy the liberty that justified it. As even a Northerner like Wendell Phillips said during the secession crisis, "A Union is made up of willing states, not of conquered provinces. There are some rights, quite perfect, yet wholly incapable of being enforced. A husband or wife who can only keep the partner within the bond by locking the doors and standing armed before them, had better submit to peaceable separation."[12] By the 1850's Northerners as well as Southerners spoke of "this confederacy" when they meant the Union and in doing so they gave popular voice to Calhoun's view that there was no nation, but only a collection of states joined in convenient and free Union. Indeed, few men spoke of the nation at all; almost invariably it was simply the Union.

At no time was the dilemma of American nationhood more clearly delineated than in President James Buchanan's response to the secession of the lower South during the secession winter of 1860–61. A staunch Jacksonian Democrat who had witnessed the firm Unionist stand of his predecessor in the crisis of 1832, Buchanan in 1861 was nonetheless acutely aware of the popular conviction that the United States was not held together by force. As a result he could not bring himself to resist secession by arms, but neither could he, as an old Jacksonian, countenance secession as a legal remedy under the Constitution. In retrospect and despite the criticism that historians have heaped upon Buchanan's "indecision," the truth seems to be that probably a majority of Americans—taking Southerners into the count—agreed with Buchanan's view. The idea of a centralized state maintaining itself by force simply was not, to most Americans, the proper basis of Union.

If most Americans, North and South, in 1860 emphasized a Union of limited authority, there was still a large—and as events would show, a growing—minority who envisioned the United States as a nation, a people united by ties of tradition, history, and emotion. (Ironically enough, many of these people drew their inspiration from Southern leaders of an earlier and more nationalistic time, like Jefferson, Andrew Jackson, and Henry Clay.) To this romantic nationalism Lincoln appealed in his first inaugural address when he spoke of "the mystic chords of memory, stretching from every battlefield and patriot grave to every living heart and hearthstone all over this broad land. . . ." His decision to sustain Fort Sumter tested which view of the Union would prevail, for, as Southern Unionists had warned, to use coercion would cause the upper South to join the new Confederacy. One North Carolina Unionist editor wrote in January, 1861 that he did not believe in secession, but he "would never, as a Southern man, suffer a Southern state to be driven into sub-

---

[12]Quoted in Paul C. Nagel, *One Nation Indivisible. The Union in American Thought 1776–1861* (New York, 1964), p. 257.

jection by armed force, as long as we could stagger under a musket."[13] Even some ardent Northern Republicans, like Horace Greeley, at first counselled that the "erring sisters" be permitted to go in peace, rather than use coercion. Lincoln's decision to hold the Union together by military power marked a new stage in the evolution of American nationhood.

From the war that followed upon Lincoln's decision, a nation emerged where none had existed before. Both Lincoln and his successor Andrew Johnson contended that the war was fought to preserve the Union, but the fact of the matter was that the old Union died when the war began. The old Union had left a loophole for secession; the new Union made secession hereafter intellectually unthinkable and politically impossible.

It was more than a nationalistic conception of the Union that made the change. Of great importance were the nationalizing demands that the war placed upon the institutions of the country. When the Lincoln government undertook to suppress the rebellion, the country was like a jellyfish in organizational structure and internal skeleton. England, Allan Nevins points out, was better organized to fight Napoleon half a century earlier than the United States was to suppress secession.[14] This invertebrate character was even more evident than at the time of the Revolution, for in the interim the country had tripled in extent and seventy-five years of rapid economic growth and democratic individualism had watered down rather than strengthened social cohesion. In 1860 there were no large business enterprises, yet massive amounts of goods had to be produced quickly to equip the great army and navy that would be needed; railroads were still primitive by European standards and differences in gauges made them less useful as long distance haulers than the lines on maps would suggest. There were no medical or legal societies, no business organizations, no farmers' or workers' groups to which the government could turn for advice, assistance, or much-needed expert personnel. The complicated organization required to fight a major war had to be constructed from the ground up. And when it was done a new nation emerged, tied together by the communications, organizations, and bureaucracy generated by the demands of war.

The new nationalism was evident even as the war was being fought. Americans had always been proud of their freedom and prosperity, but few of them had thought in modern nationalistic terms. Loyalty to the Union was common, but loyalty to the nation was a new idea. As Ralph Waldo Emerson said in 1864, "Before the War our patriotism was a firework, a salute, a serenade for holidays and summer evenings. . . . Now

---

[13]Dwight Lowell Dumond, ed., *Southern Editorials on Secession* (New York, 1931), p. 386.

[14]Allan Nevins, *The War for the Union* (New York, 1959) I, 243.

the deaths of thousands and the determination of millions of men and women show that it is real."[15] The measure of that reality was the evocation of an emotional attachment to the nation—that is, the creation of a modern sense of nationhood. It is not accidental that Edward Everett Hale's emotionally nationalistic story "A Man Without a Country" appeared in 1863, just when many Americans were feeling for the first time the emotion of nationalistic fervor. At the close of the war James Russell Lowell commented that before 1860 there had not been "that conscious feeling of nationality, the ideal abstract of history and tradition, which belong to older countries," but now the war had changed that. "Here at last is a state whose life is not narrowly concentered in a despot or a class, but feels itself in every limb; a government which is not a mere application of force from without, but dwells as a vital principle in the will of every citizen. . . . Loyalty has hitherto been a sentiment rather than a virtue."[16]

The marks of a new government of strength to which Lowell referred were all around. In prosecuting the war the Lincoln administration was compelled to take measures that no federal government before had dared to assume, but which thereafter no national government could fail to use. Issues that had been sources of deep constitutional dispute in the years before 1861, now became matters of mere expediency. During the war the protective tariff was raised to new levels, to become a standard Republican campaign plank. Though Democrats in later years, as during the war, would challenge the wisdom of protection, they no longer argued, as they had before 1860, that it violated the constitutional limits on federal power. In the name of winning the war, the finances of the nation felt the centralizing power of the new, vigorous federal government. Congress authorized the printing of almost $400 million worth of "greenbacks" to help pay for the war. This currency was the first paper money issued by the federal government in its history, the backing of which was only the credit and prestige of the government. A national banking system was established to replace the unsystematic state banks; a newly imposed federal tax virtually drove out of circulation the paper money issued by the state banks. The nation's first income tax was enacted along with the first conscription law. Never before had the federal government resorted to such a denial of individual liberty as when it enacted conscription. And the bloody riots that broke out in protest in a number of Northern cities measured in violence the novelty of the experience for Americans.

Undoubtedly the most telling instance of the new nationalism was the destruction of slavery itself. Only a few years before, almost all

---

[15]Quoted in Merle Curti, *The Roots of American Loyalty* (New York, 1946), p. 169.
[16]*Ibid.*, p. 170.

Americans were in agreement that slavery in the Southern states enjoyed a constitutional sanctuary forever. Lincoln himself, in his inaugural address, as a means of forestalling the secession of the upper South, reiterated his conviction that the federal government had no constitutional authority to deal with slavery in the South. Yet within two years, under the exigencies of the war, Congress and then the President abolished slavery in those states in rebellion. The immediate practical effect was nil, to be sure, since federal forces did not yet control affairs in those states. But in the long perspective, those first blows against slavery determined the future and provided yet another instance of the new national power in Washington.

If the war produced a revolutionary effect upon federal power, in other ways it made Americans less radical. For one thing, the new emphasis upon organization, system, and institutions as means for preserving the Union constituted a repudiation of the individualistic, anti-institutional, almost anarchistic outlook exhibited by many reformers of the antebellum years. Men like Emerson and Theodore Parker and movements like Transcendentalism had sung the praises of the individual while questioning the value of organized society with its emphasis upon conformity. Tradition, these reformers proclaimed, was the enemy of progress. The abolitionists, too, had found established institutions faulty if only because they justified the bondage of the slave. Some of the more radical anti-slavery men had even repudiated the Constitution itself as a "covenant with death and an agreement with hell," because it sanctioned slavery.

But when the war became an anti-slavery struggle, organization and established institutions of society were no longer to be scorned. Reformers and social critics who for years had believed that reform could be achieved only by the disruption of institutions, suddenly found themselves, perforce, working to strengthen them in order to preserve the Union and eradicate slavery. After the Civil War American reform lost much of the semi-anarchistic, anti-institutional outlook, which had been so striking in the pre-war years.

To make that observation is only to say that reform now became respectable. During the 1850's many Northern and Southern conservatives had despaired for the future of the Republic as they witnessed unrestrained individualism attacking the organizations and institutions of society. Some, like Francis Lieber, a professor of political science at Columbia College, actually hoped for a war in order to stun the nation back to its senses and social responsibility. The war had the further effect of making clear to conservatives that reform and social change could be supported without at the same time seeming to advocate anarchy or repudiating social institutions. It was not accidental, as George Fredrickson has pointed out, that the conservative elite of the North wholeheartedly supported the Sanitary Commission.[17] The Commission was organized early in the war to provide medical and other aid to the Union soldiers. Like the Army, the Sanitary Commission was one of the new nation-wide organizations that sought to achieve reform *through* institutions, rather than by repudiating them. It also demonstrated that reform could be tough-minded, practical, and devoid of the sentimentality that many conservatives had found objectionable in the reform activities of the 1840's and 1850's. Some of the older reformers, on the other hand, found the new humanitarianism of the Sanitary Commission overly organized and lacking in concern for individuals. Walt Whitman, for example, whose primary drive as a volunteer army nurse was compassion for the soldiers, loathed the male nurses of the Commission, whom he called "hirelings." The purpose of the Sanitary Commission was eminently practical—to return the men to battle as soon as possible, for the winning of the war was the Commissioners' principal object. The means was the institutionalization of medical care and the bringing of efficiency to a hitherto haphazard service. As a consequence, the Commission usually resented the "meddling" and sentimentality of a Clara Barton or a Walt Whitman.

In another way the war moderated the American revolutionary tradition. It destroyed the simple connection between revolution and the Good that Americans had assumed ever since 1776. Down through the years since their own revolution most Americans, both Northern and Southern, had applauded each effort of a suppressed European nationality to be free of its alien master. Thus Americans supported the Greeks and the Latin Americans in the 1820's and the Hungarians in 1848 when they revolted against their oppressors. For many Americans, especially Democrats, who constituted a majority of the voters in the North, and for many Southerners, of course, the secession of the South was 1776 all over again. Among European liberals, too, it was commonplace to regard the secession of the South as an effort by a new people to achieve self-determination and freedom. Such liberals wished success to the Confederacy just as they had wished success to similar struggles for self-determination in central and eastern Europe. Indeed, it was just that analogy that proved embarrassing to many Northerners, when, in 1863, the Poles rose in rebellion against their Russian overlords. It was difficult for some Northern newspapers that supported the war against the South to explain how they could, at the same time, support the Polish revolt in the name of self-determination. When the Russian fleet arrived at New York, the *New York Times*, an ardent supporter of the Lincoln Administration, abandoned the Polish cause entirely in the interest of friendship with

[17]George M. Fredrickson, *The Inner Civil War: Northern Intellectuals and the Crisis of the Union* (New York, 1965), Chap. 7.

the Russians. After the secession of the Southern states it was no longer possible to assume that a people who declared themselves a separate nation should automatically be granted the right of self-determination.

Some political thinkers, like Francis Lieber, argued that Southern secession was illegitimate because it was against a democratic government, against which there was never any justification for violence. In making his point, however, Lieber was compelled to repudiate the Jeffersonian justification for revolution, for Jefferson had drawn no distinction between forms of government in his advocacy of periodic revolutions. The old Jeffersonian love of revolution was undoubtedly romantic as well as impractical, but it had been a symbol of the more profound idea that all governments tend to become rigid and unresponsive to the will of the people (regardless of their form of origin). After the Civil War Americans would never again exhibit that insouciant attitude toward revolution that Jefferson and his generation had exemplified.

"The Civil War," wrote Henry James in 1879, "marks an era in the history of the American mind. It introduced into the national consciousness a certain sense of proportion and relation, of the world being a more complicated place than it had hitherto seemed, the future more treacherous, success more difficult. At the rate at which things are going, it is obvious that good Americans will be more numerous than ever; but the good American, in days to come, will be a more critical person than his complacent and confident grandfather. He has eaten of the tree of knowledge."[18] Other men, too, who lived through the war found the world and their fellow men changed by the conflict. The devotion and courage of the soldiers, the sacrifices of the civilians, and the martyrdom of Lincoln provided a new dimension of human experience as well as setting a new standard of loyalty that transcended self and family. Twenty years after the war, Oliver Wendell Holmes, Jr. vividly recalled that "through our great good fortune in our youth our hearts were touched with fire. It was given us to learn at the outset that life is a profound and passionate thing."[19] A half century after the war, William James, the brother of the novelist, talked of the need for a "moral equivalent of war" in times of peace. James thought he found that equivalent in a new form of service by youth to the nation, analogous to the Civilian Conservation Corps of the New Deal or the Peace Corps and Vista of the 1960's. Still other men, also unable to forget the courage, manliness, and discipline that the war evoked, cast about for ways to call forth those virtues again. One way was through competitive athletics, which became common for the first time on college and university campuses in the 1880's. Henry Lee Higginson, a Boston philanthropist,

---

[18]Henry James, *Hawthorne* (New York, 1879), p. 144.
[19]Quoted in Fredrickson, *Inner Civil War*, p. 219.

hoped to rekindle the fire to which Holmes referred, when he gave an athletic field to Harvard, to be called, appropriately enough, Soldiers Field.

Southerners, too, found the war a sobering experience, for they had lost it. As C. Vann Woodward has pointed out,[20] no other Americans have suffered defeat on the battlefield. Defeat was to make them a little less sure of the future, a little less confident that things would turn out all right, a little less assured that man could control his destiny. The war for them reinforced rather than effaced the differences between the Southerner and the Northerner even as it forced the sections together again under the old flag.

The new nationalism bred by the war displayed its power in the Reconstruction of the South. In swift, clean strokes the Fourteenth Amendment cut down the states and destroyed the old Union. Its very first clause, in which Negroes were made citizens, not only repudiated the Dred Scott decision of 1857, but also for the first time clearly specified United States as well as state citizenship. In its potent second clause, the amendment prohibited the states from depriving any citizen of the United States of his rights or privileges, thereby erecting a whole new series of rights that were derived from the nation's as distinct from the state's authority. In the twentieth century this single clause has been the textual basis of a whole body of judicial interpretation protecting citizens against state power. Freedom of religion, freedom of speech, and freedom for black children to attend schools with white have all been shielded against contrary state action by this one clause. The decline of the states in the federal system can be dated from the Fourteenth Amendment.

The very idea of a reconstruction of the South was a manifestation of a new view of the American Union. At the time of his death Lincoln still talked of restoring the South to the Union as rapidly as possible, with no other social and political changes than the abolition of slavery and the repudiation of secession. His successor, Andrew Johnson, less flexible and more Southern than he, almost achieved that goal at the end of 1865. But for most Northerners the war, in destroying the old Union, made it impossible for the South to return unchanged to political and constitutional power. The underlying assumption of Radical Reconstruction policy as it evolved in 1866 and 1867 was that only by a social revolution in the South could a repetition of secession be averted. Since it had been the different society of the South that was the seedbed of the rebellion, only by transforming that society could the old Union be reconstituted as "One Nation," as Charles Sumner phrased the goal.[21]

20C. Vann Woodward, *The Burden of Southern History* (Baton Rouge, La., 1960), pp. 19–21.
21The words appear in Charles Sumner's essay, "Are We a Nation?" quoted in Hans Kohn, *American Nationalism; An Interpretive Essay* (New York, 1957), p. 127.

Most Radicals, it is true, did not accept Wendell Phillips' plan for an indefinite occupation of the South. But they followed his conception of reconstruction when he described it as "primarily a social revolution. You must plant at the South," he advised, "the elements which make a different society."[22]

Under the Radical program the slave system was to be replaced by civic equality for the Negro and the removal of the great planters and Confederates from the political leadership of the region. Hopefully, loyal Southern whites, Negroes, and Northerners would create a new society modeled after that of the North. And the constitutions which these Reconstruction leaders in the South drew up for the Southern states reflected their revolutionary intent as well as their Northern bias. Popular education was introduced, women's rights over their property expanded, many local officials for the first time made subject to popular election, and railroad and industrial development encouraged. Moreover, many of the carpetbaggers who went South after the war saw themselves engaged in a mission to a benighted and undemocratic South, long retarded by slavery. One carpetbagger, Adelbert Ames, who became Governor of Mississippi, recalled later: "That I should have taken a political office seems almost inexplicable. My explanation may seem ludicrous now, but then it seemed to me that I had a mission, with a large M. Because of my course as military governor, the colored men of the state had confidence in me, and I was convinced that I could help to guide them successfully, keep men of doubtful integrity from control, and the more certainly accomplish what was every patriot's wish—the enfranchisement of the colored men and the pacification of the country."[23]

What better way to remove the source of national disruption forever than to bring the Republican Party into the South, based upon the votes of the former slaves? With such a political revolution the conservative and unprogressive plantation society of the antebellum years would be beyond restoration. Not until the Second World War, when Americans determined to remake German and Japanese society in the image of western political and social democracy, would Americans undertake as thoroughgoing a social transformation as they sought to achieve in the South after 1865. Ironically enough, the demand made upon the South that attracted the most attention then and later—equality for the Negro —was the one least derived from Northern experience.

Prior to the Civil War Americans differed profoundly as to the merits of slavery and the nature of the Union. But many anti-slavery Northerners in seeking to end slavery gave little thought to what should be

[22]Quoted in James McPherson, *The Struggle for Equality; Abolitionists and the Negro in the Civil War and Reconstruction* (Princeton, N.J., 1964), p. 370.

[23]Quoted in James W. Garner, *Reconstruction in Mississippi* (New York, 1901), p. 290n.

the status of the freed Negroes. Undoubtedly one reason the future was so little anticipated was that in the North, where slavery no longer existed, Negroes were neither numerous nor economically important. For Southerners, however, the institution of slavery was the principal means of keeping in subordination a people who constituted a quarter of the population of the South. Abolition would strike not only at their pocketbooks, but at their conception of social order as well. Northerners prior to 1861 would not engage in the debate over slavery on these terms, but when the war brought slavery to an end, it was evident that all along the basic question had been the future of the Negro in American society.

Some of the leading abolitionists like William Lloyd Garrison, Theodore Weld and Angelina and Sarah Grimké, it is true, left no doubt that they believed in the complete equality of the Negro with the white man. But their views were not representative of the millions of Northerners who supported the war against slavery, either in 1868 or after. More typical was the view of a man like James Pike, a Republican journalist and vociferous antebellum opponent of slavery. Pike believed Negroes to be racially inferior and unworthy of inclusion in a white man's society. He advocated that they be herded together into some remote corner of the country and denied any influence. Other anti-slavery men thought the only solution was colonization abroad—usually to Africa—though thirty years of the experiment in Liberia had shown that most Negroes refused to leave their native soil in America for an unknown life on an alien continent. Even Abraham Lincoln was unwilling to grant equality to Negroes, despite his conviction that slavery was wrong. While President he continued to seek places and means to colonize the freed slaves outside the country, on the assumption, as he told a group of Negroes in 1862, that black men would never be accepted as equals by white Americans. Ultimately, Lincoln's practical outlook compelled him to abandon his attempts at colonization, but his frequently expressed doubts that Negroes could live in equality with white men in the United States accurately reflected the attitudes of millions of his fellow citizens in the North.

Lincoln's doubts rested on the undeniable social fact that the North, like the South, did not treat the Negro equally. All the Northern states, it is true, had abolished slavery by the 1850's; yet only six states permitted Negroes to vote and only Massachusetts allowed Negroes to attend the same schools as whites. In fact, in most of the states of the North Negroes received no public education at all, though they were expected to pay taxes, obey the laws, and live peacefully. Throughout the North Negroes were relegated to special sections in or excluded entirely from omnibuses, trains, hotels, restaurants, theaters, and other public places. Moreover, in times of tension Negroes were the object of vicious physical assaults, usually without any provocation except their color, as during the draft riots in New York City in 1863, when scores of Negroes were maimed and dozens murdered by mobs. Although 200,000 Negroes served honorably in the Union Army and Navy during the war, resentment against Negroes ran high in the military services. Soon after the Emancipation Proclamation was issued one Indiana soldier wrote: "As soon as I get my money . . . i am coming home let it be deserting or not, but if they dont quit freeing the niggers and putting them in the North i won't go back any more . . . it is very wrong to live with niggers in freedom."[24] Northern public figures during the war, as before, did not hesitate to express their conviction that Negroes could not be accorded equal rights with white men. Indeed, as late as January, 1865 the Democrats in the House of Representatives fought hard to prevent the passage of the Thirteenth Amendment, which would finally abolish slavery throughout the Union. As it was, the amendment passed by only two more votes than the necessary two-thirds. In 1867, the very same year that the Radical Republican Congress was imposing Negro suffrage upon the South, the states of Ohio and Kansas turned down proposals for Negro suffrage, though the number of Negroes in both states was politically inconsequential. When Negroes were voting in the South as a result of the Radical Reconstruction policy, more than half of the Northern States still withheld the ballot from black men.

In the context of these Northern attitudes and practices, the revolution in public policy that took place between 1865 and 1870 is all the more remarkable. For in the course of those five years the American people wrote into the Constitution, with the Fourteenth and Fifteenth Amendments, the complete equality of black and white, both at the polls and in civil rights.

How was such a revolution in law and outlook effected? Part of the explanation is undoubtedly to be found in the desire of Republicans to have their party be the agency for the remolding of the South. For if that party was to remain in power and to consummate the revolution it thought necessary in the South, it would have to secure votes there. As Thaddeus Stevens, one of the leaders of Radical Reconstruction, told the House in January, 1867, unless Negroes received the right to vote, loyal whites in the South would be outvoted. Furthermore, he pointed out, Negro suffrage was necessary to "assure the ascendancy of the Union party. . . . I believe that on the continued ascendancy of the party depends the safety of this great nation."[25]

But those who believed in and worked for the idea of Negro equality had a second reason for their espousal of Reconstruction. They drew inspiration from the traditional American belief in equality. When Americans spoke of equality they had in mind at least two meanings.

[24]Quoted in Bell Irvin Wiley, *Life of Billy Yank* (Indianapolis, 1952), p. 112.
[25]Quoted in Ralph Korngold, *Thaddeus Stevens* (New York, 1955), p. 382.

The most familiar kind was equality of opportunity; indeed, it was this form of equality that Lincoln invoked when he opposed slavery because it set limits to the opportunities open to Negroes. But along with equality of opportunity Americans also cherished a belief in the equality of worth of each individual. Alexis de Tocqueville saw this form of equality being practised in the age of Jackson when he reported that Americans could not abide invidious social distinctions. They will accept many things, he said, but they will not accept aristocracy. Mrs. Trollope also noticed the same attitude, though with more distaste. She reported that Americans disliked being domestic servants because such a station implied servility and denied equality. Politically the American idea of equality of worth expressed itself in the drive for universal manhood suffrage, in which each man's vote was equal, regardless of his wealth, education, or any other personal qualification.

Historically, to be sure, Americans have not applied the idea of equality, of either kind, to all people. Nativists during the 1850's, for example, tried to prevent immigrants from being treated equally with the native born, but that attempt was scotched before the decade was out. For most of the nineteenth century, however, Indians, Negroes, and women were all denied equality of both kinds, just as in earlier years men without property had been denied the suffrage or the opportunity to hold office. Yet, despite the unevenness with which Americans have interpreted equality, it is clear that the principle has always carried great persuasive power for them. Appeals to it cannot be easily brushed aside. During and immediately after the Civil War, abolitionists and other advocates of Negro equality successfully appealed to that egalitarian tradition. The stirring war against slavery and the need to make the results of the war permanent coincided with great tradition. As a consequence equality for the Negro was written into the Constitution.

As events turned out, though, the inclusion of the Negro in the doctrine of equality was more a promise than a commitment. Considering the long history of the American belief in Negro inferiority, any other result would have been a miracle. Even for abolitionists the conception of full equality for Negroes was essentially a matter of faith, for there was little social evidence to support it. In both North and South the Negro was at the bottom of the social and economic scale. The abolitionists, however, began with the assumption that Negroes were human beings who had been ruthlessly suppressed for generations. In spite of the Negroes' low position, the abolitionists possessed the faith that once slavery was removed the human potentiality of the black man would realize itself in tangible social achievement. One abolitionist, appalled at the ignorance and lack of morals he found among the newly freed slaves of the South, clearly expressed both that faith and the social obstacles to its realization: "They, the freedmen, are not angels," he wrote to a fellow abolitionist in 1863, "they are not even civilized men. . . . We must deal with them as children in intellect, but men in instincts and passions. . . . It is useless to disguise the difficulties, or to throw a false halo of romance about the negro. It is the highest proof of genuine sympathy and interest, to admit all the disagreeable features of the work, to realize all the difficulties and *still to go on*."[26]

Although abolitionists might have faith in the human potentialities of the Negro, most pragmatic Americans did not. For them to be convinced required tangible proof—that is, social achievement. For many reasons the requisite achievement did not come. The burden of slavery was too heavy to be quickly overcome, the opposition of white Southerners too consistent and determined, and the support from Northern Republicans too meager. In fact, as early as 1872 liberal members of the Republican Party in the North were already calling for the abandonment of the social revolution in the South on the ground that it had failed. Men like Horace Greeley and Carl Schurz, who had been strong supporters of early Reconstruction policy, now turned against it. By 1876 the Republican Party as a whole reached much the same conclusion as it became evident that the North was not prepared to force equality of the Negro upon the South.

The Radical experiment in social revolution was abandoned for another reason besides the weakness of the Northern commitment to Negro equality. Just as in the full flush of the war, Americans had taken up a new position on the Negro, so they had assumed, as we have seen, an extremely nationalistic position in regard to the power of the federal government. Together, these had constituted the Radical experiment to remold Southern society. By the middle seventies the war was ten years in the past; yet the Radical experiment had produced few results. The Southern whites were more adamantly set against Reconstruction policy than ever; by 1874 over half of the former Confederate states were already under Democratic regimes. Only by a persistent exertion of federal power in the South for an indefinite length of time could the few remaining Radical regimes be sustained. This unprecedented road, however, the country was not prepared to take. Not even the great majority of Northern Republicans cared to defend the degree and duration of centralized control that would be necessary for the full carrying out of the Radical policy in the South. The end came in 1877 with the withdrawal of the last federal troops from the South, much to the relief of most Northerners as well as white Southerners.

When faced with a choice between a federal government that would dominate the internal affairs of the states for an indefinite period and one under which local self-government by Southern whites would be

[26]Quoted in McPherson, *Struggle for Equality*, pp. 174–75. Emphasis in original.

restored, Americans chose the latter. Local self-government, Americans were saying, was a more important social and political value than the renovation of the South or the civic equality for the Negro. They also were announcing that there were limits to the new war-born powers of the federal government.

In cultural terms the ending of Radical Reconstruction meant that the United States was not to be a unified, homogeneous nation, but a federation of regions still, in which each section would be free to pursue its own social patterns. Indeed, it was the decision to limit the national authority and to permit cultural diversity that explains the rapidity and ease with which "The Road to Reunion" was traveled after 1876. Since, for the remainder of the century, the dominant Northern attitude was that white Southerners ought to be permitted to shape their society without interference, Southerners could fit their divergent culture into the national framework without strain.

One consequence of the South's freedom from national interference was the removal of the Negro from the mainstream of Southern life through disfranchisement, segregation, and confinement to the occupation of farm laborer. The acceptance of that consequence by the nation was symbolized by the decision of the Supreme Court in *Plessy* v. *Ferguson* in 1896. In that decision the court accepted segregation in public facilities so long as the accommodations were equal, arguing that "Legislation is powerless to eradicate racial instincts or to abolish distinctions based upon physical differences, and the attempt to do so can only result in accentuating the difficulties of the present situation."[27]

The imprimatur of a Northern-dominated Supreme Court upon Southern segregation, ironically enough, only deepened the division between the two cultures. Northern society, to be sure, did not accept the Negro as an equal any more than Southern society. The social practices of the North denied the Negro equal access to public places like bathing beaches, hotels and restaurants. Moreover, Negroes held the lowliest jobs there too because white men would neither hire them for anything better nor work beside them. But it is significant that the North did not follow the Southern states in writing segregation into law. Indeed, some of the Northern states actually enacted civil rights acts as gestures—they were little more than that—in support of Negro equality. More important, Negroes continued to vote freely in the North and legally-segregated schools gradually disappeared. In the South, on the other hand, the tendency was in the opposite direction: to separate white and black as much as possible by law.

It is quite true that to the Negro then and later the difference between legal and practical segregation may not be great. But from the standpoint

[27]163 *U. S. Reports* 551.

of the historian attempting to discern the social values of a society, a legal commitment is a significant statement. There is surely a difference in values between a society that legally discriminates against Negroes, as was true in the South, and one that legally proclaims equality even though it practices discrimination, as happened in the North. For law is an expression of social values; it sets social goals and by its very existence influences the direction in which the society will move. In fact, without the enactment of the Fourteenth and Fifteenth Amendments during the Reconstruction period, the movement for real equality for Negroes in practice as well as in law would have been constitutionally without foundation in our own time. By the close of the nineteenth century the South still held out against the inclusion of the Negro within the meaning of equality.

The disfranchisement and segregation of the Negro by law in the South was not the only manifestation of the persistence of the two cultures. Less ambiguous evidence is to be found in the failure of the movement to create a "New South." After Reconstruction enterprising Southerners like Henry Grady, Daniel Tompkins, and Richard Edmonds, and many others campaigned vigorously and unceasingly for the industrialization of their region. Although there was a quickening of industrial activity in the South in the 1880's, the results by 1900 were disappointing. At the opening of the new century Dixie was still an agricultural region, beset by a growing burden of farm tenancy, both black and white, and falling even farther behind the North in industrial growth. Indeed, as Clement Eaton has pointed out, in 1900 the South produced a smaller proportion of the nation's manufactures than it had in 1860.

The devastation of the war undoubtedly accounted in part for the slow economic growth of the South. But modern examples of rapid recovery from even more extensive destruction, as in Germany and Japan after World War II, suggest that war damage alone is not enough to account for the retardation. A more convincing explanation is to be found in the persistence of those attitudes and circumstances that had set the South apart from the rest of the nation in the days of slavery. Slaves may have constituted a poor market for manufactures, but poverty-stricken Negro tenant farmers did not provide a much better one. And a segregated, uneducated Negro population and a poorly educated white population offered little hope for a changed situation in the future. As before the war, the South found itself caught in a vicious economic circle. The limited economic opportunities of the region meant that the efforts of the leaders of the New South to attract immigrants into the region came to nothing, though the incoming tide of newcomers reached new heights in the North during the 1880's. Socially and religiously the South remained outside the mainstream of American society; it had few immigrants, few Jews, and few Catholics. Furthermore, without substantial industrial growth the South continued to be without many large cities, though the decade of the 1880's saw spectacular urban growth in the Middle West and on the Pacific coast. Although advocates of a New South were articulate and could capture the attention of Northerners, the fact of the matter seems to be that the great majority of Southerners were simply not convinced of the virtues of an industrial order. This lack of conviction is evident, for example, in the attacks by Populists and other leaders of farmers upon the advocates of a New South and Northern capitalists and upon the whole idea of an industrial South. Moreover, as late as the 1920's a group of Southern intellectuals like the Vanderbilt Agrarians could still get a hearing for their forthright repudiation of industrialization for the South.[28]

The divergence between the cultures may have originally been brought about by slavery and the plantation, but a generation after slavery had been eliminated the two cultures still prevailed. Indeed, by the close of the nineteenth century the gulf between the two may well have widened because of the South's military defeat and the "angry scar" of Reconstruction. Much later, in the middle of the twentieth century, the task of reducing the differences would be taken up again. This time the agencies at work would be more powerful than ever: the economic impact of World War II, which brought massive federal and private investment in the South, widespread communications media like radio, television and the movies, which spread a single culture throughout the nation, and the Second Reconstruction initiated by the Supreme Court and implemented by the administration of Lyndon Johnson.

[28]See *I'll Take My Stand* by Twelve Southerners (New York, 1930), which is the manifesto of the group.

CLYDE GRIFFEN
Vassar College

the

progressive

ethos

With the vantage of the Twenties, the distinguishing feature of reform in the Progressive era was an ethos, a unifying spirit, which did not long survive the first World War. Secular and religious versions of the nineteenth-century evangelical Protestant hope of realizing the Kingdom of God on earth permitted prewar Americans seeking different kinds of change to think of themselves as sharing in a larger crusade. At the height of progressive enthusiasm in 1912, the journalist Walter Weyl described a new social spirit which "in a curiously cautious, conservative way, is profoundly revolutionary.... Reform is piecemeal and yet rapid. It is carried along divergent lines by people holding separate interests, and yet it moves toward a common end. It combines into a general movement toward a new democracy."[1]

Contrasts with the Twenties are dramatic. The chief casualty of disillusionment following the war "to make the world safe for democracy" was that ethos which allowed reformers with separate interests to learn

[1]Walter Weyl, *The New Democracy* (New York, 1964), pp. 165, 167.

from each other and to cooperate in pushing particular measures. In 1912 Theodore Roosevelt—no stranger to paranoia about danger from the Left—could say, "... many of the men who call themselves Socialists to-day are in reality merely radical social reformers, with whom on many points good citizens can and ought to work in hearty general agreement, and whom in many practical matters of government good citizens can well afford to follow."[2]

After the Bolshevik Revolution and the American "Red Scare" of 1919, Christian Socialists and other proponents of welfarism were suspect. As early as 1919 settlement worker Lillian Wald reported that old and generous friends were withdrawing financial support because she was "'socialistically inclined.' Poor things I am sorry for them—they are so scared. It is foolish since . . . I am at least one insurance against unreasonable revolution in New York."[3] By 1920 some erstwhile progressives were joining businessmen in campaigns, such as that of the National Civic Federation, to root out radicalism within the churches, labor unions, and organizations of the foreign-born.

The dissipation of support for reform was more rapid than awareness of it, however. In the immediate aftermath of war everything seemed possible to the dedicated minority of professional social workers, social gospel clergymen, and leaders of voluntary reform associations who had developed more ambitious notions of reform than most prewar progressives. Some continued to hope for an early realization of their dreams as late as 1924 when LaFollette went down to defeat and Massachusetts rejected the child labor amendment, but most came earlier to a recognition that they were engaged in a long, uphill struggle. Their development of new programs and new concepts for social reform during the Twenties was ignored by most Americans or looked upon as subversive.

The blurring of the lines between radicalism and reform in prewar progressivism had been matched by a blurring of religious differences. A sense of sharing a vision of Christian democracy had obscured for

[2]Theodore Roosevelt, *Autobiography* (New York, 1913), p. 542.

[3]Quoted in Clarke A. Chambers, *Seedtime of Reform: American Social Service and Social Action, 1918–1933* (Minneapolis, 1963), p. 25. Chambers' first chapter describes the frustration in the Twenties of the hopes of progressives concerned with social justice for an early realization of their aims. But his book emphasizes continuity in reform through the "small band [who] kept the faith," pioneering new methods and goals. Continuity, especially the survival of progressivism in Congress, also is the theme of Arthur Link, "What Happened to the Progressive Movement in the 1920's?" *American Historical Review*, LXIV (July, 1959). The present essay, by contrast, emphasizes the difference in national receptivity to reform efforts in the progressive era and the Twenties. Recognizing continuities, it is more impressed by the dissipation in the Twenties of the ethos of the prewar reform coalition and consequent loss of support from important elements of that coalition and from the wider public which responded to its appeals.

reformers that growing schism between liberal and fundamentalist Protestantism which roughly paralleled divergence between urban and rural mores. In the early Twenties William Jennings Bryan personally tried to keep alive a unifying emphasis on Christian ethics and brotherhood, insisting that there was no conflict between his social progressivism and his religious fundamentalism. But the loss of tolerance among progressives was all too evident in the fight at the Democratic convention of 1924 on the issue of censuring the Ku Klux Klan.

Many of the components of the old progressive coalition were present and dissatisfied during Normalcy. But, as historian Henry May observes, "What was lacking was the old idealistic cement, the thing that had made representatives of opposing interests sing hymns for Roosevelt or wipe their eyes over a Wilson peroration."[4] The idealism which did remain, especially among the minority who elaborated new programs for reform during the Twenties, changed gradually in emphasis. Postwar progressives continued to combine traditional appeals to moral sentiment with a stress on fact-finding and scientific analysis, but the balance changed as the latter waxed in importance and the former waned. The religious enthusiasm and rhetoric with which prewar reformers expressed their vision of democracy to a Bible-reading generation became the exception rather than the rule.

The dissipation of support for reform coincided with an evident decline in the place and influence of religion in the lives of urban middle class Americans. The churches continued to prosper in membership and especially in finances, but a host of signs indicated that religious affiliation had become a conventional expectation rather than a primary commitment. Religious illiteracy and secularism increased. Symptomatically, whereas Sunday School enrollment among Protestant denominations showed an average increase of nearly 40 per cent between 1906 and 1916, the increase between 1916 and 1926 was only 10 per cent. Customary symbols of the nation's commitment to Christianity like faithful church attendance, grace before meals, and family devotions were no longer usual in respectable homes. Furthermore, as Winthrop Hudson notes in his study of American Protestantism, "Religion, which had been one of the principal subjects of serious and intelligent discussion in the literary monthlies and quarterlies, now became conspicuous by its absence, and was usually resurrected only to serve as a target for the satirical shafts of a Mencken."[5]

Protestantism lost the momentum that fed its prewar optimism about

[4] Henry May, *The End of American Innocence* (New York, 1959), p. 394.

[5] Winthrop Hudson, *The Great Tradition of the American Churches* (New York, 1963), p. 196. See also C. E. Olmstead, *History of Religion in the United States* (Englewood Cliffs, New Jersey, 1960), pp. 542–45 and Bureau of the Census, *Religious Bodies: 1926*, I (Washington, 1930), pp. 51–52.

ushering in a new era of brotherhood and righteousness, of establishing the Kingdom of God on earth. In 1912 the chairman of the concluding congress of the Men and Religion Forward Movement had exulted, "There are more gifts for the cause of Christ, in money and lives, today, than ever before."[6] Never had so many American churchgoers been so actively involved in so many efforts to improve the world, from modest attempts to provide kindergartens, parks and playgrounds for the children of urban tenements to ambitious campaigns to end child labor. Churchmen mobilized great drives to Christianize America and the world, such as the Laymen's Missionary Movement and—in the immediate aftermath of war—the Interchurch World Movement. But by 1921 it was apparent that lay support for these drives had largely evaporated.

Coincidence in the fortunes of Protestantism and reform was not an accident. Progressivism was the sensitive conscience of American Protestantism during its most expansive and optimistic era, a time when American idealism was practically synonomous with Protestant idealism and vice versa. Progressives could appeal effectively to Americans with no predisposition toward reform because the progressive vision and rhetoric derived from Protestant values pervasive among the native-born Progressives gave those values an interpretation which made them a cutting edge for social change, but their interpretation was made easier by fundamental changes in American religion and popular culture in the nineteenth century. The general direction was apparent in antebellum moral, humanitarian, and utopian ventures fostered by the perfectionist tendency of revivalism. The emphasis on right behavior rather than right belief in revivalism—and subsequently in theological liberalism—made Protestantism highly susceptible to reform impulses.

As the Twenties revealed, the churches became victims of their own success in shaping American values. The intellectual framework of a distinctively Christian perspective had been eroded by the simplifying influence of revivalism and by the accommodation of new currents in secular thought since the Civil War. Instead of being the beginning of a golden age as so many Protestants had thought, the progressive years were the culminating expression of a culture which had accepted Protestant moralism but lost the piety which vivified it.

For the historian this aftermath, this loss of a sense of the distinctively Christian, poses a large temptation to discount the importance of evangelical Protestantism in shaping the progressives' perspective. Aware-

---

[6]*Messages of the Men and Religion Movement*, I (New York, 1912), p. 9. On the relationship between evangelical Protestantism and American culture, see, in addition to Hudson, H. Richard Niebuhr, *The Kingdom of God in America* (New York, 1937), Sidney Mead, *The Lively Experiment* (New York, 1963), and W. G. McLoughlin, "Pietism and the American Character," *American Quarterly*, XVII (Summer, 1965), 163–86.

ness of the subsequent development of American society makes it seem more plausible to emphasize the relation of progressive reforms to interest groups, to the growing academic and professional concern for planned social change, or the search for new means of social control by an urban middle class. Because a scientific emphasis was the wave of the future, it is all too easy to overlook the continuing influence of the older ethos during the progressive years even on the professional and managerial mind and to conclude, mistakenly, that modernity became fully characteristic of that mind before the war.[7]

Necessary as the new professionalism and the concerns of interest groups are to an explanation of reform in this period, they do not account for the peculiar slant in the progressives' way of looking at and talking about their world. The most overt expression of this perspective is found in their expectation for the immediate future, their vision of a new democracy and a new Christianity. The favorite slogan of liberal Protestantism, the Brotherhood of Man under the Fatherhood of God, expressed a deeply felt sense of common cause and hope for men of widely different convictions. The range of meanings given to both democracy and Christianity made it possible for progressives to accommodate the methods and values of an emerging urban, bureaucratic, and relativistic society without seeming to abandon those of an older America of smaller communities and simpler, more secure faith.[8]

Progressivism began with the belief that righteousness could be restored by the exposure of wrong-doing and appeals to conscience and civic pride. Hard experience with backsliding from the converted and the resilience of the unconverted led most progressives to put less emphasis on moral crusades and more emphasis on careful formulation and enforcement of particular measures for change. Between 1900 and 1917 the shibboleths of reform, especially among the younger generation, became scientific investigation of social problems and efficient administration of their remedies. But before 1917 few reformers abandoned the older faith that something approaching a moral perfecting of society

---

[7]Samuel P. Hays, *The Response to Industrialism, 1885–1914* (Chicago, 1957) and Robert Wiebe, *Businessmen and Reform* (Cambridge, 1962), especially pp. 206–12. Wiebe's recent book, *The Search for Order, 1877–1920* (New York, 1967), is an extreme example of this tendency to push the emergence of a modern mentality backward in time and to discount the lingering influence of evangelicalism on the attitudes of urban professionals and businessmen.

[8]On progressivism as a mood, a perspective, and a preoccupation with realizing certain values, see May, *End of American Innocence*, Chaps. 1–3; Richard Hofstadter, *The Age of Reform* (New York, 1955), Chap. 4; George Mowry, *Era of Theodore Roosevelt* (New York, 1958), Chaps. 2, 5; Paul Glad, "Progressives and the Business Culture of the 1920's," *Journal of American History*, LIII (June, 1966), 77–78; and especially Richard M. Abrams, "The Failure of Progressivism," paper read before the Organization of American Historians, Cincinnati, Ohio, April 28, 1966.

was possible through appeals to the nation's conscience. Even men most inclined to rationalism in their approach to reform, like Herbert Croly and Louis Brandeis, pointed Americans toward the most demanding moral aspirations.

Progressives shared a sense of living in a peculiarly hopeful time when brotherhood, justice, and righteousness were about to be realized to a degree never thought possible before. The key to social progress was simple—a matter of right values—but no previous generation had had sufficient faith or understanding of society to carry out with any fullness the related ideals of Christianity and democracy. Progressives believed with Walter Rauschenbusch that organized Christianity in the past "has accepted as inevitable the general social system under which the world was living at the time, and has not undertaken any thoroughgoing social reconstruction" implementing the teachings of Jesus. Most of them also agreed with Rauschenbusch that "to undertake the gradual reconstruction of social life consciously and intelligently would have required a scientific comprehension of social life which was totally lacking in the past."[9]

Looking at their immediate past, progressives shared a sense that the possibilities of human nature for joyous and wholesome living had not been fostered in the Gilded Age, with its extremes of vulgar materialism and over-refined, ascetic idealism. They saw themselves as more open to new ideas, more tolerant of differences, and freer from puritanical rejection of innocent pleasures than their mugwump predecessors in reform. They prided themselves on bringing to reform a realism and practicality that they believed the genteel reformers, Populists, and other crusaders of the late nineteenth century lacked. Their calling was to show that "practical idealism" and "applied Christianity" could remake society, that goodness need not be ineffectual.

A book on *The Church and Society*, published in Macmillan's Social Progress Series in 1912, typifies the progressive coupling—without any sense of disparity or incompatibility—of an exalted vision of the future with an emphasis on immediate practicality in the means of reform. The author, R. Fulton Cutting, a founder of New York City's Bureau of Municipal Research, rejoices in the "audacious optimism" of the Laymen's Missionary Movement in looking forward to an "evangelization of the world in this generation" and himself proposes a "saturation of Society by Christianity through its public functionaries. . . ."

Cutting emphasizes throughout the book the previous "failure on the part of the Church to recognize that government is the most potent factor in social uplift and that inefficient administration can manufacture more social ill than a generation of social programs can remedy." As his con-

[9]Quoted in Donald B. Meyer, *The Protestant Search for Political Realism* (Berkeley, Calif., 1960), p. 17.

cluding illustration of what can and should be done, he describes the
various methods by which New York City clergymen have aided the
Bureau of Municipal Research's efforts to secure an adequate city budget
for schools, playgrounds, juvenile courts, hospitals and for the prevention
of crime, disease, and abuses in housing. He praised especially the
ministers' "two budget Sundays to show New York congregations the
religious and moral significance of scientific budget making. . . ."[10]

The juxtaposition of a practical piece-meal approach to reform with
a religious or quasi-religious vision of democracy is the most satisfactory
test of a progressive. Like any attempt to isolate a dominant type of
reformer among the many seekers after change in early twentieth century
America, this definition leaves us with borderline cases. But it also
clarifies distinctive emphases.

This definition separates progressives from businessmen concerned
only with reforms favoring their own economic interests, such as the
shippers who supported railroad regulation and the city bankers outside
of Wall Street who supported a federal reserve plan.[11] It also separates
progressives from political leaders of the foreign-born and representatives
of organized labor. The latter cooperated with progressives on measures
to improve the lot of the working class, but did not share native-born
Protestant America's preoccupation with assimilating alien elements and
eliminating class divisions.[12]

This definition distinguishes the progressive outlook both from the
lack of emphasis on "the art of the possible" among genteel reformers
of the Gilded Age and from the explicit rejection of monism in religion
and morality by younger intellectuals. The progressive did not share the
genteel faith that preaching of right doctrine by the intelligent minority
would of itself ultimately bring political righteousness. They regarded
as pious hope the conviction—as expressed by George William Curtis—
that "it is after all, 'the Remnant' that avails, even though it be the
reviled Mugwumps."[13]

The older generation of reformers had not paid enough attention
to realities; some of the younger generation, at the other extreme, adopted
a thoroughgoing relativism which made the study of what is the pre-
condition for a satisfactory formulation of what ought to be. In *A Preface
to Politics* in 1913, the young Walter Lippmann described the idealism
and moralizing of many progressive reformers as the triumph of past

10Robert Fulton Cutting, *The Church and Society* (New York, 1912), pp. 10, 26,
28, 176–79.

11Wiebe, *Businessmen and Reform.*

12Irwin Yellowitz, *Labor and the Progressive Movement in New York State, 1897–
1916* (Ithaca, N. Y., 1965).

13G. W. Curtis to H. C. Potter, December 2, 1884, Henry Codman Potter MSS
(Archives of the Protestant Episcopal Diocese of New York).

taboo over present need, of routine over creativity. Lippmann called for an experimental ethic which recognized that "truth is a thousand truths which grow and change...."[14]

In practice, progressives often moved toward relativism in their explanation of behavior, but they did not abandon the older faith in a secure and coherent moral universe. They escaped that sense of being adrift which Lippmann described for the rebels of his generation: "We are unsettled to the very roots of our being.... There are no precedents to guide us, no wisdom that wasn't made for a simpler age."[15] The progressives were a transition generation. The Protestant middle class culture in which they grew up—their education, in the broadest sense—allowed them to adapt to new ideas and situations without seeing clearly how far they were departing from the world view of their childhood. This essay is intended as a brief history of that education, beginning with the influence of revivalism in shaping the culture into which they were born and then describing the kind of preparation their world provided in the years between the Civil War and the beginning of the twentieth century.

The chief features of the progressive vision of democracy were anticipated in the "awakened" Protestantism of the three decades after 1850, the period in which most progressive leaders were born. Revivalism in the age of Jackson had simplified piety, rendering it more susceptible to influence by popular attitudes and by secular thought. To understand this transformation is to understand how American Protestantism could become almost synonymous with American idealism, both in its more self-justifying and complacent moods and in its times of self-criticism and reforming zeal.

By the middle of the century revivalism had become the usual means of breathing new life into the churches of most denominations.[16] Viewed simply as a technique for encouraging conversions, it was neutral theologically and could be used alike by the orthodox Calvinist, the perfectionist Methodist, and the evangelical Unitarian. In practice, revivalism after the 1830's undermined theological orthodoxies of every kind by making theology itself seem less important. It promoted a religion of the heart as against the head by insisting that the struggle for the soul of the sinner was won or lost in the heart alone.

This disjunction of emotion and intellect had not characterized the teaching of early leaders of revivalism like Lyman Beecher and Asahel Nettleton. They appealed to heart and mind simultaneously, regarding

---

14Walter Lippmann, *A Preface to Politics* (Ann Arbor, Mich., 1962), p. 94.

15Walter Lippmann, *Drift and Mastery* (Englewood Cliffs, N. J., 1961), p. 92.

16On antebellum revivalism see W. G. McLoughlin, *Modern Revivalism* (New York, 1959); Timothy Smith, *Revivalism and Social Reform* (New York, 1957); Whitney Cross, *The Burned-Over District* (Ithaca, N. Y., 1950); and Charles Cole, *Social Ideas of the Northern Evangelists* (New York, 1954).

revivalism as an auxiliary to the church's normal life of instruction and prayer rather than as its central feature. The shift in emphasis in the 1830's reflected the influence of Finney and his imitators in making the churches' success in inducing conversions the test of their spiritual health. Henry Ward Beecher carried this to its logical conclusion. He recalled without any embarrassment in 1882, "I gradually formed a theology by practice, by trying it on, and the things that really did God's work in the hearts of men I set down as good theology, and the things that did not, whether they were true or not, they were not true to me."[17]

As the size of the harvests increased, optimism mounted as to the possibility of saving the entire nation. As early as 1829 one religious observer commented that "the same heavenly influence which, in revivals of religion, descends on families and villages . . . may in like manner . . . descend to refresh and beautify a whole land."[18] Such optimism, spurred especially by the nationwide revivals of 1857, gave impetus to post-millennialism in the churches. The increase in benevolent and humanitarian activities was further evidence that God was ushering in His Kingdom.

The harvests also had a levelling effect. They made social differences between men and ideological differences between denominations seem of less consequence. The vision of an entire nation saved replaced the idea of the Elect as a minority. Concerned primarily with success in inducing conversions, revivalists of various denominations banded together in prayer meetings to conduct intensive and sustained efforts on a larger scale than a single preacher could manage.

A centrifugal tendency continued—indeed the splitting off of new sects occurred with greater frequency in an age of religious excitement—but the divisions increasingly seemed less important than a broader common identity. The latter was encouraged by the fact that so many American sects, including the numerous Methodists and Baptists, lacked a well-defined ecclesiastical tradition. With little sense of a distinctive history of their own, they tended to make Jesus and the primitive church normative. Appealing to the same models, they found it easy as theological differences became less important to stress the Brotherhood of Man under the Fatherhood of God. Christian democracy was nourished by the democracy of revivalism.[19]

17Quoted in Hudson, *Great Tradition*, p. 173.

18Quoted in Perry Miller, *The Life of the Mind in America from the Revolution to the Civil War* (New York, 1965), p. 11; on millennialism, see the review article by David Smith, "Millennarian Scholarship in America," *American Quarterly*, XVII (Fall, 1965), 535–49.

19On the way in which Protestant churchmen through "establishment and control of both public and private schools . . . stamped upon neighborhoods, states, and nation an interdenominational Protestant ideology which nurtured dreams of personal and social progress," see Timothy L. Smith, "Protestant Schooling and American Nationality, 1800–1850," *Journal of American History*, LIII (March, 1967), pp. 679–80.

Revivalism everywhere tended to make the Christian life seem simpler and more congenial to the many. Emphasis on the loving mercy of God in accepting sinners transformed the image of the Christ into an increasingly sentimentalized Jesus, friend and teacher, exemplified in Washington Gladden's hymn of 1879, "O Master, Let Me Walk With Thee." Ethics became a matter of the heart more than the head. Anxious to avoid a utilitarian line of argument which they deemed dangerous to revealed religion, the academic moral philosophers who most influenced evangelical America divorced ethics, in theory, from rational consideration of the consequences of behavior to the individual and to society. They espoused a modified Scottish realism which held that intuition or conscience was the proper guide to right action.[20]

The moral philosophers' appeal to intuition suggests their confidence that individual consciences would agree on what was virtue and what was vice. Judging from the readers and histories, Sunday School tracts and manuals on how to get ahead in life, this confidence was fully justified. Educational and other popular books endlessly enumerated and illustrated the virtues of benevolence, self-reliance, humility, sincerity, perseverance, orderliness, frugality, reverence, patience, honesty, purity, punctuality, charity and so on.[21]

There was nothing new in the virtues themselves, but there was in this era, as in other revivals of pietism, a tendency to take them literally. They were interpreted as demanding far more of human nature than the churches in more complacent eras would suppose. The requirement of purity was construed in favor of puritanism; benevolence became unceasing attention to the moral and spiritual improvement of other men whether they desired it or not.[22]

The moral absolutism of the school readers was offset to some extent by an emphasis on success, an opportunistic bias which was most marked in manuals on how to get ahead in life. The difference in moral emphases between those Americans who responded most to this opportunistic bias and those who like the progressive reformers responded more literally to the moral idealism of their education is exemplified in an episode reported by the young Wisconsin lawyer, Robert LaFollette. He had defended successfully a tramp accused of shooting with intent to kill,

[20]Wilson Smith, *Professors and Public Ethics: Studies of Northern Moral Philosophers Before the Civil War* (Ithaca, N. Y., 1956).

[21]On the moral consensus as seen in schoolbooks, see Ruth Elson, *Guardians of Tradition* (Lincoln, Nebraska, 1964); as seen in the literature of success, see Irvin Wyllie, *The Self-Made Man in America* (New Brunswick, N. J., 1954).

[22]The pietism and moralism which Queen Victoria symbolized in nineteenth-century England was an outgrowth of the evangelical revival there, reminding us that the influence of revivalism was not peculiar to America. English evangelicalism influenced American abolitionism; a little later, the American Dwight L. Moody won his first great success as a revivalist on a tour of Britain. See Frank Thistlethwaite, *The Anglo-American Connection in the Early Nineteenth Century* (Philadelphia, 1959).

but the praise of his performance by local lawyers and politicians made him uneasy. "They seem to consider that I did a smart thing—that I was sharp in the management of the matter and keen in the argument—but they don't seem to think that I did it all because I thought he was innocent—that I was simply fighting a fight for the truth."[23]

The progressives grew up with a moral consensus so clear and unquestioned that they tended to assume this consensus was characteristic of human nature wherever it was permitted to develop freely. This assumption easily fostered righteous indignation against violators of the consensus; personalities with an authoritarian warp carried this to the blind intolerance of "sinners" which not infrequently appears in progressive crusades against intemperance, gambling, and prostitution. But the most universal consequence of consensus was a security about fundamental values and what constituted the good life. Remembering that security with an oversimplifying nostalgia, George Creel wrote, "Life presented no soul-tearing problems necessitating a call for psychiatrists, for there were things that decent people did and things they did not do. And all knew what they were."[24] This sense of security about values makes it much easier to understand John Dewey's faith that ethics could be made an empirical science and also why Dewey's ethical pronouncements so often proved to be the same as those of liberal Christianity.

The pervasiveness of this antebellum moral code owed much to the great expansion of publishing which reinforced preoccupation with self-improvement among the literate middle class. Conformity even on "minor morals", as manners often were termed, was encouraged by the increasing number of books devoted to them—twenty-eight in the 1830's, thirty-six in the 1840's, and thirty-eight in the 1850's. The development of a mass audience for a much broader kind of self-improvement was whetted by that spontaneous upsurge of adult education, the Lyceum movement, in which groups of citizens and whole communities organized themselves into local associations for intellectual advancement. In the 1840's a technological revolution in printing and an expanding transportation network made it easier for publishers to exploit that audience. Hot competition sprang up in cheap editions of new English and American books.[25]

The significance of this revolution for the education of the progressive generation is hard to overestimate. A nation-wide popular culture emerged in the 1840's and 50's, spurring the levelling tendency of American society by making "culture" available to the many. The best-sellers of that "culture" included the banal works of lady novelists like Mrs.

23Quoted in Belle and Fola LaFollette, *Robert M. LaFollette*, I (New York, 1953), 46.

24George Creel, *Rebel at Large* (New York, 1947), p. 24.

25On the emergence of mass culture, see Carl Bode, *The Anatomy of Popular Culture* (Berkeley, Calif., 1959); for the best-sellers, see F. L. Mott, *Golden Multitudes* (New York, 1947) and James Hart, *The Popular Book* (New York, 1950).

E. D. N. Southworth as well as the more lasting contributions of Washington Irving and Fenimore Cooper, but even so it was a levelling upward sufficient to encourage all but the fastidious that an entire people could be elevated spiritually, morally, and intellectually.

The sentimentality of so much of the new popular culture encouraged a belief in the levelling upward of society in much the same way as revivalism's emphasis on a religion of the heart did. All men were capable of pure and exalted feelings, whatever their capacity for reasoning. Throughout the novels, the chromos, the ballads, and the melodramas, the ties of love, in weal and woe, are omnipresent. The family circle was the consummate symbol of love. In Donald Mitchell's bestseller of the Forties, *Reveries of a Bachelor*, subtitled a *Book of the Heart*, the Bachelor characteristically sits by his fireside entertaining visions of an ideal wife, of his own unselfish devotion to her and to his children, and of the solace she provides when his friends, relatives, and finally he himself die.[26]

The very democracy of this emphasis on feeling reinforced the Evangelical tendency to hold up an ideal of human relations associated with the family and friendships as the ideal for society at large. The emotional penumbra which surrounded the ideal of the Brotherhood of Man for so many progressives makes more sense in the light of their exposure to a popular culture idealizing those relationships. This idealization was all the more potent because it came at the very time when the nuclear family in a mobile society was increasingly vulnerable to disruption of its integrity and authority and, simultaneously, more important as a source of emotional support for the individual.

Preoccupation with the immediate family circle in popular culture reflected the situation of the family in Western society by the mid-nineteenth century. Compartmentalization of work, home life, and education replaced for increasing numbers of men the usual experience of the past where these activities occurred largely under the same roof. In middle class homes the gradual withdrawal of the family into privacy was almost complete. Even servants within the household had separate living quarters. Whereas before, the child was educated by the larger world which was incorporated within or moved easily in and out of the household, he now was increasingly insulated at home and at school from the workaday world of adults.[27]

---

[26]Bode, *Anatomy*, pp. 212–13.

[27]On changes in the family in the western world see Philippe Aries, *Centuries of Childhood* (London, 1962), especially the conclusion; in America, see Bernard Bailyn, *Education in the Forming of American Society* (Chapel Hill, N. C., 1960), especially pp. 22–27; W. E. Bridges, "Family Patterns and Social Values in America, 1825–1875," *American Quarterly*, XVII (Spring, 1965), 3–11; Richard L. Rapson, "The American Child as Seen by British Travellers, 1845–1935," *Ibid.*, XVII (Fall, 1965), 520–34. For many Americans transiency offset this tendency to insulation. Residence in board-

As the number of parental surrogates readily available decreased, the concentration of attention and affection on the immediate parent-child relationship increased. The result was a strong tendency toward indulgence. Corporal punishment in the discipline of children was replaced increasingly by appeals to their love for their parents and their shame in disobeying them, a replacement encouraged by a developing literature of child nurture. By the 1850's the new pedagogy had vanquished, in theory if not always in practice, the Puritan idea that the child's sinful will must be broken at an early age.[28]

Not all of the progressives benefitted in their own childhoods from the new and milder pedagogy, but they were profoundly influenced by the premium which the literature as well as the domestic arrangements of their time placed on familial intimacy and love. Woodrow Wilson was descended from a succession of Scotch Presbyterian ministers, ruling elders, or professors of theology who gloried in the logical exposition of their faith and distrusted mere emotionalism in religion. But the books that his father, also a Presbyterian clergyman, read aloud to his family—most often the novels of Dickens and Scott—did nothing to perpetuate the distinctive rational piety of his forebears.

Nor did the effusive expression of affection between parents and children encourage perpetuation of the Calvinist emphasis on the awesomeness and inscrutability of God the Father. Rather, the love of the dear Saviour Jesus for his flock—increasingly revivalism's chief appeal to the sinner—was made believable to young Wilson in the evident devotion of his parents to "our precious son" and "darling boy". It was natural for the mature Wilson to describe Christianity as a personal relationship with God, a gospel of love to which "you are drawn by the knowledge that if you come you will be received as a son. Nothing but yearning draws you."[29] Almost without exception the progressive reformers took ideal qualities associated with the home, in fact or in evangelical precept, and held them up as a standard for the wider world.

The best testimony to the success of evangelicalism in infusing American culture with a profoundly idealistic moralism is to be found among

---

ing houses and hotels gave children an experience of human variety and fellowship wider than that of family, social class, or locality although it did not significantly alter the developing pattern of compartmentalization of work, education, and home life. See Daniel Boorstin, *The Americans: the National Experience* (New York, 1965), pp. 145–47. But this very rootlessness also increased yearning for secure and intimate relationships and helps explain the immense popularity of sentimentalized views of family life and friendship.

[28]On the new pedagogy and literature for children see Bernard Wishy, *The Child and the Republic* (Philadelphia, 1968).

[29]Woodrow Wilson, "The Young People and the Church" (1904) in R. S. Baker and W. E. Dodd, eds., *College and State: Educational, Literary and Political Papers by Woodrow Wilson*, I (New York, 1925), 485.

those progressives whose religion placed them outside the mainstream. Jews like Henry Morgenthau, Senior, and Louis Brandeis (before 1912) believed in the desirability of assimilation. In Morgenthau's case, his evident anxiety to become as American as possible resulted in a self-image which is almost a parody of evangelical gentility.

In his autobiography Morgenthau reports that the gift of William Penn's "No Cross, No Crown" by a Quaker doctor inspired him to compose "twenty-four rules of action, tabulating virtues that I wished to acquire and vices that I must avoid. . . . The fact is that I acquired an almost monastic habit of mind and loved the conquest of my impulses much as the athlete loves the subjection of his muscles to the demands of his will." He expresses thanks for having grown up in the era when Emerson led American thought and New England provided so many examples of moral idealism, firing his boyish imagination with "a vision of a life of unselfish devotion to the welfare of others."[30]

Any generation would have found it difficult to come to terms with the new social order produced by industrialization and urbanization after the Civil War. But the problem was exaggerated for a generation raised with so refined a moral idealism and such high hopes for the future as that born in the late 50's, 60's, and 70's. It escaped the chastening and sobering experiences of soldiering; more important, the war made no significant difference in the popular culture in which the progressives grew up. The two antebellum decades have been called the "Sentimental Years," but as Robert Roberts has noted "the implication of sentimentalization of human relationships could with equal accuracy be applied to the Gilded Age."[31]

The direction Protestantism took in the postwar years tended to reinforce this sentimentalization rather than to call it into question. Dwight L. Moody and a number of other urban revivalists preached an otherworldly fundamentalism unsympathetic to visions of the Kingdom come on earth, but they did nothing to challenge the pre-war idealization of personal relations and its projection as a standard for society. More important, the dominant tendency of urban middle class evangelicalism was not toward fundamentalism but toward a theological liberalism optimistic about the future of American society, whether from a gospel of wealth or a social gospel standpoint.

The response of the more sophisticated urban churches to Darwinism was the clearest indication that Protestantism had lost its intellectual rigor and any significant detachment from secular culture. With remarkable ease, clerical and lay reconcilers such as John Fiske, Henry Ward Beecher, and Lyman Abbott devised a variety of syntheses of

[30]Henry Morgenthau, *All in a Lifetime* (New York, 1922), pp. 15, 16, 94.
[31]H. Wayne Morgan, ed., *The Gilded Age: A Reappraisal* (Syracuse, N. Y., 1963), p. 194.

evolutionary thought and Christocentric theism. Few of them involved serious grappling with the issues a naturalistic interpretation of human evolution posed for Christian theology. Instead they offered fairly simple ideas of animal and human progress, arguing that God was continuously working in and through natural law to bring about this progress. Irreconcilable doctrines or biblical accounts became metaphors rather than literal truths.

This accommodation by Protestant intelligentsia to prevailing winds of secular doctrine was repeated on a much lower level by a general confusion of religion and culture. In rural and small-town America that confusion is seen most clearly in Chautauqua—which Theodore Roosevelt called the "most American thing in America." The Chautauqua movement grew out of a Methodist minister's summer program, begun in 1874, for training Sunday School teachers. A regular program of education, cultural uplift, and entertainment was soon added. By 1900 these summer sessions at Lake Chautauqua had attracted so many imitators that promoters put Chautauqua on the road, pitching tents for a five or six day program in town after town across the country.

Religion degenerated into a vapid religiosity in that enthusiastically received class of inspirational speakers whom the Chautauqua managers privately labelled "mother, home, and heaven." Among the favorite items on tent programs were William Jennings Bryan's "Prince of Peace" lecture and the Rev. Russell Conwell's sanctification of the pursuit of riches, entitled "Acres of Diamonds." They shared popularity as well as the platform with such "uplifters" as the Chicago Lady Entertainers singing "My Grandfather's Clock" and "Blest Be the Tie That Binds" and chalk-talker Ash Davis with his reproduction of the "Statue of Liberty Enlightening the World."[32]

The most educated, especially in the big cities, were more restrained than Chautauqua. But both the more perfunctory and conservative kind of urban churchgoers and the social gospellers were moving in a similar direction to that of Chautauqua. They, too, identified Christ with their particular view of American culture and those views were not so far apart as they seemed superficially. The Clarence Days who treated religion as a necessary propriety frequently could be persuaded to support institutional methods in their affluent parishes in an attempt to make them more attractive to workingmen. Among the clergy a promoter of the gospel of wealth, Russell Conwell, and a moderate social gospeller, W. S. Rainsford, were pioneers in the movement to make the individual parish a neighborhood social center as much as a place of worship. Their

32On the mentality of rural and small-town Protestantism, see Paul Glad, *The Trumpet Soundeth* (Lincoln, Nebraska, 1960); on Chautauqua, see Victoria and Robert Case, *We Called It Culture* (Garden City, N. Y., 1948) and Harry Harrison and Karl Detzer, *Culture Under Canvas* (New York, 1958).

churches, the Baptist Temple of Philadelphia and St. George's Episcopal Church in New York City, offered a wide variety of facilities and services, including gymnasiums, employment bureaus, singing, sewing, and dramatic clubs, and agencies selling food and fuel to the poor at cost.

The same Bishop Lawrence who is forever quoted for his gospel of wealth dictum in 1900 that "Godliness is in league with riches" also helped author the 1904 Report of the Episcopal Church's Standing Commission on the Relations of Capital and Labor which reflected the social gospel. This report argued that, given present commercial conditions, labor must be organized to "maintain such a standard of wages, hours and conditions as shall afford every man an opportunity to grow in mind and in heart."[33] The participation of conservatives like Lawrence in statements such as this swelled the tide of optimism during the progressive years about the possibility of meliorating social ills. It encouraged the illusion that an immensely active and prosperous Protestantism moved as one in ushering in the Kingdom.

The very vagueness and sentimentality of postwar Protestantism made it easier for reformers to claim its support for progressive causes. For the genteel middle class most influenced by it, it also heightened the shock of confronting the uglier realities of the new social order. Discovering industrial conflict and urban poverty was unsettling enough to a generation educated to a lofty idealism, but there was also the disillusionment of discovering how frequently men with the highest moral pretensions betrayed them in their behavior.

The grossest violations of traditional ideals were not the most disturbing. The financial and political misdoings of Jay Gould and Jim Fisk or the blackmail of distillers by the Whiskey Ring within the Grant administration could be chalked off to bad men. But it was not easy to explain away the discovery that some of the most respectable people profitted from illegal activities like prostitution and gambling conducted on properties they owned. Yet, as Lincoln Steffen's series of articles published as *The Shame of the Cities* illustrated, that was the discovery of reformers in city after city as they tried to wipe out commercialized vice and corruption in politics.

Nor was it easy to explain away the pious John D. Rockefeller who contributed munificently to a host of Baptist philanthropies but apparently saw no contradiction in driving independent oil refiners out of business by methods which, as set forth in Ida Tarbell's series of articles, shocked progressives everywhere. Theodore Roosevelt spoke to the experience of his generation when he said, "the longer I have lived the more strongly I have felt the harm done by the practice among so many

---

[33]"Report of the Standing Commission on the Relations of Capital and Labor at the General Convention of the Protestant Episcopal Church held in Boston in October, 1904" (Pamphlet in H. C. Potter MSS), p. 2.

men of keeping their consciences in separate compartments; sometimes a Sunday conscience and a weekday conscience . . . sometimes a conscience for their private affairs and a totally different conscience for their business relations."[34]

Expressing their dismay was easier for the generation that went progressive than finding a model of the idealist with which to identify. Civil service reform tended to attract that portion of the middle class most imbued with evangelical notions of righteousness, but also most vulnerable to charges of irrelevance and ineffectuality during the Gilded Age. Their ideal of the good citizen emphasized purity of motive and scrupulousness in means to a degree which men of affairs, and especially hard-headed politicians, found totally unrealistic. Senator Roscoe Conkling of New York called the reformers "the man milliners, the dilettanti and carpet knights of politics . . . they forget that parties are not built up by deportment, or by ladies' magazines, or gush."[35]

While young progressives were learning that preaching principles was not sufficient for the political success they sought, a Harvard philosopher —also raised in the world of middle class idealism—was criticizing the philosophies that world found most congenial. Significantly, William James used the word "refinement" to characterize rationalistic and idealistic philosophies which satisfied a desire for a simple, clean and noble world by leaving out the contradictions of real life.

The unhappy result, said James, was that such desperately needed qualities as faith in man's capacity to shape his destiny, tender concern for others, and a sense of reverence for the wonder of the universe became identified with a philosophy which was a "monument of artificiality." In sheer reaction those who loved facts were inclined to adopt a point of view which was irreligious, materialistic, and fatalistic. What James wanted, and sought to offer in his formulation of pragmatism, was a philosophy which was at once grounded in experience and receptive to the highest human hopes.[36] What the progressives wanted was a comparable approach to social reform.

The initiation of the progressive generation into the problems and possibilities of their world was a peculiarly encouraging education for middle class reformers. It was an exposure to the disturbing realities of social injustice, economic waste, and political corruption, but an ex-

[34]Theodore Roosevelt, *Realizable Ideals* (New York, 1911), pp. 3–4; on the concern with hypocrisy in English middle class culture which was also profoundly influenced by evangelicalism, see Walter Houghton, *The Victorian Frame of Mind* (New Haven, Conn., 1964).

[35]Quoted in Matthew Josephson, *The Politicos* (New York, 1938), pp. 246–47; on the reputation of genteel reform see Richard Hofstadter, *Anti-Intellectualism in American Life* (New York, 1963), Chap. 7; the foundation of the reputation in fact can be seen in Geoffrey Blodgett, *The Gentle Reformers* (Cambridge, Mass., 1966).

[36]William James, *Pragmatism* (New York, 1955), pp. 28, 56–57.

posure within the context of a substantial hopefulness that these could be changed by means consonant with middle class values.

As a younger generation coming of age in a time of social unrest, the progressives not surprisingly showed a greater readiness than their elders to investigate that unrest, to explore the world beyond the confines of their middle class upbringing. Some went to live in alien territory like the settlement house workers. But many more made occasional forays into it as did the young New York assemblyman, Theodore Roosevelt, when he accepted Samuel Gompers' challenge to accompany him into the tenements to see the conditions under which cigars were made. The progressives came to pride themselves on not flinching from the most unpleasant facts. Some of them were so conscious of having been insulated in their middle class upbringing from the harsher facts of society that they tended, if anything, to identify reality with the more sordid, corrupt, or conspiratorial behavior they discovered.

The progressives also were more open than their elders to seeing things from fresh perspectives, as Jane Addams saw the immigrant or, Fremont Older, the corrupt politician, or Ben Lindsey, the juvenile offender. Lindsey, the Kid's Judge whose Denver courtroom became a model for progressives, attributed his own interest in the influence of environment on delinquency to one case. The anguish of a toothless old woman whose boy Lindsey had just sentenced to state reform school for stealing lumps of coal from the railroad tracks unsettled the judge and led him to look into the family's circumstances. He found that home was a cold room in a tenement where the father, a smelting worker, was dying of lead poisoning without receiving any compensation from his employer. With this perspective, he found it impossible to think of the boy as bad or sinful by nature, still less to be treated the same as hardened criminals. Lindsey began to explore the possibilities of rehabilitation rather than punishment, of exposing the wards of his court to a new environment of better care and education.[37]

But the fresh perspective of Lindsey's generation was only in small part a matter of youthful openness to experience. The popular writers and academicians who most influenced progressives emphasized the influence of environment on behavior; by the turn of the century the earlier evangelical view that "sin" and deficiency of character explained poverty had been largely discredited. The common denominator of the progressives' mentors was an optimism about man's ability to translate his social ideals into reality.

The writers with the largest audience before 1900 made the ideal of the Brotherhood of Man under the Fatherhood of God the foundation of their discussion. The most widely read book on social policy was Henry George's *Progress and Poverty*, a best-seller in the 80's and 90's and the

[37]Eric Goldman, *Rendezvous with Destiny* (New York, 1952), pp. 121–23.

only book largely devoted to economic theory ever to win such success. Only a minority were converted to George's panacea of a single tax on land, but all carried away his message that poverty was not the result of God's will, of Nature, or of individual sin, but of society's failure to destroy monopoly and special privilege.

For the minority who did accept George's panacea as well as his vision of progress, response to the book often was akin to that experienced in revivals. Brand Whitlock said that, in reading George's books, Tom Johnson, the reform mayor of Cleveland, "had a spiritual awakening, experienced within him something that was veritably, as the Methodists would say, a 'conversion'."[38]

Edward Bellamy's best-selling utopian novel, *Looking Backward*, took antimonopolism to a collectivist conclusion that George found abhorrent. But Bellamy's import for the middle class which read him so eagerly was much the same as George's. Christian solidarity and decency could be reinforced by proper social arrangements rather than being contradicted as they were under the present social system.

George and Bellamy could be dismissed as amateurs, but their optimism was backed by a growing body of academic social analysis which claimed scientific support for the idea that man can direct social change to rational purposes. Economists and sociologists like Richard T. Ely, John R. Commons, Simon Patten, Albion Small, Henry Carter Adams, and Edward A. Ross, rejected the determinism which laissez-faire conservatives like William Graham Sumner read into evolution. They reinterpreted Darwin or drew upon European social analysis, especially the German historical school of political economy, to develop a justification for more centrally directed public policy making.[39]

The fact that a number of these new professional investigators identified themselves as reform-minded Christians, promoting the social gospel within Protestantism and emphasizing the importance of ethics as a dimension of their discipline, was reassuring. The most influential, Ely, insisted that "Christianity which is not practical is not Christianity at all" and altered the scope of that practicality by asserting, "God works through the State in carrying out His purposes more universally than through any other institution."[40]

This relation with the social gospel helped to obscure the shift

[38]Brand Whitlock, *Forty Years of It* (New York, 1925), p. 155; on the quasi-religious character of American social and economic thought, conservative as well as reformist, see T. E. Cliffe Leslie, "Political Economy in the United States," *Fortnightly Review*, October 1, 1880 and Goldman, *Rendezvous With Destiny*.

[39]On the anti-Spencerian sociologists and economists, see Sidney Fine, *Laissez-Faire and the General-Welfare State* (Ann Arbor, Mich., 1964), Chaps. 7 and 8 and Jurgen Herbst, *The German Historical School in American Scholarship* (Ithaca, N. Y., 1965), especially Chaps. 6 and 7.

[40]Quoted in Fine, *Laissez-Faire*, p. 180.

from a religious to a scientific perspective in reform which already was underway. Under the auspices of Christian professionals, the specific furnishings of progressive minds more often came from contemporary developments in the sciences of man, society, and nature than from religious sources. Frederick Howe, Woodrow Wilson, Walter Weyl, Albert Shaw and others were exposed directly to the new social sciences in the universities, but many more progressives learned from them. Both LaFollette and Roosevelt said that Ely affected their thinking. Roosevelt is reported as observing that Ely "first introduced me to radicalism in economics and then he made me sane in my radicalism."[41]

The new professionalization and specialization of inquiry which shaped progressive realism was most clearly evident in the natural sciences and in engineering. In a society which valued learning for its utility in mastering the environment, there was a natural stimulus for the newly emerging class of professional investigators to become advisors to government, private interest groups, and the nation at large on the practical implications of their subjects. In some cases, notably the four national societies representing civil, mechanical, electrical and mining engineers, the very esprit de corps of the professionals early came to include a mission to teach society how to use its resources more efficiently. Individual scientists and engineers employed by the federal government went far beyond their assigned duties in helping to initiate policies or to create the public sentiment needed to enact legislation they desired. For example, Frederick Newell, chief hydrographer for the United States Geological Survey, agitated throughout the 1890's for a new irrigation policy.[42]

The professionals' concern for efficient use of resources produced the conservation movement, one of the greatest contributions of progressivism. As Samuel Hays has shown, the men who pushed the changes in national policy on irrigation, forest reserves, public land, mineral resources, and inland waterways did not do so out of the hatred of monopoly and special privilege which motivated many progressives. Their primary commitment was to efficiency, not to the extension of democracy. Indeed, the kind of planning and coordination they desired was hard to reconcile with the emphasis on grass roots control, decentralization of power, and encouragement of individualism in progressivism of the New Freedom variety.

41*Ibid.*, p. 240.

42For the activities of Newell and of other Federal officials who promoted conservation—such as Gifford Pinchot and Overton Price in the Bureau of Forestry, botanist Frederick Coville and engineer Elwood Mead in the Department of Agriculture, W. J. McGee in the Bureau of Ethnology, and Joseph Holmes and Marshall Leighton in the Geological Survey—see Samuel P. Hays, *Conservation and the Gospel of Efficiency* (Cambridge, Mass., 1959).

A concern with administrative efficiency and expertise, often with elitist overtones, can be found among other progressives. But it would be grossly misleading to emphasize conflict between the expansive democratic sentiments so frequently expressed and the nascent planning mentality most clearly evident among professionals in conservation, municipal reform, and the scientific management movement. During the progressive years the conflict was more often potential than actual. Louis Brandeis, for example, was a strong believer in leadership by intelligence, but as progressivism swelled to flood tide and his own political influence increased he became optimistic about the people's ability to choose good leaders and about the value of interaction between public and expert opinion.[43]

Wisconsin under LaFollette illustrates the kind of balance usually struck in the progressive years. As Governor, LaFollette sought to enact a reform program grounded in a realistic appraisal of needs and so well-devised that it could withstand searching opposition. His innovation, admired by progressives everywhere, was in the extent to which he drew upon the expertise available at his State University in drafting bills and in staffing State boards. The shape of particular reforms reflected the opinions of the expert, as did the civil service reform bill LaFollette asked Professor John R. Commons to draft. The broad social vision which permeated the reform movement in the State was LaFollette's.[44] The progressives might be as elitist at heart as some of the experts who served them, but it was the reformers' vision of a new democracy which gave the era its distinctive quality.

The old and the new coexisted in progressivism. Exposure to, even training in, the new inductive techniques of the social sciences did not immediately overcome the older evangelical propensity for moralizing issues. The habit of polarizing behavior into righteousness and iniquity, was strongest among those closest to the older evangelical mentality, but it was not confined to them. An anticlerical progressive like Brand Whitlock could interpret a party platform and campaign promises as the most serious of moral obligations. He declared, "I suppose no greater moral wrong was ever committed in America" than the Democrats' passage of a high tariff in 1893 betraying their appeals to workingmen in 1892 which called for downward revision.[45] Protectionism as such was still an "evil" to Whitlock in 1925, echoing Woodrow Wilson's moralistic approach to the tariff question in the campaign of 1912. Describing discussion of the problem of monopoly in business, in which the tariff was so crucial a factor in his view, Wilson had said, "America began

[43] Samuel Haber, *Efficiency and Uplift: Scientific Management in the Progressive Era* (Chicago, 1964), pp. 78–79.

[44] R. S. Maxwell, *LaFollette and the Rise of the Progressives in Wisconsin* (Madison, Wis., 1956), Chap. 9.

[45] Whitlock, *Forty Years*, p. 89.

to display a broken field ... groups contending for new ways to settle new questions; whereas there is but one way to settle questions, new or old, and that is by the old way of righteousness, of righteousness and justice."[46]

Wilson's campaign approach to the tariff problem was the moralizing of nineteenth century free trade and anti-monopolism, not the concern with efficient development of resources characteristic of scientific management. To be sure, the tendency to moralize issues exists in every generation. What makes it so conspicuous among progressives is its prominence *despite* their evident desire to escape the naiveté of genteel reform. It contrasts sharply with the remarkable modernity of intellectuals like Arthur Bentley, Charles Beard, and Thorstein Veblen in going beyond the forms of government, business, and the university to expose how these institutions actually worked.[47] The relationship of progressivism to the moral universe of nineteenth century Protestantism is so striking precisely because progressivism also anticipated in varying degrees the attitudes of planning and scientific management.

If a moralizing tendency continued to limit the new progressive realism, so also did the incredible surge of optimism about the future of the nation and mankind that became so pronounced around 1907 and 1908. It is true that this optimism was most extravagant among the spokesmen for small-town and especially midwestern America, the world which clamored for the sunshine and sweet verities of Chautauqua. The perennial Nebraska optimist, Bryan, heralded the coming to realization of the centuries-old dream of the brotherhood of men in talks and articles after 1906. Bryan's Kansas neighbor, Republican progressive William Allen White, was just as exuberant in 1909, claiming that American institutions were becoming progressively "reflections of the spirit of Christ .... I think there never has been a time in the world when ... this good will was so much a part of human institutions, political and commercial and religious."[48] But even so skeptical a product of the new learning as Walter Weyl temporarily lost his doubts about the efficacy of middle class reformism in describing *The New Democracy* in 1912.

Yet however much their moralizing and optimism seem limitations on

46Woodrow Wilson, "An Unweeded Garden," October 18, 1912 in John W. Davidson, ed., *A Crossroads of Freedom* (New Haven, Conn., 1956), p. 463.

47On the anti-formalism and pragmatism of progressive intellectuals, see Morton White, *Social Thought in America* (New York, 1949) and Charles Forcey, *The Crossroads of Liberalism* (New York, 1961).

48White to W. E. Barton, December 20, 1909 in Walter Johnson, ed., *Selected Letters of William Allen White, 1899–1943* (New York, 1947), p. 104. If, retrospectively, we are inclined to think that the progressive generation generalized a host of small and in many cases transient improvements into a bad case of wishful thinking, it is well to remember that the seeming tide of betterment was sufficiently impressive to modify even the attitudes of some skeptical intellectuals like Walter Weyl and the social gospeler, Walter Rauschenbusch.

their realism in retrospect, the progressive reformers found these qualities no handicap in overcoming the Gilded Age image of the reformer as an ineffectual wishful thinker. Quite the contrary, these characteristics enhanced their appeal to contemporaries still receptive to an evangelical appeal to further the coming of the Kingdom. Combined with the progressive emphasis on practicality they helped make the reformer seem like a sensible citizen who had more conscience and vision than his fellows. Theodore Roosevelt led the way, in this as in so much else, by bringing to reform a high sense of adventure as well as respectability. No one was more conscious than Roosevelt of the importance of identifying idealism with healthy red-blooded, high-spirited American manhood. Nothing upset him more than the idea that Americans might become divided "into two camps, one camp containing nice, well-behaved, well-meaning little men, with receding chins and small feet . . . who if they are insulted feel shocked and want to go home; and the other camp containing robust and efficient creatures who do not mean well at all."[49]

Roosevelt himself practiced as well as preached the strenuous life, from boxing to big-game hunting. He was the young dude from polite society who appeared in evening clothes at a district political club meeting behind a saloon and got away with it. Genteel reform had never been so persuasive nor so much fun. And other progressives echoed Roosevelt. Franklin K. Lane held "with old Cicero 'that the whole glory of virtue is in activity.' " Of a friend's career, he commented, "What a fine life—all fight interwoven with fun and friendship."[50]

Almost universally progressives reacted against the elements of fussiness, narrowness or preciosity in genteel reform. Just before the turn of the century Woodrow Wilson hoped out loud for "a generation of 'leading people' " who would replace the sentimentalists and busybodies in suggesting "the measures that shall be taken for the betterment of the race. . . . They would bring with them an age of large moralities, a spacious time, a day of vision. Knowledge has come into the world in vain if it is not to emancipate those who may have it from narrowness, censoriousness, fussiness, an intemperate zeal for petty things."[51] Progressives like Brand Whitlock wanted to avoid the "unctuous, holier-than-thou connotation" that reform had; they "wanted a healthfully gayer world, not one puritanically bleaker."[52] But even the more traditionalist among reformers tended to make much of the importance of humor, tolerance, and innocent pleasure.

[49]Roosevelt, *Realizable Ideals*, pp. 42–43.

[50]A. W. Lane and L. H. Hall, eds., *The Letters of Franklin K. Lane* (Boston, 1922), pp. 6–7.

[51]Woodrow Wilson, *On Being Human* (New York, 1916), pp. 41–42.

[52]Allan Nevins, ed., *The Letters and Journal of Brand Whitlock*, I (New York, 1936), p. xliv.

The fact that Whitlock identified the word "reform" with a puritanism which he regarded as active in his own time does indicate, however, that there were important differences in interpretation of the bogey-word, "puritanical." To Whitlock the moral reformers—those who were most concerned with prohibition and elimination of prostitution, gambling and corruption in government—were a different breed altogether. In Ohio, he noted, "the charge is freely made that an agreement or some understanding has existed between the Anti-Saloon League and the corporations by which, in return for temperance legislation, the corporations are to be let alone . . . such a feeling exists here among those who look more to economic reform than to personal reform for results."[53]

The charge had some foundation in hard experience. In retaliation for Mayor Samuel M. ("Golden Rule") Jones' failure to attack the saloons, the clergy of Toledo rallied behind the business interests in efforts to defeat him. Their idea of reform did not include efforts to bring about brotherhood by abolishing the use of billyclubs by the police or to end municipal corruption by instituting public ownership of utilities. The godly pastors went so far as to invite the Rev. Samuel P. Jones, ardent prohibitionist and revivalist, to come to town for the purpose of exposing the unrighteousness which flourished under Mayor Jones, no relation.[54]

But the evident differences between the older kind of moral reform and the unconventional humanitarianism of "Golden Rule" Jones or more conventional proponents of regulation of business can easily be exaggerated. A good many progressives did not see the sharp conflict Whitlock defined for the very good reason that during the progressive years the lines between moral and economic reformers, to use his distinction, were often blurred. Some of each kind found it possible to work together in various crusades. The Anti-Saloon League, the Women's Christian Temperance Union, and the Prohibition Party, for example, broadened their reformism shortly after the turn of the century. By 1902 the W. C. T. U. Declaration of Principles affirmed belief in a living wage, an eight hour day, and courts of conciliation and arbitration as well as, generally, in "the coming of His Kingdom" and "the gospel of the Golden Rule."[55]

Certain reforms like the crusade against child labor attracted both those with a concern largely limited to protecting the physical, mental and moral health of the nation's future citizens and those with an ideal of social justice seeking major changes in the condition of all laborers, their wages, working conditions, homes, and educational and recrea-

[53]Whitlock to Norman Hapgood, April 8, 1908 in *Ibid.*, I, 92.

[54]McLoughlin, *Revivalism*, pp. 314–26.

[55]See James Timberlake, *Prohibition and the Progressive Movement* (Cambridge, Mass., 1963), especially pp. 33–38.

tional opportunities. Socialists like Florence Kelley and Robert Hunter were prominent in the membership of the New York Child Labor Committee in its early days; but there were also moderates like the lawyer, George Alger, who saw the committee's work as the moral obligation of a society whose "professional and business life . . . has for its essential qualities, not decadence, but rather regeneration, in which moral forces have not lost ground but are receiving a sure and constant increase of power."[56]

In other types of reform, such as improvement of municipal government, the preoccupation of business interests with improving efficiency of services they needed and with reducing taxes tended fairly early to alienate those with a broader concern for social justice. As the Chicago Civic Federation lost its first flush of enthusiasm for a wider civic renaissance after 1894, Jane Addams lost interest in the Federation, maintaining only a nominal connection.

Another kind of division among reformers was even less common in the early years of progressivism. Most progressives began with an assumption of common values and an ideal type of citizen to which Americans should conform. But among urban progressives concerned with social justice, an important and growing minority were coming to question the moral code they had inherited and the desirability of attempting to impose it upon immigrants with different values. New currents in philosophy, notably pragmatism, encouraged this tendency toward cultural pluralism as against Americanization.

Among most prewar reformers the tendency toward questioning the older morality did not go much beyond purging solemnity, overscrupulousness, and intolerance from an idea of the good life which was native and Protestant in its sense of what was wholesome, innocent, and therefore desirable. For example, despite their rejection of the prudery of gentility in favor of the earthier fraternal democracy of Walt Whitman, "Golden Rule" Jones, Brand Whitlock, and their friends did not oppose the precepts of evangelical morality as such. Full rebellion against the older morality was not characteristic of progressivism.

It is no accident that the most popular American songs of the twentieth century celebrating an ideal of innocent romance and decent fun in a rural or small-town setting were written in the first decade. "In the Good Old Summertime" (1902), "In the Shade of the Old Apple Tree" (1905), "School Days" (1907), and "Down by the Old Mill Stream" (1910) appeared in the years when Americans were beginning to move away from the more restricting qualities of nineteenth century evangelical

[56]Jeremy P. Felt, *Hostages of Fortune: Child Labor Reform in New York State* (Syracuse, N. Y., 1965), p. 217. On the pluralism of progressive reform and especially the contrast between "social justice" and "moral" or "good government" reformers, see Yellowitz, *Labor and the Progressive Movement*, Introduction, and Daniel Levine, *Varieties of Reform Thought* (Madison, Wis., 1964), pp. 109–17.

and small-town culture. Yet at the same time Americans were nostalgic for the simplicity, security, and warmth that past represented by contrast with a more complicated urban and industrial existence. The songs captured a social ideal just before the actuality and the sense of innocence associated with it vanished forever.

This ideal of democratic brotherhood, of a relaxed and good-natured neighborliness, appears in George Creel's reminiscence of the Golden Age before the world war. His account of how "those two blessed small towns [Independence and Odessa, Missouri]...helped to drive home the essential meaning of Americanism" assumes mythic proportions, embodying all the chief progressive values.

"There, throughout my formative years, I saw democracy in action—not just a word but something you could *feel*. No dividing line between the rich and poor, and no class distinctions to breed mean envies. The wealthiest merchant stood behind his counter, and the banker walked home of an evening with the round steak for supper tucked under his arm.... When Mother came down with a fever, the neighbors flooded in with broths and extra sheets and blankets, and in turn I ran my legs off carrying little delicacies to sick friends. ' "Miz" Jones, here's something Mamma thought you might relish.' "[57]

The progressives were pre-Freudian not so much in failing to recognize the importance of sexuality as in believing that there was no necessary and warping conflict between demands of civilization and the instincts of the human animal. They knew how sadistic and perverse in their pleasures human beings could become, but the mark of their faith was the belief that their ideal of normality and goodness was human nature itself. As William Allen White said in 1926 in an introduction to Fremont Older's poignant memoir of how he gradually lost his faith in the ability of man to change much, Older "rose up in the days following the Civil War, full of ideals, full of aspirations, full of that rampant love of man and belief in man's decency which was the motive of his time...that old-fashioned notion that men are good, that they want to be decent, that they would like to be honest, aspiring, neighborly and affectionately helpful."[58]

It was the vision of a new democracy realizing inherited notions of decency, of a brotherhood of man perfecting small-town notions of neighborliness, that distinguished the progressives. Faith in its possibility reflected a common appraisal that the vision had never really been given a full and fair trial, that even the approximations to true democracy and brotherhood in some of America's small towns never characterized the nation as a whole.

The vision did not depend upon agreement in ideas about reform but it did involve certain consistent themes. One was the broad goal of a

---

[57]Creel, *Rebel at Large*, p. 24.
[58]Fremont Older, *My Own Story* (New York, 1926), pp. x–xi.

classless society. Progressives opposed privileges for the rich, but most of them also were uneasy about, and many were adamantly opposed to, reforms which favored a special class—even such contemporary under-dogs as the factory worker or the farmer. The ideal went beyond a wish to obliterate group antagonisms and to encourage mobility according to individual merit. It verged constantly on a social ideal in which all difference of opinion on fundamentals disappeared, in which social harmony was achieved by that impulse to conformity de Tocqueville feared in egalitarianism. Woodrow Wilson stated it baldly when he described the public schools as "the genuine melting pot of equality into which when children entered they came out Americans, adjusted to the conditions of our life, acquainted with each other, having a common impulse and common training, a common point of view."[59]

The second major theme of the vision directly reflects the evangelical preparation for progressivism. Christianity, at least in its primitive form, appears as a primary source for the ideal of democracy and as a continuing standard of judgment for any failures in realizing that ideal. Reminiscing about an episode of church membership as a young woman, Jane Addams offered as part of her rationale for joining a church her increasing and "almost passionate devotion to the ideals of democracy. . . . When in all history had these ideals been so thrillingly expressed as when the faith of the fisherman and the slave had been boldly opposed to the accepted moral belief that the well-being of a privileged few might justly be built upon the ignorance and sacrifice of the many?"[60]

There was nothing accidental in Herbert Bigelow's use of parables, biblical quotations, and generally a quasi-religious appeal to middle of the road supporters to stay in line for the initiative and referendum at the Ohio Constitutional Convention in 1912. "Oh, my friends, we are striking down tyranny. We are forging the greatest tools democracy ever had. . . . Our task is a profoundly religious one."[61] Later in the same year the Progressive Party, as Amos Pinchot observed, deliberately went "into battle singing hymns and announcing that we will stand at Armageddon and battle for the Lord. From the very beginning, we have framed our campaign rather as a crusade than as a political fight."[62]

"Golden Rule" Jones had anticipated this fusion of religiosity and democracy when he told his employees in 1900, "We are to see in the near future a wave of revival that shall sweep over this country and,

[59]Woodrow Wilson, "Human Rights," September 18, 1912, in Davison, ed., *Crossroads*, p. 194.

[60]Christopher Lasch, ed., *The Social Thought of Jane Addams* (Indianapolis, Ind., 1965), pp. 21–22.

[61]Quoted in H. L. Warner, *Progressivism in Ohio, 1897–1917* (Columbus, Ohio, 1964), p. 322.

[62]Amos Pinchot to Theodore Roosevelt, December 3, 1912 in Pinchot, *History of the Progressive Party*, Helene M. Hooker, ed. (New York, 1958), p. 184.

indeed, the civilized world, that shall be, in the best sense of the word, a revival of real religion; the setting up of a social and political order that will enable every man and woman to be the best kind of a man or woman that he or she is capable of being. The noble, the patriotic thing for each now is to do his best to spread the truth of Equality, of Brotherhood, that alone can bring the better days."[63]

More remarkable than this relating of democracy and the religion of Jesus was the assumption that, ultimately, most social and economic questions could be reduced to moral questions to which Christianity had a clear answer. Progressives of every type, from Bryan and the W. C. T. U. to Samuel M. Jones and Lincoln Steffens, made the Golden Rule and other precepts of Jesus the key to solving all the problems of mankind. Bryan had no hesitation, for example, about defining God's law of rewards and deducing anti-monopolism therefrom. Even those who disagreed with Bryan in politics could say, as the Springfield, Massachusetts, *Republican* did in 1908, "of lay preaching such as Mr. Bryan's we need more and not less. The message of the pulpit can gain converting power in secular lips as it is seen that the ideals of the 'sacred office' are convertible into terms of everyday good citizenship . . . and that the life and words of Jesus Christ still constitute the great solvent of problems that vex the community, the nation, and the great family of nations."[64]

At the extreme of anticlericalism Lincoln Steffens came to an equal appreciation of the teachings of Jesus. Writing to Congressman William Kent in 1910, he explained that his drift toward Christianity had been slower than Kent's and directly occasioned by his search for remedies to the social questions his muckraking posed. "I studied socialism, anarchism, the single tax, and finally (from time to time), the Bible. And I was amazed at the teachings of Jesus. They seemed to me to be new . . . I think their freshness was due in part to the irreverent way in which I read the New Testament, but also to the fact that Christianity is seldom taught in the Christian churches. However that may be, I find that Jesus saw what we see; he understood, as his disciples don't, the evils, their causes; and he had a cure."[65]

The Jesus that commanded Steffens' respect was not the sweet Jesus of evangelical pietism. He was Jesus the Carpenter, the first democratic reformer, fashioned from more than a half century of biblical criticism and from the imagery of Christian Socialists and labor organizations. Steffens himself noted that the scholars "are separating the authentic from some of the bogus stuff in the book and enabling one to get a clearer,

63Samuel M. Jones, *Letters of Love and Labor* (Toledo, Ohio, 1900), pp. 7–8.

64Springfield (Massachusetts) *Republican* as quoted in *The Commoner Condensed*, VII (Chicago, 1908), 132.

65Steffens to William Kent, April 19, 1912 in Ella Winter and Granville Hicks, eds., *The Letters of Lincoln Steffens*, I (New York, 1938), 243.

liver, more human sense of the Son of Man." This new image of Jesus was a fitting symbol for a progressivism self-consciously trying to fuse a realism of outlook and method with its Christian and democratic idealism.

So moderate a progressive as William Allen White wrote to Theodore Roosevelt in 1912, "I do not like the idea of the pale, feminine, wishy-washy, otherworldly Christ that has grown out of the monkish idea of religion. I have always thought that Paul was an old standpatter who came in and captured the Christian caucus and ran it into the organization."[66] White liked a book by the Christian Socialist Bouck White, entitled *The Call of the Carpenter* (1911), which depicted Christ as the sturdy and deliberate strategist of "proletarian" emancipation within the Roman empire. The Kansas editor added, however, that he wished the book "had been written more in the spirit of Tolstoy."

The confusion of Christ with American culture was almost complete. In 1912 a massive evangelistic campaign by laymen from the major Protestant denominations culminated in a Congress which showed how far the churches themselves participated in the confusion. The Men and Religion Forward Movement had begun in 1910 under the auspices of lay brotherhoods of the Baptist, Methodist, Presbyterian, Episcopalian, and Congregational denominations as well as the International Sunday School Association, the Gideons, and the International Committee of the Y. M. C. A.

The 1912 Congress reported that in a year and a half of preparation and six months of the campaign itself there had been an attendance of 1,491,245 at 7062 meetings. Reports were published on Evangelism, Social Service, Christian Unity, Men's and Boys' Work, Rural Churches, and Publicity, emphasizing the importance to the churches of relying on experts in each of these endeavors. In his opening address the chairman said, "This wonderful age of ours, instead of pushing away from God and Christ, has by its discoveries and scientific attainment, rather brought us back to the simplicity of the gospel. . . . The harvest is white to the gathering."[67]

Two of the reports struck the major themes. That on Evangelism noted that "religious questions have become so closely related to ethical theories and moral issues that the line of demarcation between the secular and religious, as such, has been erased." That on Social Service noted that in the last six months "social service had become a household phrase to laymen who before would have looked upon it with suspicion." Walter Rauschenbusch went further, claiming that the "social gospel has now come to be one of the dogmas of the Christian faith." The

[66]White to Roosevelt, January 16, 1912 in Johnson, ed., *Letters*, pp. 130–31; for the image of Jesus as reformer, see especially Upton Sinclair, ed., *The Cry for Justice* (Philadelphia, 1915), Book VII.

[67]*Messages of the Men and Religion Movement*, I, 9.

churches were urged to develop councils or federations in the cities, with working committees specializing in tuberculosis, the county jail, work house, juvenile court, housing and sanitation, industrial peace and unemployment, the social evil, substitutes for the saloon, etc. These committees should work closely with municipal agencies and should "combine the love of social science with the love of man."[68]

There were a few uneasy voices at the Congress. One clergyman who described himself as an experimentalist and an institutionalist said nevertheless that he was worried about the tendency to submerge religion in reform. " ... if we are seeking for these things along so-called altruistic or humanitarian lines, then I say in the fear of God, let us be mighty cautious about this social service movement."[69] The warning went unheeded. By 1914 concern with religious experience and personal conversion had declined to such a point that Billy Sunday protested, "some people are trying to make a religion out of social service with Jesus Christ left out."[70]

Almost a century before, Charles Finney, the greatest antebellum revivalist, had prepared the way unwittingly for the fusion of Protestant Christianity and American culture, a fusion susceptible to interpretations favoring the social gospel or the gospel of wealth, reform or the status quo. His most flamboyant successor in the work of inducing religious harvests now sounded the alarm to save the gospel. But except in the most superficial sense of a reaffirmation of supernaturalism, Billy Sunday's religious fundamentalism was not a return to a gospel transcending culture. Sunday's amalgam of piety, popular prejudices, and laissez-faire conservatism simply substituted 100 per cent Americanism for the crusade to make the nation and the world safe for democracy.

The very vagueness of the vision and rhetoric of a Christian democracy created a semblance of national unity of purpose, encouraging the progressive generation to minimize divisions between various kinds of reformers and conservatives within and without the churches. In the Twenties that vision and rhetoric no longer attracted many native middle class Americans and the divisions had become all too obvious.

[68]*Ibid.*, III, 219; II, 107, 122.
[69]*Ibid.*, I, 59.
[70]Quoted in McLoughlin, *Revivalism*, p. 399.

LOREN BARITZ

State University of New York at Albany

the

culture

of the

twenties

In his elegant and searching survey of the material implications of the work done at the Paris Peace Conference, John Maynard Keynes concluded that "we are at the dead season of our fortune." He believed that the war had produced the kind of emotional exhaustion that restricted vision, feeling, and thought to the limits of the self. According to Keynes, having implicated themselves so fully in the public realm during the war, men, especially in England and America, could no longer be moved by public events of whatever magnitude or intensity. In turning to the peace, such men turned from society; the men of a wounded world demanded the time now to attend to themselves. Thus it was, as Keynes put it in the final sentence of his book, that "the true voice of the new generation has not yet spoken, and silent opinion is not yet formed."[1] If Keynes was right, that "true voice" when it became

[1] John Maynard Keynes, *The Economic Consequences of the Peace* (New York: Harcourt, Brace & World, Inc., 1920), pp. 297–98.

150

audible might tell of somewhat unaccustomed things, might find the perhaps autonomous, perhaps isolated, perhaps alienated self a continuingly satisfying subject. Even if that should occur, however, the voice of the Twenties would not tell of things never before heard in ways never before imagined. It did occur, and it had a history.

Thinking of the mid-Twenties, F. Scott Fitzgerald later remembered that "life . . . was largely a personal matter."[2] Fitzgerald, along with other writers, artists, and intellectuals who flourished then, had a deep sense of the uniqueness of that decade. Fitzgerald himself claimed to have found the most descriptive and characteristic label: he had baptized those years "The Jazz Age."[3] And Gertrude Stein, following a lead given her by the manager of a garage in Paris, gave Hemingway another, and more important, characterization: "All of you young people who served in the war," she said. "You are a lost generation."[4]

The decade's writers seemed to agree with Keynes' worried prophecy. Regardless of the attribute emphasized, many of the most articulate spokesmen of the time eventually concluded that they had occupied a parenthesis in historical time, one that opened with the Armistice and closed with the crash. The feeling of having come from nowhere and of being headed toward no discoverable destination was described with sufficient power to convince later generations that at least the cultural life of the decade had in fact swung free in time. The writers of the lost generation who occupied the jazz age in convincing themselves that they were rootless and aimless seem also to have convinced others.

Though an important part of the brief in defense of their uniqueness is true, it is too simple. Thinking for the moment only of Keynes' description of the retreat into privacy, and of Miss Stein's intended meaning about the loss of identity that came from war, one can easily—perhaps too easily—cast up an intellectual and emotional geneology that would presumably prove that the ideas and tonalities of the Twenties had long been familiar in the American and European landscapes. The literature of disillusion has its own history, as does that of the feeling of cultural isolation. One needs only to open the American ledger to the pages devoted to Poe and Melville to see how rich and how clear that background is. The sense that the present generation has wearily climbed beyond earlier ones, that the present must suffer because of the stupidities of the past, that the son must break free from the father or lose his own

2F. Scott Fitzgerald, *The Crack-Up*, Edmund Wilson, ed. (New York, 1945), p. 70. Copyright 1945 by New Directions Publishing Corporation. Reprinted by permission of New Directions Publishing Corporation.

3F. Scott Fitzgerald to M. Perkins, May 21, 1931, FSF, *Letters*, Andrew Turnbull, ed. (New York: Charles Scribner's Sons, 1965), p. 225.

4Ernest Hemingway, *A Moveable Feast* (New York: Charles Scribner's Sons, 1964), p. 29.

authenticity, has characterized perhaps every single decade of the American story from the Puritans forward. The celebration of the private self and recoil from society may be found at the very heart of what most of the New England transcendentalists had tried to say. None of this came new-born and fully developed from the forehead of Fitzgerald or anyone else.

It has been shown that a significant part of the generation immediately before World War I was itself in rebellion against many of the same aspects of middle class American life that the men of the Twenties were to find inhibiting, stultifying, and suffocating.[5] This must mean that the war did not, as was so often assumed at the time and since, produce that pervasive wave of disillusion and, on occasion, pessimism that always seemed to rise to the surface of the Twenties. If similar disillusion existed before the war, how could the war be considered as its cause? The impeccable logic of that question may not turn out to be conclusive, as we will see.

The stage was properly set by four quite different works that were all published in 1920. To understand the mood and thrust of each is to open the larger themes of that decade. In *Hugh Selwyn Mauberley*, Ezra Pound, with an electric condensation of rage and outrage, utterly rejected the war, repudiated the peace, and condemned that civilization whose rottenness was the cause. The corrupt complacencies of the antebellum world were replaced with new crimes. The political leaders of the world at peace were liars, and the young men who had died for their European countries had died "For an old bitch gone in the teeth."[6] The war, in Pound's view, was simply a catastrophic waste that was made necessary because of the power held by those pretty Victorians and Edwardians on both continents who would bleed the younger generation in order to conserve the corruption of the old.

Though Pound's temperature was higher than most, he spoke for a wide circle of articulate young people. The impact of that view on America was severe. George Santayana, in *Character and Opinion in the United States*, another work published in 1920, believed that recent experience had aged America, had functioned as a kind of puberty rite that symbolized the passage to adulthood, the passage from innocence to

---

[5]See, for example, Henry F. May, *The End of American Innocence* (New York, 1959), *passim*; Christopher Lasch, *The New Radicalism in America, 1889–1963* (New York, 1965), pp. 253–54. The surge of poetry in the Twenties similarly began with the prewar generation; see Conrad Aiken, "Poetry," in Harold E. Stearns, ed., *Civilization in the United States* (New York, 1922), p. 217.

[6]Ezra Pound, *Hugh Selwyn Mauberley*, reprinted in Frederick J. Hoffman, *The Twenties* (New York, 1955), p. 438. From *Personal: The Collected Poems of Ezra Pound* (New York: New Directions Publishing Corporation), copyright 1926, 1954 by Ezra Pound.

experience, from callowness to a sense of tragedy. As he saw it, America had been taught that it could no longer pretend to self-determination: "Hitherto America has been the land of universal goodwill, confidence in life, inexperience of poisons. Until yesterday it believed itself immune from the hereditary plagues of mankind."[7]

The impact of that cultural shock on an individual can be found in Fitzgerald's youthful and excited first book, *This Side of Paradise,* also published in 1920. On the last page of that novel, the narrator muses about the men at Princeton: "Here was a new generation, shouting the old cries, learning the old creeds, through a revery of long days and nights; destined finally to go out into that dirty gray turmoil to follow love and pride; a new generation dedicated more than the last to the fear of poverty and the worship of success; grown up to find all Gods dead, all wars fought, all faiths in man shaken."[8] If Santayana was right, the discovery that America was susceptible to ugliness and pain meant, for the young Fitzgerald, an instant world-weariness. American faith when shaken once seemed completely destroyed. Pleasure was the residual goal, along with the glamor and private power that formed the foundation of the Jazz Age.

Sinclair Lewis' *Main Street* completes this quartet of works published in the first year of the Twenties. It was in many ways, despite its occasionally cardboard characters, the single most premonitory work. In the context of the three other works, Lewis' intention can be put this way: Was the past dead in fact? Had the war been rejected? Had America gone through its rites of passage? Were Gods and faiths dead? There were places in America, he answered, where none of that was true in even the slightest degree. In the American small town the terrible education suffered by an intellectual or artistic elite was simply unavailable.

The mentality of non-metropolitan America had not had to agonize about the tragic in modern life. The pieties and faiths of a more comfortable past remained untouched and unyielding. Lewis telegraphed his attitude at once, in the opening lines of the foreword to the novel: "Main Street is the climax of civilization. That this Ford car might stand in front of the Bon Ton Store, Hannibal invaded Rome and Erasmus wrote in Oxford cloisters."[9] The small town and small city, against which so many American intellectuals, artists, and writers revolted in the Twenties, seemed—at least superficially—sufficiently secure not to take particular notice of the latest noise from America's bohemia. Evidently closed to

[7]George Santayana, *Character and Opinion in the United States* (Garden City, N.Y.: Doubleday Anchor, 1956), p. 89.

[8]F. Scott Fitzgerald, *This Side of Paradise* (New York: Charles Scribner's Sons, 1920), p. 282.

[9]Sinclair Lewis, *Main Street* (New York: Harcourt, Brace & World, Inc., 1920), "foreword."

new possibilities, to alternatives, the village, as Lewis sketched it, continued to define itself as both the center and goal of the universe.

Carol Kennicott, the often simultaneously rebellious and acquiescent heroine of *Main Street*, confessed that American mythology had acquainted her with only two traditions about the village. The first told that the small town was the essential repository of all virtue, the single habitat of "clean, sweet marriageable girls."[10] Ambitious boys might forsake their parental homestead in search of success or sophistication, but they would ultimately come to their senses, return to the village, rediscover the childhood sweetheart, marry, settle down, and live happily ever after. The other tradition described the town as rich in local color, picturesque, and infinitely amusing in its "whiskered rusticity." The truths that Carol discovered about Gopher Prairie reveal what most of America's creative people thought of the American village, and consequently, of the American past:

> It is an unimaginatively standardized background, a sluggishness of speech and manners, a rigid ruling of the spirit by the desire to appear respectable. It is contentment . . . the contentment of the quiet dead, who are scornful of the living for their restless walking. It is negation canonized as the one positive virtue. It is the prohibition of happiness. It is slavery self-sought and self-defended. It is dullness made God.
>
> A savorless people, gulping tasteless food, and sitting afterward, coatless and thoughtless, in rocking-chairs prickly with inane decorations, listening to mechanical music, saying mechanical things about the excellence of Ford automobiles, and viewing themselves as the greatest race in the world.[11]

Though Carol believed that the prairie had a perhaps magnificent future, she finally concluded that she had somehow to resist its present. Urging a young man to break away, to go East, she also urged him to return in order to explain what the citizens of Gopher Prairie should do with the land they were clearing, "if," she said, "we'll listen—if we don't lynch you first!"[12]

What Carol demanded of her husband and of Gopher Prairie was the substitution of one kind of sublimation for another. Thinking of the wives of American villagers as a part of the oppressed classes of the world,[13] she thought "we want a more conscious life." She felt unable to continue living a life of postponement as "the politicians and priests and cautious reformers (and the husbands!)" continually advised. She

---

10 *Ibid.*, p. 264.

11 *Ibid.*, p. 265.

12 *Ibid.*, p. 343.

13 Cf. F. Scott Fitzgerald to his daughter, Oct. 5, 1940, in *Letters*, 96: " . . . I think the faces of most American women over thirty are relief maps of petulant and bewildered unhappiness."

demanded her own Utopia, and now: "All we want is—everything for all of us!"[14] She knew she would fail, and explained that that was why she would never be content. She did not have secret yearnings for the heady atmosphere of bohemia; she wanted everything, to be sure, but everything that would still comport with her own sense of decorum, a sense not entirely different from her husband's.

To encounter provincial America only in the writings of those who had declared war on it is finally to see merely a bizarre, pathetic, and infinitely comic phenomenon. Ludwig Lewisohn, Sherwood Anderson, and, above all, H. L. Mencken could conjure up the simple yokel whose five thumbs made him a lower order of creature, but that view is disabling in respect to the yokel's political strength. The American province, to put it most simply, was also committed to war, had a vast and dangerous arsenal, and won almost every major battle it had entered. It was in virtual control of America's public life during the Twenties, and the dismay of the writers and artists cannot be fully understood in any other context. They could dream of a world free of the province, but the present provincial hegemony made it impossible to predict what that world would be like. "Who knows," Walter Lippmann asked, "having read Mr. Mencken and Mr. Sinclair Lewis, what kind of world will be left when all the boobs and yokels have·crawled back in their holes and have died in shame?"[15] And those creatures would refuse to crawl away without a bitter fight. One example will make the point; a newspaper editor and supporter of the Prohibition Party designed his early tirade to catch virtually all of the vibrations in America's provincial civilization:

> Besodden Europe, worse bescourged than by war, famine and pestilence, sends here her drink-makers, her drunkard-makers, and her drunkards, or her more temperate but habitual drinkers, with all their un-American and anti-American ideas of morality and government; they are absorbed into our national life, but not assimilated; with no liberty whence they came, they demand unrestricted liberty among us, even to license for things we loathe; and through the ballotbox, flung wide open to them by foolish statesmanship that covets power, their foreign control or conquest has become largely an appalling fact; they dominate our Sabbath, over large areas of country; they have set up for us their own moral standards, which are grossly immoral; they govern our great cities, until even Reform candidates accept their authority and pledge themselves to obey it; the great cities govern the nation; and foreign control or conquest could gain little more, though secured by foreign armies and fleets.[16]

14Lewis, *Main Street*, p. 201.

15Walter Lippmann, *A Preface to Morals* (New York, 1929), p. 16.

16Alphonso Alva Hopkins, quoted in Andrew Sinclair, *Prohibition: The Era of Excess* (Boston: Little, Brown and Company, 1962), p. 19.

Mencken's "yokel" might amuse the sophisticated, but the yokel might have found the sometimes frantic parody comic too. He must have known something about political power because, though he had to fight, he almost always won. The fight, for him, was to implement that phrase of Harding's: "not heroics but healing; not nostrums but normalcy; not revolution but restoration." As the intellectual could reject the war because the peace had not gone far enough, provincial Americans apparently grew restive because it had gone too far. The public policy the villager and burgher demanded was designed to recreate a known and presumably safer but seriously threatened earlier America. The legislation sought was intended to recreate that supposedly more congenial time when values were clearer, when religion was more secure, when intellectuals were supposedly more housebroken, when the farmer was supposedly dominant in the fields cleared from God's country.

William Jennings Bryan, the complete spokesman of rural and sometimes of provincial America, could seem thoroughly ludicrous to some, but he too knew something. He knew that the nation had changed, that urbanization and industrialism together with enormous immigration were generating political, economic, and even moral forces that were repugnant to the idyllic, Protestant, and democratic America he envisaged. He knew that something more important than the publication of the four books mentioned above occurred in 1920: for the first time in American history, according to the census bureau, more Americans were living in cities than in the countryside and villages combined. That single fact may explain some of the urgency in the battle of the small town and small city against continued uncontrolled change.

The massive power of non-metropolitan America may best be understood by viewing national policy and significant social phenomena as designed to arrest change or not, as intended to recapture the alleged simplicity and morality of a past but still desired rural civilization. "Foreign" influences in national or religious terms, urban power together with its pathology in crime and corruption, and the intellectual life constituted the dark trinity which the villager and the burgher were determined to destroy.

In simple economic terms, the American farmer suffered depression throughout most of the decade; in simple occupational terms, the Republican presidents represented business, not farmers or villagers. But in a wider perspective, the provincial mentality was virtually incarnate in Harding and Coolidge, and Hoover, too, spoke with and for the village in the special circumstance of his rival's thoroughly urban, Catholic, and wet background. It is true that rural political insurgency continued to sputter through the Twenties, but the dominant issues were no longer political. The collapsing alliance between old-time urban and rural reformers, the failure of national leadership, prosperity, exhaustion, boredom, and fear of change, together with Wilson's own example of defeat, all combined to wound if not destroy the earlier Progressive movement.[17] The small city—Zenith, Sinclair Lewis called it—exercised its power over the nation through its values, attitudes, and ideals; though it would be beset from perhaps desperate farmers on the one side, and the urban middle classes along with intellectuals on the other, it could generally rely on enough support in all quarters to ensure victory.

In their terms, the most abstract battle fought by villagers and their allies in small cities was the place and role of the United States in world affairs. Whether they were simple isolationists is an on-going debate.[18] We know, obviously, that the League of Nations was repudiated, though American participation, such as it was, increased throughout the decade. The Kellogg-Briand Pact intended to outlaw war through the moral pressure of world opinion. And American corporate interests extended to virtually every corner of the world. But public policy was not planned in the major cities; Zenith's George Babbitt, with his realtor's reflexes, could smile indulgently at the wishful thinking of the Kellogg-Briand Pact, could smile unreservedly in appreciation of the expansion and extension of American business (and therefore approve high protective tariffs), and he could bristle with indignation over the League with its supposed threat of "furrin" control.

The key to provincial desires and power, one that opens the door to almost everything else, is prohibition, the single most revealing phenomenon of the time. It too, appropriately, went into effect in the first year of the decade, and was to last almost fourteen years. That "noble experiment" was preeminently the creature of the provincial, middle class, Protestant, white, American. The alignment over the Eighteenth Amendment in the House of Representatives shows what happened. One-hundred and ninety-seven representatives supported the Amendment; 129 were from towns of less than ten-thousand, and 64 came from villages of less than 2500. One-hundred and ninety representatives opposed the Amendment; 109 came from cities of over twenty-five thousand. "In fact," as the movement's most acute historian put it, "national prohibition was a measure passed by village America against urban America."[19] The war brought urban allies to the villager because of the

---

[17]See, for example, Arthur S. Link, "What Happened to the Progressive Movement in the 1920's?" *American Historical Review*, LXIV, 4 (July, 1959), 833–51; Richard Hofstadter, *The Age of Reform* (New York, 1960), esp. pp. 272–301; Arthur M. Schlesinger, Jr., *The Crisis of the Old Order* (Boston, 1957), pp. 11–124.

[18]McGeorge Bundy, "Foreign Policy: From Innocence to Engagement," in A. M. Schlesinger, Jr. and Morton White, eds., *Paths of American Thought* (Boston, 1963), pp. 293–308; George F. Kennan, *American Diplomacy* (Chicago, 1951), pp. 55–73; William Appleman Williams, "The Legend of Isolationism in the 1920's," *Science and Society*, XVIII (Winter, 1954), 1–20.

[19]Sinclair, *Prohibition*, p. 163.

identification of beer with the Kaiser, of alcohol with unpatriotic waste and selfishness during a national crisis. That alliance made the ratification of the Eighteenth Amendment possible. After The Volstead Act and with peace, the urban-village coalition broke showing the determined core of prohibitionism to be where it always was: in the Methodist and Baptist churches, in villages and towns all across the nation, among Southerners fearful of drunken Negroes and employers wanting sober laborers and afraid of drunken agitators, among nativists who believed that swarthy and alien types would commit their worst excesses if given access to booze. An historian caught the basic strategy of the prohibitionists: "The emotion which they exploited was fear: The fear of sin and God; the fear of race against race and skin against skin; the fear of venereal diseases; the fear of idiot children; the fear of violence suppressed by conscience and loosed by liquor; and the dark sexual fears of civilization."[20] The rich and middle class urbanite could get liquor if he wanted it, but he had to contribute to Al Capone to do it, thereby confirming the dry villagers in all of their suspicions about urban corruption, the wages of sin, and the menace of foreigners. Nothing less than the protection of God and country was involved in prohibition, and the provincial American was militant.

Those same goals became the battle cry of the renewed Ku Klux Klan whose membership rose to approximately four million in the Twenties. Prohibition and the Klan both aimed at restoring the values of an earlier America, values which were eroding under the waves of immigrants, cities, irreligion, science, and modernity in general. A dentist from Texas, Hiram Wesley Evans, became the national leader, the Imperial Wizard and Emperor, of the Klan in 1922, and a few years later published an article which showed that he viewed his organization as the only effective defense of traditional America, as a brake on noxious change, and as the true locus of patriotism.

Klansmen, according to Evans, "have enlisted our racial instincts for the work of preserving and developing our American traditions and customs."[21] He argued that the Klan had succeeded in limiting its earlier violence and internal corruption, and had now thrown its full weight against the results of the melting pot which, he said, the Klan considered "a ghastly failure" whose "very name was coined by a member of one of the races—the Jews—which most determinedly refuses to melt."[22] No alien and no "alien idea" could be tolerated in the America he envisaged.

[20]*Ibid.*, p. 46.

[21]Hiram Wesley Evans, "The Klan's Fight for Americanism," *The North American Review*, CCXXIII (March–May, 1926), 35. Reprinted in Richard M. Abrams and Lawrence W. Levine, eds., *The Shaping of Twentieth-Century America* (Boston, 1965), p. 386.

[22]*Ibid.*, p. 40.

In order to purge successfully, the Klan had broken with liberalism because that ideology "had provided no defense against the alien invasion, but instead had excused it—even defended it against Americanism. Liberalism," Evans said, "is today charged in the mind of most Americans with nothing less than national, racial and spiritual treason."[23] The Klan supposedly opposed the Catholic Church on political rather than religious grounds, and, following the lead of Madison Grant and Lothrop Stoddard, opposed the Negro and Eastern European Jews on racial grounds, and Western European Jews on religious grounds. All constituted a direct menace for the white, Protestant, Anglo-Saxon, American villager. Knowing that he and his kind were under some kind of attack for being villagers, Evans took the offensive:

> We are a movement of the plain people, very weak in the matter of culture, intellectual support, and trained leadership. We are demanding, and we expect to win, a return of power into the hands of the everyday, not highly cultured, not overly intellectualized, but entirely unspoiled and not de-Americanized average citizen of the old stock.... This is undoubtedly a weakness. It lays us open to the charge of being 'hicks' and 'rubes' and 'drivers of second hand Fords.' We admit it.... The Klan does not believe that the fact that it is emotional and instinctive, rather than coldly intellectual, is a weakness. . . . [Emotions and instincts] are the foundations of our American civilization, even more than our great historic documents; they can be trusted where the fine-haired reasoning of the denatured intellectuals cannot.[24]

Evans was responding to all of the strains in the provincial mentality: the alleged moral superiority, evangelical and fundamentalist religion, anti-intellectualism, racism, nativism, and hypertrophy of patriotism. The imposition of quotas based on national origin (favoring those nations in which the villager's own family had probably originated) in the new immigration policies of the Twenties shows that Evans was, in many ways, merely giving voice to attitudes which small town America could and did enact into the law of the land. That the pressures for immigration restriction came from diverse interests and sections means that, once again, the villager and small city American could rely on outside support on specific issues. Intellectuals would protest that the idea of the great, blue-eyed blonde Nordic was a groundless "myth,"[25] but, groundless or not, it contributed to the blood knowledge of the Klan, as well as to national attitudes toward immigration.

That myth lurks also in the background of the Red Scare of 1919 and

[23]*Ibid.*, p. 42.
[24]*Ibid.*, p. 49.
[25]See, for example, C. E. Ayres, "The New Higher Criticism," *The New Republic*, XLV (Dec. 9, 1925), 85–86.

the early Twenties, and the subsequent Palmer raids. A. Mitchell Palmer, the Attorney General, invented and initiated neither the fright nor the retribution. He was himself an expression of and vulnerable to the pressures from Zenith. Sharing the growing fear of revolution that would be caused by recent immigrants, Palmer once described those aliens arrested in his raids: "Out of the sly and crafty eyes of many of them leap cupidity, cruelty, insanity, and crime; from their lopsided faces, sloping brows, and misshapen features may be recognized the unmistakable criminal type."[26] The east side of New York was the most favored lair of the Leon Bronstein, alias Trotsky, type dedicated to the overthrow of Zenith, hence nation, hence God. At the very beginning of the decade, on January 2, the Palmer raids reached their height with over 6000 people taken into custody in the ensuing weeks.[27] If the alien could be deported, as legislation of May, 1920 provided, and prevented from entering, as the new immigration policies provided, the old-stock American with his ideals and values would presumably be safer.

The alien threat was supposedly proved by the arrest and conviction of two semi-literate Italian radicals, Sacco and Vanzetti, confessed pacifists and draft-dodgers. Arrested for murder they were convicted of being aliens, because the issues dominating the trial were patriotism and radicalism. Again sophisticated men protested, as Felix Frankfurter did: "By systematic exploitation of the defendants' alien blood, their imperfect knowledge of English, their unpopular social views, and their opposition to the war, the District Attorney invoked against them a riot of political passion and patriotic sentiment; and the trial judge connived at—one had almost written, cooperated in—the process."[28] The fears of the American provinces, whether Muncie or elsewhere, determined that Sacco and Vanzetti should be executed.

Those fears, as the Klan understood perfectly well, included the basic fear that alien gods would stalk the land, along with alien beer and ideologies, unless the Nordic American fought back. Religious fundamentalism was perhaps the most authentic expression of that native fight, and Fundamentalism was a ligament that held Prohibition, the Klan, and nativism together. Billy Sunday's "booze sermon" demanded more than abstinence; he called for the deportation of foreigners involved in bootlegging, as well as other dissenters who refused to kiss the American flag.[29] Mencken (in the *American Mercury*) and Sinclair Lewis (in *Elmer Gantry*) poured scorn on the evangelists who wrapped the cross in the flag and carried it in a bible, who baptized by the thousands, and who

[26]Quoted in Stanley Coben, *A. Mitchell Palmer* (New York, 1963), p. 198.

[27]*Ibid.*, p. 227.

[28]Felix Frankfurter, "The Case of Sacco and Vanzetti," *The Atlantic Monthly*, CXXXIX, 3 (March, 1927), 421.

[29]Sinclair, *Prohibition*, p. 290.

attacked booze, Darwin, and anarchy all in the same long breath. But Fundamentalism, as an intense folk movement, could fight back, claiming, as the Klan claimed, that too much education and piety were mutually exclusive.[30]

Fundamentalism's best champion was William Jennings Bryan, and his chosen field for his final battle was Dayton, Tennessee. The Scopes trial, with Bryan and Clarence Darrow facing each other, had to do with whether it was a punishable crime to teach evolution in the public schools, but it also had to do with the continuing struggle between small and large cities. Bryan had protested against the theory of evolution since the beginning of the twentieth century, but the fears that became exacerbated during the Twenties convinced him that direct action was then required. The silver-tongued orator shared so much of the provincial mood that he, too, adopted the usual aggressive apology for the lack of literary felicity of his adherents, and he, too, mounted an attack against cleverness and mind which must kill God. Early in the decade he accused that generation of "mind-worship—a worship as destructive as any other form of idolatry."[31] The head and the heart were at war, and meant, to him, that America's folk religion was being subverted by most of the dark forces of the city:

> A scientific soviet is attempting to dictate what shall be taught in our schools and, in so doing, is attempting to mould the religion of the nation. It is the smallest, the most impudent, and the most tyrannical oligarchy that ever attempted to exercise arbitrary power.[32]

H. L. Mencken chortled, Darrow referred to Bryan's "fool ideas," but Bryan was more than the incredible figure that journalists and intellectuals exploited. Until he died a few days after the Scopes trial, he was the voice of non-metropolitan America, especially so with regard to Fundamentalism.

The political and social power of the non-urban American means, of course, that he was something other than the silly clown that emerged from Mencken's pages. But Mencken also knew that provincial America had muscle, that he and fellow cosmopolites could not control the legislature. These words, obviously, are his: "Our laws are invented, in the main, by frauds and fanatics, and put upon the statute books by poltroons and scoundrels."[33] But others, too, understood the pervasive pub-

---

[30]Norman F. Furniss, *The Fundamentalist Controversy* (New Haven, Conn., 1954), esp. pp. 39–41.

[31]Quoted in Lawrence W. Levine, *Defender of the Faith* (New York: Oxford University Press, 1965), p. 279.

[32]*Ibid.*, p. 289.

[33]H. L. Mencken, *Notes on Democracy* (New York: Alfred A. Knopf, Inc., 1926), p. 129.

lic power of the small town, and wrote that it was necessary at least "secretly" to acknowledge that fact:

> The civilization of America is predominantly the civilization of the small town. The few libertarians and cosmopolites who can continue to profess to see a broader culture developing along the Atlantic seaboard resent this fact, though they scarcely deny it. They are too intelligent, too widened in vision to deny it. They cannot watch the tremendous growth and power and influence of secret societies, of chambers of commerce, of boosters' clubs, of the Ford car, of moving pictures, of talking-machines, of evangelists, of nerve tonics, of the *Saturday Evening Post*, of Browning societies, of circuses, of church socials, of parades and pageants of every kind and description, of family reunions, of pioneer picnics, of county fairs, of firemen's conventions without secretly acknowledging it. And they know, if they have obtained a true perspective of America, that there is no section of this vast political unit that does not possess—and even frequently boast—these unmistakably provincial signs and symbols.[34]

Clearly enough, it was the strength not the pathos or mere uncongeniality of the provinces that made the writers and artists react in the ways that they did. If it was simply the latter, parody would have sufficed; but expatriation and high art aimed at the provinces are symptoms of the power of the enemy.

One result of the political power of the American small town and small city was the decision on the part of many intellectuals and writers simply to withdraw from politics. The disgust with that political process which has led to war and to Versailles also contributed to political quiescence. Whether the enemy was Babbitt or Woodrow Wilson, or—more likely—both, the result was the same: Fitzgerald's life as a "personal matter."

Joseph Freeman, later to become an editor of a politically radical journal, remembered a canoe trip he had taken with a friend; reciting Plato and Swinburne, neither could list the terms of the Treaty of Versailles.[35] And much more extreme, but more indicative, George Jean Nathan, Mencken's partner in parody, exploded:

> The great problems of the world—social, political, economic and theological —do not concern me in the slightest. If all the Armenians were to be killed tomorrow and if half of Russia were to starve to death the day after, it would not matter to me in the least. What concerns me alone is myself, and the interests of a few close friends. For all I care the rest of the world may go to hell at today's sunset.[36]

34Louis R. Reid, "The Small Town," in Stearns, ed., *Civilization* (1922), p. 286.
35Joseph Freeman, *An American Testament* (New York, 1936), p. 154.
36George Jean Nathan, quoted in William E. Leuchtenberg, *The Perils of Prosperity* (Chicago, 1958), p. 150.

The phenomenon of political retreat was sufficiently widespread to engage the attention of at least two important social analysts. By 1927 Walter Lippmann concluded that the combination of party splintering and affluence gave rise to bewilderment, complacency, and cynicism. It was, he argued, one thing to feel disgust with politics, but another to be able to avoid it; affluence made the difference. Social questions concerning the Klan, prohibition, Fundamentalism, immigration, evolution, and xenophobia continued to interest the electorate as phases in the war between province and city, but they were issues usually outside the formal political process. The economic boom, according to Lippmann, allowed these social issues to exist outside of politics,[37] as it allowed President Coolidge to announce that America's business was business.

John Dewey, in the same year, considered other reasons for that apathy. He also believed that the public was politically bewildered, but he concluded that the public had lost its political existence. The inability to identify with concrete issues resulted in the retreat from politics; the increasing complexity of American life made such concrete issues increasingly hard to find and, more important, created a crippling discrepancy between current political needs and the traditional political machinery. That discrepancy made the traditional actions and pronouncements of political leaders seem increasingly irrelevant to what people cared most about.[38]

> The present era of 'prosperity' may not be enduring. But the movie, radio, cheap reading matter and motor car with all they stand for have come to stay. That they did not originate in deliberate desire to divert attention from political interests does not lessen their effectiveness in that direction. The political elements in the constitution of the human being, those having to do with citizenship, are crowded to one side. In most circles it is hard work to sustain conversation on a political theme; and once initiated, it is quickly dismissed with a yawn. Let there be introduced the topic of the mechanism and accomplishment of various makes of motor cars or the respective merits of actresses, and the dialogue goes on at a lively pace.[39]

That complexity, furthermore, made decisions often too technical and specialized to create a devoted public, with the result that the public atomized. For that reason, no genuine community could be created, and that fact made a further advance in democratic efficiency impossible.[40] A genuine public, held together by political conviction and involvement, was a necessary and anterior condition to meaningful reform. As things stood, politics had degenerated into a mere reflex: "Only habit and tradi-

---

[37]Walter Lippmann, "The Causes of Political Indifference To-Day," *The Atlantic Monthly*, XXXIX, 2 (Feb., 1927), 261–68.

[38]John Dewey, *The Public and Its Problems* (New York, 1927), pp. 122–23, 134–35.

[39]*Ibid.*, p. 139.

[40]*Ibid.*, pp. 157–58.

tion, rather than a reasoned conviction, together with a vague faith in doing one's civic duty, send to the polls a considerable percentage of the fifty percent who still vote."[41]

By now it is clear that Lippmann and Dewey had more in mind than the political withdrawal of scholars, writers, and artists. They were addressing a national problem that was manifested almost everywhere. The provincial American could retire with the conviction that he was the master of the legislature; the intellectuals and artists could thumb their noses at the public sector as they set out to explore what they believed to be more important terrain. But between the country village and Greenwich Village the rest of America lived. Relatively affluent, basically unchallenged, middle-class urban Americans constituted the middle term between the little old lady in Dubuque and the literary exile in Paris. That middle term was the world of the jazz age, the flapper, speakeasy, and the rest. Reaching both forward and backward it knew it was not truly of either world. It was the booming New Era, the roaring twenties. But it too was caught by the power of the village; it had to consume its booze secretly lest the village law would cause embarrassment.

Urban America was not so far from its own rural or village past that the Red Scare would pass it by, that the Anti-Saloon League could find only a few urban adherents, that anti-immigration was a dead issue, that xenophobia generated no pressure. That middle America, as it were, would laugh with Mencken, frown with Sinclair Lewis, but without full certainty. It made best-sellers of both *Main Street* and *Elmer Gantry* along with Emily Post's *Etiquette* and, more revealing, Bruce Barton's *The Man Nobody Knows*. The most popular tunes, "Dinah" and "Ol' Man River," recalled the rural past, though Chaplin's popular comedies were invariably urban in spirit if not in setting.

That urban America, feeling somewhat free of older sexual restraints, could tolerate the fashions of the flapper. Held's cartoon character inspired that craze and was a point-by-point repudiation of the earlier ideal of femininity, the Gibson girl. The Gibson girl had flowing hair, the flapper bobbed hers; shoulders, breasts, and the waist line were emphasized before the war, but the flapper bound her breasts flat and wore loosely fitted blouses; legs were voluminously covered by the Gibson girl, and the flapper raised her hemline above her knees and rolled her stockings below them.

The matter of sex created a vast urban market for a new publishing adventure. The sex "confession" and picture magazine made several fortunes. And yet, enough of the older morality survived to create incredible but by now familiar attitudes, as a letter an editor sent as instructions to his authors will show:

[41]*Ibid.*, p. 135.

I intend to keep—a sex magazine, but sex need not necessarily mean dirt. I want to stick to elementals, sex-elementals—the things closest to the heart of the average woman or girl, whatever her ignorance or sophistication. Above all, I mean to lift the moral tone of the magazine. I believe that to treat sex trivially is to diminish its dramatic value, while sober treatment enhances it. Characters may do anything they please but they must do it from some lofty, or apparently lofty, motive. If a girl falls, she must fall *upward*.[42]

The ostensible freedom of the flapper, her flat rejection of the modishness of the past, was countered by the village matron's firm conviction about the relevance and applicability of earlier standards and usages. The villager had to embark on no quest for spiritual authority; morality, purity, and the home were, for him, unshaken though under criticism from the city. One civilized man struggling to keep his spirit alive while he was teaching at Ohio State, encountered, to his obvious dismay, that provincial type: "thin-lipped, embittered by the poisons that unnatural repression breeds, with a curious flatness about the temples, with often, among the older men, a wiry, belligerent beard." He saw them with their ladies, "shallow-bosomed, ill-favored wives—stern advocates of virtue— walking on Sunday self-consciously to church."[43]

For intellectuals and artists, the brutality of the war that led only to the repugnant peace, together with the political prominence of provincial America, seemed to force them into themselves, seemed to produce precisely what Keynes had feared. Feeling betrayed by history in war and peace, and assaulted by the present in prohibition, anti-evolution, and the rest, they tended to withdraw from society, actually to become exiles or to become unpolitical, perhaps anti-social, and probably alienated strangers at home. The lost generation was created by the war and non-urban America.

For the urban middle class, the brutality of the war could be forgotten in the bubbly ambience of the jazz age. Babe Ruth, mah jong, and crossword puzzles could, apparently, capture and hold attention. But affluence was the key; Fords and movie stars made their significant contribution to the de-politicization of the urban middle class. The sense, however, that the New Era was an intense moment of personal liberation, of sexual freedom for women as well as men, evidently places the urbanite at least partly in the camp of the exiles. The past was as dead, disabling, and irrelevant to the urbanite as to the exile, as the flapper showed when she contradicted Gibson in such perfect detail. Also besieged by the village, the middle class could acquiesce more easily than

[42]Quoted in Ernest W. Mandeville, "Gutter Literature," *The New Republic*, XLV (Feb. 17, 1926), 350.

[43]From *Up Stream* by Ludwig Lewisohn, (New York: Liveright Publishing Corp., 1922), p. 186.

the exiles. But enough feeling of futility was generated to induce the city dwellers to embark on Fitzgerald's quest for cash and success. Privacy was the result, and, though for dramatically different reasons, the flapper and the exile both turned their backs to society in their respective celebrations of the autonomous and inviolate individual. And neither could find a usable social past.

The search, not for a usable past, but for an alternative to the past is another of the revealing symptoms of the decade. The resulting conflict of generations gave at least one disillusioned intellectual grounds for measured optimism: "The most hopeful thing of intellectual promise in America today is the contempt of the younger people for their elders; they are restless, uneasy, disaffected." From that clash of old and new, the young would "attempt to create a way of life free from the bondage of an authority that has lost all meaning, even to those who wield it."[44] That this was an echo of a similar charge made by the pre-war generation—by Randolph Bourne in 1915, for example—should not obscure the fact that the special circumstances of the Twenties gave a new urgency and intensity to the paean to youth, and the condemnation of age. Those circumstances similarly created the sense that since all guideposts were down the future could be newly charted. But those guideposts had once kept men from getting hopelessly lost; they once had given a certain security; they once signified that at least part of the world was known. Freedom from the past was liberating, but also perhaps frightening.

The villager had succeeded in preventing a free experimental method in politics, to John Dewey's dismay. Sanctifying the political institutions of the nation, the American villager was preventing significant change, maintaining control, and participating in a widespread human process: "As supernatural matters have progressively been left high and dry upon a secluded beach, the actuality of religious taboos has more and more gathered about secular institutions, especially those connected with the nationalistic state."[45] That is simply a different way of saying that the small town had succeeded in dominating political institutions, thereby making the political process as such an anachronism for most intellectuals and artists.

Walter Lippmann's *A Preface to Morals* was a key text that tied together the themes of the irrelevance of politics and society, the fearfulness of an unmapped terrain, and the concomitant retreat into self. He explained that the death of God left men without satisfying explanations of what they were compelled to do, had left them unable to refer to a universe teleologically organized. When an earlier American believed

---

[44]Harold E. Stearns, "The Intellectual Life," in Stearns, ed., *Civilization*, p. 149; cf., however, Lewis Mumford, "The Emergence of a Past," *The New Republic*, XLV (Nov. 25, 1925), 18–19.

[45]Dewey, *The Public and Its Problems*, p. 170.

that the unfolding of events was a manifestation of the will of God, he could say:

> Thy will be done.... [sic] In His will is our peace. But when he believes that events are determined by the votes of a majority, the orders of his bosses, the opinions of his neighbors, the laws of supply and demand, and the decisions of quite selfish men, he yields because he has to yield. He is conquered but unconvinced.[46]

Where the small town could control events, other Americans were conquered but unconvinced by those who preached its values. Where the small town could control events, other Americans were freer, but that freedom brought with it complications. Lippmann believed that the Twenties, for the first time in human history, made authoritative belief impossible for large masses of men. Massive and radical irreligion (always excepting provincial America) contributed to the destruction of those older guideposts that left men now free to walk new but obscure and therefore dangerous paths. Worrying that men's greater difficulties would only begin when he was free to do as he pleased, Lippmann got under the surface of the times:

> The evidence of these greater difficulties lie all about us: in the brave and brilliant atheists who have defied the Methodist God, and have become very nervous; in the women who have emancipated themselves from the tyranny of fathers, husbands, and homes, and with intermittent but expensive help of a psychoanalyst, are now enduring liberty as interior decorators; in the young men and women who are world-weary at twenty-two; in the multitudes who drug themselves with pleasure; in the crowds enfranchised by the blood of heroes who cannot be persuaded to take an interest in their destiny; in the millions, at last free to think without fear of priest or policeman, who have made the moving pictures and the popular newspapers what they are.[47]

By the end of the decade, Lippmann said, the problem for young urban America was no longer that of mounting an attack on the stupidities, pieties, and inhibitions of their close-kneed parents. That attack had already succeeded. The square dance was no longer audible over the bounce of the Charleston. The privacy of the back seat of their cars gave the young an opportunity to be sexually freer than ever before. Their rebellion for greater moral freedom had been won, but the young, according to Lippmann, had now to deal with the sobering consequences of that success: "When he has slain the dragon and rescued the beautiful maiden, there is usually nothing left for him to do but write his memoirs and dream of a time when the world was young."[48] The distinguishing

46Lippmann, *Preface to Morals*, p. 9.
47*Ibid.*, p. 6.
48*Ibid.*, p. 17.

characteristic of the young generation of the Twenties was therefore not merely the fact of rebellion against the ethical and moral codes of the past, but its disillusionment with its own rebellion. Such modern men, repelled by the village, bewildered by the present, were radically alone; following Fitzgerald's sigh over a world whose past faiths and Gods had died, Lippmann now probed a little deeper into the mood of the young:

> They have seen through the religion of nature to which the early romantics turned for consolation. They have heard too much about the brutality of natural selection to feel, as Wordsworth did, that pleasant landscapes are divine. They have seen through the religion of beauty because, for one thing, they are too much oppressed by the ugliness of Main Street. They cannot take refuge in an ivory tower because the modern apartment house, with a radio loudspeaker on the floor above and on the floor below and just across the courtyard, will not permit it. They cannot, like Mazzini, make a religion of patriotism, because they have just been demobilized. They cannot make a religion of science like the post-Darwinians because they do not understand modern science. They never learned enough mathematics and physics. They do not like Bernard Shaw's religion of creative evolution because they have read enough to know that Mr. Shaw's biology is literary and evangelical. As for the religion of progress, that is preempted by George F. Babbitt and the Rotary Club, and the religion of humanity is utterly unacceptable to those who have to ride in the subways during the rush hours.[49]

The meaninglessness of society, the absurdity of a purposeless nature, and the richly textured mood of combined pleasure and isolation, all coalesced to encourage exploration of the increasingly fascinating world of the ego. Having just heard about Freud, the modern man learned that there were things about himself that even he did not know. The several pressures of the decade pushed him inward. His own moods and motives, preferences and aversions, were hugely more interesting than the antics of villagers, and more interesting, too, than maintaining vigilance against an older generation that was too preoccupied with making money to counter-charge. "His inferiority complex and mine, your sadistic impulse and Tom Jones's, Anna's father fixation, and little Willie's pyromania"[50] were, in Lippmann's view, the substitute for tradition. Personal rather than social history became relevant, and psychoanalysis was the new way to make the past usable, the past of the individual not the group. Sherwood Anderson summed this up in *Dark Laughter*: "If there is anything you do not understand in human life consult the works of Dr. Freud."[51] Guilt replaced conscience, and Freud taught the rebels

49*Ibid.*, p. 18.

50*Ibid.*, p. 114.

51From *Dark Laughter* by Sherwood Anderson (New York: Liveright Publishing Corp., 1925), p. 230.

lesson after lesson showing reason after dark reason why the rejection of the parental code was essential to health. As the parent became the metaphor of the past, the child became that of the present. Such personifications could not and were not intended to disguise what was happening: the individual and his past was replacing the world and its history.

The massive presentism that resulted was reflected in the works of some of the leading intellectuals of the decade. The presentism of the "New History" of Robinson and Beard, the institutional economics of Veblen that demanded a repudiation of classical economics, and Dewey's "reconstruction in philosophy" that rejected his empirical and classical predecessors in philosophy—all attempted to start afresh, to re-design their tools for modern tasks, and to bring serious thought to bear seriously on the pervasive present.[52]

The idea of progress was one of the casualties of the war, the peace, the village, and Freudianism. A humanistic celebration of the steady and irrevocable march of civilization to higher and higher plateaus of achievement became increasingly difficult for those who were now questioning the value of civilization itself. Emil Coué might make his incantation: "Day by day in every way I am getting better and better,"[53] but, for some, Coué's popularity merely proved that vulgarity was profitable. Edison and Ford showed that technological progress was possible, but the war showed that men were not necessarily or even probably served well as a result.[54] Cumulative disciplines would continue to make progress, but who would win in a struggle for survival between Darwin and Bryan? Social theories might grow increasingly sophisticated and ingenious, but Clemenceau, A. Mitchell Palmer, and Judge Webster Thayer (in whose court Sacco and Vanzetti were tried) seemed also to have something to say about how the world would be ruled, who would rule, and about the staying power of the past. The American economy could boom along with the proliferation of machines, but even the usually sanguine Dewey concluded that "we have harnessed this power to the dollar rather than to the liberation and enrichment of human life."[55] In the eyes of a widening circle of disaffected intellectuals and artists, modern America was a spiritual and cultural desert, committed to standardization and repression and blind to freedom and spontaneity. America was therefore a case study which showed that the older generation had used the idea of progress to camouflage its own failures.

[52]Morton White, *Social Thought in America* (Boston, 1957), pp. 182, 188–89.

[53]Frederick Lewis Allen, *Only Yesterday* (New York, 1946), p. 102.

[54]Clark A. Chambers, "The Belief in Progress in Twentieth-Century America," *Journal of the History of Ideas*, XIX, 2 (April, 1958), 204–8; Sidney Kaplan, "Social Engineers as Saviors," *Ibid.*, XVII, 3 (June, 1956), 369.

[55]John Dewey, *Individualism Old and New* (London, 1931), p. 91.

None of this seems to have touched Herbert Hoover, the leading and most intelligent spokesman of non-metropolitan America. He published an important little book on *American Individualism* early in the decade that is a sensitive rendition of provincial values; by listing what he does not discuss, and by contradicting what he does, one may learn what the exiles, alienates, and even the flappers thought important. His optimism was unlimited because he believed that Americans were increasingly devoted to service: "Moral standards of business and commerce are improving; vicious city governments are less in number; invisible government has greatly diminished; public conscience is penetrating deeper and deeper; the rooting up of wrong grows more vigorous; the agencies for their exposure and remedy grow more numerous, and above all is the growing sense of service."[56] (The frequent reiteration of the ideal of "service" in the decade drove Mencken wild: "When a gang of real estate agents . . . , bond salesmen and automobile dealers gets together to sob for Service, it takes no Freudian to surmise that someone is about to be swindled."[57])

More than anything else, it was Hoover's "idealism" that connected him with the American village and separated him from serious writers and artists. Unaware of or perhaps despite the very wide rejection of idealism in both cultural and philosophical meanings, Hoover asserted that "the most potent force in society is its ideals." He was able to use both the meaning and the rhetoric that was most unacceptable to the cultural leaders: "From the instincts of kindness, pity, fealty to family and race; the love of liberty; the mystical yearnings for spiritual things; the desire for fuller expression of the creative faculties; the impulses of service to community and nation, are moulded the ideals of our people."[58]

Taking notice of the radical individualism of the period, as the intellectuals did too, Hoover made a virtue of necessity. American individualism, he said, was not rampant, was unique, because it was founded on the "great ideals" of the nation. The supposedly classless nature of America cleared the way for individual achievement even while the "emery wheel of competition" was whirling. Progress, about which he evidently had no or few doubts, was a result of "the yearning for individual self-expression," and individualism "alone admits the universal divine inspiration of every human soul."[59] Absolutely rejecting the idea that nature was purposeless, that historical fatality limited human choice, and that reason was an incompetent social and even personal guide, Hoover said that good ideas could replace bad ones, that reason could

[56]Herbert Hoover, *American Individualism* (Garden City, N. Y., 1922), p. 58. Quoted by permission of the Herbert Hoover Foundation.

[57]Mencken, *Notes on Democracy*, p. 176.

[58]Hoover, *American Individualism*, p. 16.

[59]*Ibid.*, pp. 9, 21, 26.

light the way to the implementation of eternal ideals. War was a conflict of ideas; irrationality and power were left out of his analysis.[60] For Hoover, and for those whom he represented, Wilson's wartime career and the Treaty of Versailles did not prove anything about either the emptiness or danger of idealism as such.

And yet the villagers took pride in dealing with actuality, at least on a certain level. That is what Harding meant in his diagnosis of what the American electorate wanted, and that is what Coolidge meant when he called the election of 1920 "the end of a period which has seemed to substitute words for things."[61] The "words" the villager meant included the words of intellectuals and the plans of reformers; the villager did not mean to repudiate national ideals which seemed to serve well even in the hard and actual world of the assembly lines.

In philosophy idealism was repudiated by pragmatism and scientific realism. "New Realism" was formed on a rejection of the idealists' fusion of subject and object, on what was viewed as the obscurantism of idealist logic. John Dewey was the leading advocate of a new philosophy founded on exact science, not on the sovereignty of the human mind. The social implications of this philosophical recoil from idealism were drawn by one critic:

> With all its incompleteness, Dewey's philosophy is undeniably that of the America of to-day. What shall we say of the future? No nation in the world has more abused its philosophies than ours. The inspirational elements of our idealisms have become the panderings of sentimentalists. The vitalizing forces of our pragmatisms threaten to congeal into the dogmata of cash-success. The war has intensified our national self-satisfaction. We tend to condemn all vision as radical, hence unsound, hence evil, hence to be put down.[62]

The peculiarly buoyant but often fretful zest of the creative people of the decade was largely a result of the feeling not that the past had somehow to be abandoned, but that the best and most authentic expression of the time actually had already freed itself from the alleged suffocation of a social past. The individual, already almost sanctified in political and economic terms by the small town and its spokesmen, already validated by Freudianism, already placed at the center of American philosophy, was to find his most elaborate and elevated position in the art and literature of the Twenties.

What was being done to and for the individual was sometimes made somewhat obscure by talk of freedom, adjustment, self-expression, and the war against Puritanism. But under most if not all of that rhetoric

---

[60]*Ibid.*, p. 70.

[61]Quoted in Leuchtenberg, *Perils of Prosperity*, p. 89.

[62]Harold Chapman Brown, "Philosophy," in Stearns, ed., *Civilization*, pp. 176–77.

was the writers' quite open assumption: if the self could be freed from the oppression of the social past, from the repression of his private past, a new private world of self-determination would become newly accessible. That new world would still find it necessary to battle the old world of custom and tradition, but though the actual world might even probably remain unchanged, the now inviolate ego could feel for the limits of what it could do. Consigning society and history to the hell they caused and deserved, the liberated spirits of the time could themselves soar inward as they quite consciously rejected formal knowledge, economics, politics, and social service; as they quite consciously prayed at the shrine of the uncorrupted child, of the eternal present, of the equality of autonomous selves—male and female, and of freedom and paganism.[63] They were newly born into an idiot world whose power over them required their assent; refusing assent, they thought they discovered how to prevent that world from taking what they would not give. They thought they discovered how to nourish the self in a social madhouse, as E. E. Cummings showed in *The Enormous Room*. Some chose a French or English setting out of their fear or conviction that America was stultifying or otherwise dangerous, but all sought that self whose discovery was, they believed, the basis of art.

Dada was merely the verge of freedom and privacy, the extreme and essentially unformulated assault on the morbid if not moribund civilization of the time, and the appropriate reflex of that eternal present. Moving from the avowedly destructive anti-rationalism of dada to the avowedly revolutionary unconscious of surrealism, the art of that moment was of a piece with the other cultural currents. Western man with his exquisite and urgent sublimatory necessities had created mind and civilization. Both led to outrageous war. By living inward one might escape those necessities, might re-discover the body and freedom known only by the uncivilized: children, Negroes, primitives, half-wits, and other heroes of the creative sub-culture of the Twenties. Freud, after all, had already explained that mind and freedom were mutually exclusive. In their war on mind, the American writers of the period, whether in Zurich, Paris, or New York, were responding to the same impulses that dada and surrealism understood. In their war on mind, those writers were laying siege to civilization itself: society and nation, history and time. The alternative to civilization was the self, and towards that they made their sometimes unsure, sometimes nervous, often frantic, and occasionally gay way.

Writers in America easily identified the hated past with the hated village. In the beginning, they suggested, all America was a village, and

<hr/>

[63]Cf. Malcolm Cowley, *Exile's Return* (New York, 1951), pp. 60–61.

the contemporary village was a powerful reminder of the hold the past had on the present. Their enemy, with the double face of the philistine and the Puritan, was still strong enough to rule the land, though that fact mattered less and less. Of greater moment was the enemy's continued power to create and protect an environment absolutely hostile to the necessary private nourishment of those writers. One could presumably live with both prohibition and the Klan, but the hegemonic village seemed also to pollute that part of the American atmosphere that was essential to art. So Van Wyck Brooks could conclude that America demanded the premature death of her artists: "If America is littered with extinct talents, the halt, the maimed and the blind, it is for reasons with which we are all too familiar; and we to whom the creative life is nothing less than the principle of human movement, and its welfare the true sign of human health, look upon the wreckage of everything that is most precious to society and ask ourselves what our fathers meant when they extolled the progress of our civilization."[64] Frustration was the price the village demanded of the artist; public America might be shoved into a corner of one's mind, but it still had power to drive the artist to his death. As Fitzgerald asked from his ineffective refuge in Paris: "Can you name a single American artist except James and Whistler (who lived in England) who didn't die of drink?"[65] The profound irrelevance of public America did not mean that one could succeed, in Hemingway's language, in concluding "a separate peace." Internal secession, expatriation, withdrawal, isolation, and alienation were solutions, but evidently expensive for some, prohibitively so for others.

Fitzgerald is a special case. He was not importantly involved in the writers' sometimes loving and sometimes bitter attack on traditional language, as, for example, were Gertrude Stein, James Joyce, all of the dadaists, E. E. Cummings, and even Hemingway in his own way. Fitzgerald, at least at first blush, seems not to have been a man apart, seems rather to have been a perhaps simple reflection of dominant America. But his playful weariness, his brooding conviction of the hollowness of the very life he desired and depicted, and the iron inevitability of collapse in his best works, shows him, obviously enough, to be preeminently a writer of his time and place.[66] Thus it was that the poet laureate of the Jazz Age could tell his editor: "My third novel, if I ever write another, will I am sure be black as death with gloom."[67]

Fitzgerald's fascination with youth, glamor, and power was clearly real. And it is partly accurate to label him with the now stock critical

---

[64]"The Literary Life," in Stearns, ed., *Civilization*, p. 192.

[65]FSF to Marya Mannes, Oct., 1925, in FSF, *Letters*, p. 489.

[66]Cf. Henry San Piper, "Fitzgerald's Cult of Disillusion," *American Quarterly*, III, 1 (Spring, 1951), 69–80.

[67]FSF to M. Perkins, Aug. 25, 1921, in FSF, *Letters*, p. 148.

tag of the "eternal adolescent infatuated with the surfaces of material existence."[68] He made Jay Gatsby hope that hard cash could buy every desire of the insatiable heart, even the suspension of time or the eradication of the past. How is it then that, as he knew himself, his lovely, expensive, nineteen-year-old flappers came to ruin, his diamond mountains blew up, and his millionaires were damned? Fitzgerald, for all of his spiritual fraternizing with the flapper, for all of his personal needs, saw through the decade. He knew—and it was his most tense, painful, and most creative knowledge—that he, and his most living characters, were inextricably involved in an unremitting search for what would turn out to be a fraud. Although he became disillusioned with the ideas of his own youth, he consistently refused to participate in American moralism about the evil of money and the corruptibility of power. Simultaneously accepting and rejecting the flapper and her friends, he could not turn away from society, as so many of the period's other writers were to do. His search for the possibilities of the self was conducted not merely in society but in Society. Fitzgerald believed that Gatsby condemned himself to loneliness, fragility, and emptiness; this author's dependence on the self even in the face of the self's willed destruction was Fitzgerald's unique and powerful way of rendering the decade. To make and throw away a life because of an ideal of self, to be drawn towards and torn between enormous power and beatific dreams[69]—that was a fact to which he owed some of his best writing. Not rejecting society in his search for the self, Fitzgerald yet believed that the combat between them was mortal.

Hemingway's response to the Twenties was more typical of the contemporary writers' plight, as many of them understood it. Suffering what he felt to be a hideous psychic wound by the external world, Hemingway spent both his talent and his life in that period trying to learn to endure, but with some necessary dignity, with some acceptable sense of self, with some style appropriate to the problem. As the universe seemed always to be in an active conspiracy against manhood, so, for Hemingway, art was a way to fight back. Society and tradition might be rejected, but the rejection was active and necessary to his art.

Meaning was real only for the self. War, for instance, was less important than one's relationship to it, and one's experience of it. The world had come apart sufficiently, as the self perceived it, so that it was no longer necessary to demonstrate that fact. Starting with the assumption of meaninglessness, Hemingway, as other writers of the time, was convinced of the absurdity of attempting to supply meaning. Style and gesture became his personal substitute for meaning, and the struggle to clarify the contours of the self replaced the earlier American literary struggle to clarify the contours of the cosmos.

[68]Irving Howe, "American Moderns," in Schlesinger and White, eds., *Paths of American Thought*, p. 318. The following paragraph draws heavily on this essay.
[69]Lionel Trilling, *The Liberal Imagination* (Garden City, N. Y., 1953), pp. 240, 242.

Hemingway was so convinced of the emptiness of large meanings, of idealism as such, that he apparently believed it unnecessary to fight that battle. His taut language is itself an evidence of his rejection of the world of idealism, of concept, of rationalism, of civilization. Unlike American writers of the nineteenth century, he showed the results of his rejections rather than attempting to prove that they were right. Only occasionally would he become explicit, as in *A Farewell to Arms*: "Abstract words such as glory, honor, courage, or hallow were obscene beside the concrete names of villages, the numbers of roads, the names of rivers, the numbers of regiments and the dates."[70]

Personal involvement and especially risk destroyed abstraction. Perhaps one could learn through a precise scrutiny of the ego in danger or crisis, through scrutiny of probably raw nerve endings, and through awareness of the chill in the pit of the stomach. Things had a price, as Jake Barnes in *The Sun Also Rises* knew, and one had to pay: "Either you paid by learning about them, or by experience, or by taking chances, or by money." An attempt to impose or extract large meaning would necessarily destroy the involvement, and thereby necessarily obstruct learning. Endurance not progress was the point, as Barnes explained: "I did not care what it was all about. All I wanted to know was how to live in it."[71] Distance from experience would vitiate it; though life, in general terms, was not worth observing, it was worth participation if an opportunity for self-measurement could be found. So Jake Barnes explained the point of the bull fight to Brett Ashley: "the holding of his purity of line through maximum of exposure."[72] If the individual could nerve himself to will and execute maximum exposure, his personal authenticity would result in beauty, not necessarily truth. The code, the moral code, required both the risk and the gesture. The world of the other, of the non-self, was organized merely to destroy the true self, as Hemingway once explained in characteristic language:

If people bring so much courage to this world, the world has to kill them to break them, so of course it kills them. The world breaks every one and afterward many are strong at the broken places. But those that will not break it kills. It kills the very good and the very gentle and the very brave impartially. If you are none of these you can be sure it will kill you too but there will be no special hurry.[73]

Believing that, Hemingway exalted—a word he would reject—style. One could still summon courage and dignity in a meaningless world.

[70]Ernest Hemingway, *A Farewell to Arms* (New York: Charles Scribner's Sons, 1929), p. 191.

[71]Ernest Hemingway, *The Sun Also Rises* (New York: Charles Scribner's Sons, 1926), p. 153.

[72]*Ibid.*, p. 174.

[73]Hemingway, *A Farewell to Arms*, pp. 258–59.

Importantly, the style he exalted was moral—another word he would probably have rejected. His typically wounded hero achieves selfhood by facing, not trying to overcome his wound. The conditions of modern life had so radically annihilated any community, that the individual with whatever strength or will or sensitivity he could summon had finally to discover in himself a psychic refuge, a way to endure. The appropriate style of endurance tended almost always to the inarticulate and the concrete. But, as Hemingway showed it, endurance was neither acquiescence nor humiliation. The *corrida*, as a substitute for society, requires endurance gracefully achieved. In the demand for such grace Hemingway's moral code of resistance to and defiance of society and social morality becomes clear. With a perfect *veronica* the individual can introduce a transitory but genuine beauty into an ugly and meaningless world.[74] But the inherent impermanence of such beauty meant that the threshold of satisfaction would be continually receding, and the sometimes aimless and comic, often frenzied reaching out for yet a new experience that would prove that nerves were yet capable of sensation, came increasingly to characterize Hemingway's work.

The decade's intellectual and literary finale came appropriately in 1929, in a humane and gentle but anguished lament by Joseph Wood Krutch. *The Modern Temper: A Study and a Confession* was, among other things, a direct summary of the difficulties of being alive and aware during the Twenties; it was, and is, an intellectual's despair at the intensity and magnitude of an intellectual's peculiar problems during a decade of America's history when the material conditions of life for a vast segment of the population were daily improving, when life was sufficiently well-managed so that those who were repelled by public life could afford to turn away.

Krutch feared that the scientists and industrialists who were satisfied with what they had thought and built, and who, as a result, necessarily suffered a coarsening of the grain, were in fact the fittest who would not merely survive but survive to rule. Others, more sensitively tuned, seized on a now superannuated humanism, trying desperately to ignore their own disbelief. The proposed retreat into self, into imagination perhaps, depended on ironic belief, an attitude Krutch thought appropriate only to proponents of a lost cause. Power seemed to ignore humanity, and humanism was out of touch with everything, even with itself: "Both our practical morality and our emotional lives are adjusted to a world which no longer exists. In so far as we adhere to a code of conduct," Krutch explained, "we do so largely because certain habits still persist, not because we can give any logical reason for preferring them, and in so far as we indulge ourselves in the primitive emotional satisfaction—romantic

74Howe, "American Moderns," in Schlesinger and White, eds., *Paths of American Thought*, pp. 315–17.

love, patriotism, zeal for justice, and so forth—our satisfaction is the result merely of the temporary suspension of our disbelief in the mythology
upon which they are founded."[75] Deracination was the major characteristic of modernity, and that was so in emotional as well as in other terms.

Modernity was, in a sense, unconnected with the past, and, as Krutch
saw it, history was discontinuous. A more total adjustment was demanded
by his decade than ever before. Extinction was the price of failure to
understand—as the artists and writers of the period understood—and the
failure to find a way to live with unprecedented uncertainties and necessities. Science, so far from providing answers, was itself part of the problem. With growing and spreading freedom, the objects—men, women,
love—once summoned as the goal for which freedom was demanded, had
lost their significance, desirability, or meaning altogether.

Displaying something of the vogue of primitivism, new experience,
and delicately wrought anti-intellectualism, Krutch thought that the
future would fall to those who were then too deeply involved in living
and loving to have time to think about how to live and love. Such people
will come, he announced, "as the barbarians have always come, absorbed
in the processes of life for their own sake, eating without asking if it is
worth while to eat, begetting children without asking why they should
beget them, and conquering without asking for what purpose they conquer."[76]

The modern mood, as it came through the filter of Krutch's critical
intelligence, was desperate, rootless, aimless, disillusioned with everything
including disillusion, and evidently secure in the knowledge that knowledge would not help. In often wonderful prose it told of the meaninglessness of language and mind, of the need somehow to act for goals no
longer desired or believed real. It apparently longed to find a faith that
could fire the imagination, and had lost faith in the possibility of faith.
Above all (and it is strange to say of so simple a thing that it was above
all), the modern man was exhausted. Exhausted not from a particular
exertion but chronically so. The burden of needing to ask not why to
endure, but how, was murderously heavy. When men added this burden
to their other labors, they staggered into modernity.

One aspect of the grotesque humor of the Great Depression is that,
in giving men a concrete task to perform, it did not solve but at least
temporarily obscured the peculiarly modern anguish. That is probably
why many of the most articulate American writers and scholars seem to
have found new energy, new zest, and even a new joy in their work. It is
too much to say that as the stock market declined, intellectual spirits
rose. But enough is true to say that for some at least the Depression was

[75]Joseph Wood Krutch, *The Modern Temper: A Study and a Confession* (New
York: Harcourt, Brace & World, Inc., 1929), pp. 22–23.
[76]*Ibid.*, p. 237.

a relief, a chance to engage a world larger than one's own skin, a time to deal with problems that were simpler because capable of some measure of solution. It was a time when village and city could combine in common cause, when material privation seemed almost able to re-create an American community, almost coterminous with the nation. And World War II continued the happy chance to ignore the increasingly relevant legacy of the Twenties. With peace and returning affluence, with skirts rising again and traditional morality declining again, those now old questions re-asserted themselves. This time a much larger group of Americans could think of the discontinuity of history and of "a separate peace."

WARREN I. SUSMAN

Rutgers—The State University

the

thirties

So far as I am concerned, what had been the twenties ended that night. We would try to penetrate the fogs to come, to listen to the buoys, to read the charts. It would be three years before we took down a volume of *Kunstgeschichte* from our shelves to be replaced by a thin narrow book in red entitled *What Is To Be Done?*, by V. I. Lenin. Then in a few years it would be taken down to be replaced by another. And so on.[1]

The time was August 23, 1927; Sacco and Vanzetti had been executed. But for Josephine Herbst this political event, significant as it was, did not in itself mark the end of an era. For it was also on that day that she and John Herrmann were forced to abandon their twenty-three foot ketch after a difficult passage through thick fog.[2] In her brilliant memoir of the year 1927—"A Year of Disgrace"—Miss Herbst demonstrates the extraordinary complexity that results from the mixture of private misfortune and public joys, public disasters and private triumphs, personal

---

[1] Josephine Herbst, "A Year of Disgrace," in S. Bellow and K. Botsford, eds., *The Noble Savage 3* (Cleveland, Ohio: The World Publishing Company, 1961), p. 160. Copyright 1961 by The World Publishing Company. Miss Herbst's memoirs (of which two sections have thus far appeared) promise to be one of the classic accounts of the intellectual life of the 1920's and the 1930's.

[2] Herbst in *The Noble Savage 3*, S. Bellow and K. Botsford, eds., p. 160.

179

seekings and social developments. In April, for example, there were: the discovery of John Herrmann's illness and the happy preparations for the boating venture in Maine; the scandal and excitement of Antheil's *Ballet-Mécanique* at Carnegie Hall and Miss Herbst's unfulfilled longing to be moved by the music as her friends had been; and the death sentence irrevocably passed on Sacco and Vanzetti, crushing to those who had come to believe so fervently in their innocence.

This very mixture of events of different kinds and qualities provides a lesson. The past is not preserved for the historian as his private domain. Myth, memory, history—these are three alternative ways to capture and account for an allusive past, each with its own persuasive claim. The very complexities of the record raise questions about the task of reconstruction in any form. Miss Herbst, for example, is wise enough to ask:

> But is there such a thing as the twenties? The decade simply falls apart upon examination into crumbs and pieces which completely contradict each other in their essences. The twenties were not at all the museum piece it has since become where our literary curators have posed on elevated pedestals a few busts of the eminent. Even individual characters cannot be studied in a state of static immobility. It was all flux and change with artistic movements evolving into political crises, and where ideas of social service, justice, and religious reaction had their special spokesman.[3]

So complex, so varied are events and motives that Erich Auerbach shrewdly suggests, "To write history is so difficult that most historians are forced to make concessions to the technique of the legend."[4] For no matter how great the difficulties, each of us—in his private capacity or as propagandist or as historian—demands some order, some form, from the past. (In spite of her own questions about the nature of the twenties, Miss Herbst's personal reconstruction dates the "end" of the period with precision.) Yet for the maker of myths, the propagandist for a cause, the memoirist and the historian there are frequently different, compelling psychological and social needs dictating different forms and different ways of reconstruction.

Memory is often the historian's most potent ally. But hovering as it does in that strange psychological zone between nostalgia and regret it can often strike out on its own, producing not so much the ordered vision of the past the historian aims to develop as a picture of The Past (even a lurid Past) in the Victorian sense. What had seemed so right at the moment it happened becomes in retrospect not only wrong but

3Herbst in *The Noble Savage 3*, S. Bellow and K. Botsford, eds., p. 145.
4Erich Auerbach, *Mimesis: The Representation of Reality in Western Literature*, trans. by W. R. Trask (Princeton University Press, © 1953), p. 20.

criminal.[5] The personal needs of the present demand of the memoir writer a strangely skewed version of what happened.[6] In the time of Hiss trials and McCarthy accusations, the thirties appeared to be a period dominated by ideological commitment to Stalinism. Even for those who opposed "witch-hunting" there was a lesson to be learned from the "tragic innocence" of the 1930's: avoid any ideology at all cost.[7] Yet sober historical evaluation, confirming the fact of an obvious movement toward the political left by many American intellectuals, raises serious questions about how deep and how significantly "ideological" such political interest was.[8] An examination of the literature of the period reveals an enormous number of tracts, polemics, political, social, and economic analyses but when one looks for major contributions to the literature of ideology—if such a phrase can be used—the only work that seems to stand out as read by "everyone" and regarded as a "powerful instrument" is *The Coming Struggle for Power* by England's John Strachey.[9] Today it is hard to regard that work as a serious ideological contribution and the historian must be a little puzzled that a period regarded as so heavily ideological failed to produce a Lenin or a Gramsci, or indeed even a moderately significant contribution to the literature of ideology. Ideology may indeed have been important in the thirties, but many of the most brilliant and long-lasting contributions to political analysis written in the period were distinctly anti-ideological.[10]

[5]Alistair Cook, in *Generation on Trial* (New York: Alfred A. Knopf, Inc., 1952), his study of the Hiss trial, makes this point vividly, especially in his first chapter, "The Remembrance of Things Past," one of the very best essays on the 1930's.

[6]Daniel Aaron presents an excellent account of this problem based on his own research difficulties in writing his study of Communism and American writers in the 1930's in an important article, "The Treachery of Recollection: The Inner and the Outer History," in Robert H. Bremmer, ed., *Essays on History and Literature* (Columbus, Ohio: Ohio State University Press, 1966), pp. 3–27.

[7]See especially the collection of articles by Daniel Bell, *The End of Ideology* (New York: The Free Press, 1960). Most relevant are "The Mood of Three Generations," pp. 286–99, and "The End of Ideology in the West," pp. 369–76. See also Leslie Fiedler, *The End to Innocence* (Boston: Beacon Press, 1955).

[8]See Daniel Aaron, *Writers on the Left* (New York: Harcourt, Brace & World, Inc., 1961); also his previously cited article (fn. 6), as well as "The Thirties—Now and Then," *American Scholar*, 35 (Summer, 1961), 490–94. Frank A. Warren III, *Liberals and Communism: The "Red Decade" Revisited* (Bloomington, Ind.: Indiana University Press, 1966), throws further light on this question.

[9]Josephine Herbst, "Moralist's Progress," *Kenyon Review*, 28 (Autumn, 1965), 773. George K. Anderson and Eda Lou Walton, eds., have an interesting discussion of the importance of this work in their anthology *This Generation* (Revised Edition) (Chicago: Scott, Foresman and Company, 1949), pp. 545–46. Obviously, I do not mean to suggest that there were no "ideologies" or ideologists in the 1930's. I mean rather that there were several; that ideological thinking was not as striking an aspect of intellectual life as has been supposed or indeed that can be discovered in earlier periods (like the Progressive Era, for example).

[10]See footnotes 42, 43, and 44 below.

Certainly there was a movement Left; certainly there was a change in the intellectual and literary climate. As George Orwell put it when discussing the English-speaking literary community:

> Suddenly we got out of the twilight of the gods into a sort of Boy Scout atmosphere of bare knees and community singing. The typical literary man ceases to be a cultured expatriate with a leaning towards the Church, and becomes an eager-minded schoolboy with a leaning towards communism. If the keynote of the writers of the 'twenties is "tragic sense of life," the keynote of the new writers is "serious purpose."[11]

But it is all too easy to see a political thirties contrasting dramatically with an apolitical twenties. And while memory seems to demand of the figures of the 1930's a *mea culpa* for having joined the Communist Party or having been a "fellow traveller" (as that period itself demanded of the writers of the 1920's a *mea culpa* for having been duped into expatriation or into some "art-for-art's-sake" movement), history demands an examination of the deeper issues that underlay such cries of regret.

The 1960's forced memory to look again at the 1930's and this time with considerable nostalgia. Fashions in clothes and furniture return to the decade for inspiration.[12] Some of what Susan Sontag has characterized under the rubric of "camp" represents an effort to recapture the mood of the thirties, its films, its radio programs, its heroes. The literary market place suddenly rediscovers novels virtually unread and critically ignored in the period and now hailed as significant: Nelson Algren's *Somebody in Boots*, the works of Nathanael West, Daniel Fuchs' trilogy, Henry Roth's novel of immigrant life, and even Horace McCoy's "existentialist" treatment of the dance marathon craze, *They Shoot Horses, Don't They?*[13] Several anthologies of the writings of the period have appeared, each discovering a verve and importance in the literary

---

[11]George Orwell, "Inside the Whale," reprinted in *A Collection of Essays* (New York: Doubleday & Company, Inc., 1954), p. 236 in the Anchor paperback edition; quoted by permission of Harcourt, Brace & World, Inc. and Miss Sonia Brownell and Secker & Warburg, Ltd. This brilliant essay written in 1940 provides a stimulating view of the whole period.

[12]See, for example, "Making the 1930's Pay Off—At Last," *Business Week* (August 20, 1966), pp. 128–32.

[13]The original sales of the Fuchs' novels are as follows: *Summer in Williamsburg* (1934), 400 copies; *Homage to Blenholt* (1936), 400 copies; *Low Company* (1937), 1200 copies. So Fuchs reports in a new preface to the paperback edition (New York: Berkley Publishing Corporation, 1965), p. 7. These novels were also reprinted in hard covers in 1961. West's *Miss Lonelyhearts* (1933) sold only 800 copies in its original edition, according to Robert M. Coates in his "Afterword" to the Avon paperback reprint of the McCoy novel (New York: Avon Books, 1966), p. 134. McCoy's novel of 1935 may be almost regarded as a best-seller in this company: it sold 3000 copies. It was reprinted in paperback in 1948, 1955, and for the third time in 1966 (which text I am using).

output of the period previously denied or overlooked.[14] And some of the collected memories of the period reenforce significant new scholarship that reveals not only a fascination with the "proletariat" and a literature and reportage concerned with industrial workers, strikes, and coming revolution, but also a widespread agrarian utopianism, in the North as well as in the South, a deep interest in communitarian ventures that smacks more of the America of Brook Farm than of the U.S.S.R. of Five-Year Plans.[15]

The past summoned up before us by the forces of memory is important; it is part of the record that cannot be ignored. But because it serves the special functions that memory demands, because it is often colored by nostalgia or regret, the historian must be on his guard. He is obligated to seek some more solid foundation that will hold in spite of the psychological and social demands of the moment. In building this vision of the thirties the historian does not seek to debunk what the memoir writers recall or what has been written previously about the period, but rather to understand it all in a way that helps, at least, account for the complexities and contradictions, the confusions of flux and change.

In sketching this structure no fact is more significant than the general and even popular "discovery" of the concept of culture. Obviously the idea of culture was anything but new in the 1930's, but there is a special sense in which the idea became widespread in the period.[16] What had been discovered was "the inescapable interrelated-

[14]Harvey Swados, ed., *The American Writer and the Great Depression* (The American Heritage Series) (Indianapolis, Ind.: The Bobbs-Merrill Co., Inc., 1966), has a fine introductory essay and a good bibliography; Jack Salzman, ed., *Years of Protest* (New York: Pegasus, 1967), covers many issues and has especially useful headnotes. Louis Filler, ed., *The Anxious Years* (New York: G. P. Putnam's Sons, 1963), is wide-ranging and the introduction provides useful information but also some strange opinions.

[15]See Henry Dan Piper's valuable collection of Malcolm Cowley's important pieces of reportage, controversy, and criticism from the 1930's, *Think Back on Us* (Carbondale, Ill.: S. Illinois Univ. Press, 1967). On this point see especially pp. 51–55. Caroline Bird, *The Invisible Scar* (New York: Simon & Schuster, Inc., 1966), is in many ways a good social history. On this question see pp. 89–90. In addition to Paul Conkin's solid work *Toward a New World* (Ithaca, N. Y.: Cornell University Press, 1959), see the valuable essay (the third chapter) in Warren French's *The Social Novel at the End of an Era* (Carbondale, Ill.: S. Illinois Univ. Press, 1966), for important data on this point.

[16]A. L. Kroeber and Clyde Kluckhohn, *Culture: A Critical Review of Concepts and Definitions*, originally published as Volume XLVII—No. 1 of the Papers of the Peabody Museum of American Archaeology and Ethnology, Harvard University in 1952 and reprinted in paperback (New York: Random House, Inc., 1963), is the crucial work in the whole area of definition and use and a starting point for any study. It deals largely with professional social scientists, however, and does not deal with what I would call the acculturation of the concept. Charles and Mary Beard wrote an important book as part of their series of volumes on *The Rise of American Civilization*,

ness of . . . things" so that culture could no longer be considered what Matthew Arnold and the intellectuals of previous generations had often meant—the knowledge of the highest achievements of men of intellect and art through history—but rather reference to "all the things that a group of people inhabiting a common geographical area do, the ways they do things and the ways they think and feel about things, their material tools and their values and symbols."[17] The remarkable popularity of Ruth Benedict's *Patterns of Culture* (1934)—surely one of the most widely read works of professional anthropology ever published in the United States—provides us with a symbolic landmark. Its impact was significant; but more important, her analysis of the possibility of different cultural patterns and the way such patterns shape and account for individual behavior itself was part of a more general discovery of the idea itself, the sense of awareness of what it means to *be* a culture, or the search to *become* a kind of culture. "The quest for culture," one student of the problem suggests, "is the search for meaning and value."[18] It is not too extreme to propose that it was during the thirties that the idea of culture was domesticated, with important consequences. Americans then began thinking in terms of patterns of behavior and belief, values and life-styles, symbols and meanings. It was during this period that we find, for the first time, frequent reference to "an American Way of Life." The phrase "The American Dream" came into common use; it meant something shared collectively by all Americans, yet something different than the vision of an American Mission, the function of the organized nation itself.[19] It is not surprising that H. L. Mencken believed (er-

---

a final volume called *The American Spirit* (New York: The Macmillan Company, 1942). This volume, too often overlooked and much more significant than scholars have hitherto acknowledged, was the study of the idea of civilization in the United States which the authors felt was the key American idea and a molding force in the development of American civilization itself. In my own work I have argued that the idea of culture always existed somehow opposed to and in tension with the idea of civilization, but the Beards' book is significant. Kroeber and Kluckhohn also discuss the distinction between culture and civilization. In a different context, using very different material, the anthropologist Clifford Geertz has provided a very stimulating essay, "The Impact of the Concept of Culture on the Concept of Man," in John R. Platt, ed., *New Views of the Nature of Man* (Chicago: The University of Chicago Press, 1965), pp. 93–118.

[17]Robert S. Lynd, *Knowledge for What? The Place of the Social Sciences in American Culture* (Princeton, N.J.: Princeton University Press, copyright 1939, 1967 by Princeton University Press), pp. 16, 19.

[18]F. R. Cowell, *Culture in Private and Public Life* (New York: Frederick A. Praeger, Inc., 1959), p. 5.

[19]Mitford M. Matthews in his *Dictionary of Americanisms* (Chicago: University of Chicago Press, 1951) does list a use of "the American Way" as early as 1885, but his other references reinforce the opinion that it came especially into vogue in the 1930's and 1940's. There were at least four books in the period that used the phrase in a title (including a collection of essays edited by Newton D. Baker in 1936 and Earle Looker's 1933 study of F.D.R. in action). Kaufman and Hart used it as a title

roneously it appears) that the expression "grass roots" was coined in the 1930's, for during the decade it became a characteristic phrase.[20] The "promises" that MacLeish insisted were America contrast dramatically in image, rhetoric, and kind from *The Promise of American Life* Herbert Croly discussed in the Progressive Era. For Croly that promise depended on a definition of democracy and the creation of new institutional patterns divorced from history; it involved political, social, and economic readjustments. But for MacLeish the promises could be best found within history, a special kind of folk-history:

Jefferson knew:
Declared it before God and before history:
Declares it still in the remembering tomb.
The promises were Man's; the land was his—
Man endowed by his Creator:
Earnest in love; perfectible by reason:
Just and perceiving justice: his natural nature
Clear and sweet at the source as springs in trees are.

      . . .

It was Man who had been promised: who should have.
Man was to ride from the Tidewater: over the Gap:
West and South with the water: taking the book with him:
Taking the wheat seed: corn seed: pip of apple:
Building liberty a farmyard wide:
Breeding for useful labor: for good looks:
For husbandry: humanity: for pride—
Practicing self-respect and common decency.[21]

---

of a play in 1939. The play traces the history of an immigrant family in America and ends with patriotic flourishes. There is, I suspect, little significance in the fact that it was the first Broadway play I ever saw. Certainly there were more books and articles using the phrase in the 1930's than ever before. Merle Curti has some extremely interesting things to say about the idea of an American Dream in his article "The American Exploration of Dreams and Dreamers," *Journal of the History of Ideas*, 27 (July–September, 1966), 391. He believes that James Truslow Adams invented or at least publicized the phrase in 1931. George O'Neils's play of that name was produced in 1933 and showed the progressive deterioration of the ideals and character of a New England family through American history. The word culture itself begins to appear commonly. Many titles are cited in this essay. Others include Jerome Davis, *Capitalism and Its Culture* (New York: Holt, Rinehart & Winston, Inc., 1935).

20On this issue see Matthews, *Dictionary of Americanisms*, as well as Raven I. McDavid, Jr.'s revised one-volume abridgement of Mencken's *The American Language* (New York: Alfred A. Knopf, Inc., 1963), p. 183. An important book of the 1930's published as the result of a symposium organized by the Department of Agriculture, with a preface by Charles Beard which stressed the key role of agriculture as a base for any democracy in America, was M. L. Wilson, *Democracy Has Roots* (New York: Carrick & Evans, Inc., 1939). We need further studies of the rhetoric of American history.

21From "America Was Promises," *Collected Poems 1917–1952*. Copyright 1952 by Archibald MacLeish. Reprinted by permission of the publisher, Houghton Mifflin Company. Reprinted in Filler, *The Anxious Years*, pp. 225–26.

Clearly the two works differ in form and purpose. Further, it is obvious that we can discover common values and beliefs in the writings of the Progressive and the poet. But it is still proper to suggest that in the work of the thirties MacLeish actually proposes a redefinition of the promise of American life, placing great emphasis on what we might call the cultural visions: questions of life-style, patterns of belief and conduct, special values and attitudes which constitute the characteristics of a special people.

It is said all too often, that certain extremely popular works of fiction obtained their popular hold because they provided a means of escape from contemporary problems. It is not possible to deny this. But from the point of view of an increased interest in a particular life style, in patterns of belief and their consequences, as well as in the consequences of the destruction of such cultures, it becomes possible to read in a different light the enthusiastic reception given to Oliver LaFarge's *Laughing Boy* (1929), with its touching and even sentimental plea for cultural pluralism (only one of many works in the period recalling a rich American tradition of works dating back at least to Cooper in which the Indian's admired "culture" is threatened by the White Man's "civilization"), or to Margaret Mitchell's *Gone With The Wind* (1936), with its historical reconstruction of the destruction of a way of life (again, only one of many historical romances in the 1930's recounting in extraordinary detail life-styles and values different from those of the 1930's).[22]

In 1931 Stuart Chase produced a best-seller: *Mexico, A Study of Two Americas.* The book was to play an important role in the whole discussion of the nature of culture, especially "popular culture."[23] But even more important it made explicit for a large audience the very kind of distinction that became increasingly characteristic of the period. Drawing specifically not only on his own experiences but on the works of American social scientists (the Lynds' study of *Middletown* and Robert Redfield's analysis of a Mexican community), Chase sharply contrasted the urban-industrial culture of the United States and the folk-culture of a more primitivist and traditional Mexico. While the United States might well have the advantages that come with "civilization," the author of *Mexico* clearly found special benefits in the simple folkways of Tepoztlan. It was a community free of the business cycle and mechanical civilization, an "organic, breathing entity." While it had no machines, it was "im-

---

[22]Leo Gurko, *The Angry Decade* (New York: Dodd, Mead & Co., 1947), has some useful information, especially on the context of American reading in the period, although its analysis is not very penetrating. James D. Hart, *The Popular Book* (New York: Oxford University Press, 1950), is invaluable.

[23]See the perceptive essay by Reuel Denney, "The Discovery of Popular Culture," in Robert E. Spiller and Eric Larrabee, eds., *American Perspectives* (Cambridge, Mass.: Harvard University Press, 1961), p. 170.

possible for Mexicans to produce the humblest thing without form and design." Time was measured by sun and climate, not by clocks. The clock was "perhaps the most tyrannical engine ever invented. To live beyond its lash is an experience in liberty which comes to few citizens of the machine age." The villages are self-sustaining. The men want neither money nor the things money can buy. And perhaps most important, Chase frequently sees in Tepoztlan echoes of what American life itself once was before machine-age Middletown developed "a culture which has found neither dignity nor unity." "While each family harvests its own fields, community spirit is strong—as in old New England barn raisings. For machineless men generally, it is both necessity and pleasure to assist, and be assisted by, one's neighbor" or "When all is said and done, [the government, a kind of village communism] is 'a form of play.' Thus the working of the sublime principles of Jeffersonian democracy in Tepoztlan."[24]

As early as 1922 William Fielding Ogburn had defined the concept of "cultural lag."[25] But again, it was in the 1930's that the phrase and its implications became part of common discourse. "The depression has made us acutely aware of the fact that our brilliant technological skills are shackled to the shambling gait of an institutional Caliban," one of our most brilliant and widely read sociologists declared; his was an urgent appeal for a social science devoted to the study of the whole culture in the endeavor to develop the consequences of such knowledge for man.[26] And the distinguished historian Carl Becker mournfully announced that:

> Mankind has entered a new phase of human progress—a time in which the acquisition of new implements of power too swiftly outruns the necessary adjustment of habits and ideas to novel conditions created by their use.[27]

This is a far cry from the glorious hopes of a Progressive Era when "progress," "power," and indeed "efficiency" or "organization" were magic words; when it was felt that the application of the very techniques of the Communications Revolution might create a more desirable community and society.

[24]Stuart Chase, *Mexico, A Study of Two Americas* (New York: The Macmillan Company, 1931). This book, written in collaboration with Marian Tyler, begs for more extensive treatment, especially since Hart, *The Popular Book*, indicates it was a best-seller in the period. I have quoted almost at random: pp. 170, 130, 154, 171, 128.

[25]William Fielding Ogburn, *Social Change with Respect to Culture and Original Nature* (New York: Viking Press, 1922).

[26]Lynd, *Knowledge for What?*, pp. 3–4. He also speaks, in the passage immediately preceding, about what has spoiled "the American Dream."

[27]Carl Becker, *Progress and Power* (Palo Alto, Calif.: Stanford University Press, 1936), p. 91.

It is in fact possible to define as a key structural element in a historical reconstruction of the 1930's the effort to find, characterize, and
adapt to an American Way of Life as distinguished from the material
achievements (and the failures) of an American industrial civilization.
Civilization meant technology, scientific achievement, institutions and
organizations, power and material (financial) success. The battle between
"culture" and "civilization," between the quality of living and the
material, organized advancement of life was anything but new as an
intellectual issue.[28] But the theme becomes central in the 1930's and
even those older followers of the Progressive tradition who valued the
march of civilization and progress sought to emulate Thorstein Veblen
and make from an industrial civilization a meaningful culture or way
of life.[29]

However, civilization itself—in its urban-industrial form—seemed
increasingly the enemy. It stood for the electricity that was used to
destroy Sacco and Vanzetti;[30] or, as the hero of Algren's novel muses,
" 'Civilization' must mean a thing much like that mob that had threatened his father."[31] Writers as different in other ways as Reinhold
Niebuhr and Lewis Mumford wondered whether the civilization that
had triumphed was in fact worthy of the highest aspirations of man.
The increased interest in the social sciences in the period, and the
tendency to point to the failure of the natural sciences to solve man's
problems are additional evidence for a new-found cultural awareness;
we may add the growth of serious study of popular culture, of cultures
other than our own, or the remains of folk or other subcultures within
our own.[32]

Again, the effort to define precisely the nature of American culture

[28]See footnote 16. I have developed this argument at length in my paper "The
Nature of American Conservatism," which I delivered at the First Socialist Scholars'
Conference, September, 1965.

[29]I have not dwelled in this essay on what happened to Progressive ideas in the
period. Obviously, there was considerable continuity at least in some aspects of the
culture of the period. Otis L. Graham, Jr., *An Encore for Reform* (New York: Oxford
University Press, 1967), is enlightening on differences as well as similarities, but
Rexford G. Tugwell has written a most brilliant essay "The New Deal—The Progressive Tradition," *Western Political Quarterly*, 3 (September, 1950), 390–427, which
can be missed by the cultural and intellectual historian only at great peril.

[30]Herbst, "A Year of Disgrace," *The Noble Savage 3*, p. 159.

[31]Nelson Algren, *Somebody in Boots* (paperback reprint) (New York: Berkley Publishing Corporation, 1965), pp. 82–83. Originally published in 1935.

[32]In addition to works already cited, Alfred Kazin, *On Native Grounds* (New
York: Harcourt, Brace & World, Inc., 1942), has an extraordinary analysis, considering
the date of its appearance, in his section on the 1930's, especially the chapter
"America, America." We need an extended study of the newly awakened popular
interest in anthropological and archeological studies in the 1920's and 1930's which
produced not only an outpouring of scholarly discoveries and works but also a considerable popular literature as well.

itself—as it had been historically and as it was now—characteristic of so much of the writing of the 1930's is no new effort, but it appears more widespread and central than in any time previous. (This effort is also distinctly different from that which seeks to show the development of the achievements of civilization in the United States.) Constance Rourke's *American Humor* (significantly subtitled *A Study in National Character*) (1931) and her essay on "The Roots of American Culture" provide special landmarks. Miss Rourke did not devote herself to an analysis of the great contributors to Culture; she sought rather to find the significant culture patterns to which she might relate such figures and from which they could and must draw their material. And when Van Wyck Brooks emerged from long silence in 1936 with *The Flowering of New England* to begin his monumental multi-volume cultural history, he had not so much changed his way of thinking—he still sought a usable past, some meeting ground between highbrow and lowbrow—as his method of analysis. Following in some sense the lead of Miss Rourke, he attempted in his own way to discover the basic patterns of culture, basic values and attitudes, using minor and forgotten figures as well as the major writers to show the underlying structure of the culture from which they came.[33]

The issue then, is not that the 1930's simply produced a new era of nationalism.[34] Certainly few, if any, decades in our history could claim the production of such a vast literature—to say nothing of a vast body of films, recordings, and paintings—which described and defined every aspect of American life. It was not, then, simply that many writers and artists and critics began to sing glowingly of American life and its past. It was rather, the more complex effort to seek and to define America as a culture and to create the patterns of a way of life worth understanding. The movement had begun in the 1920's; by the 1930's it was a crusade. *America in Search of Culture* William Aylott Orton had called his not always friendly analysis of the phenomenon of 1933. The search was to continue throughout the decade in the most overwhelming effort ever attempted to document in art, reportage, social science, and history the life and values of the American people.[35]

[33]Brooks edited a collection of Rourke's essays and provided a most significant preface, *The Roots of American Culture and Other Essays* (New York: Harcourt, Brace & World, Inc., 1942). Vico and Herder play an important role in the new concern for culture. Brooks quotes Herder to the effect that "folk-forms were essential to any communal group, they were the texture of the communal experience and expression." All of the key words were, as we shall see, especially important in the 1930's.

[34]See the essay of Harvey Swados with which he introduces his anthology, *The American Writer and the Great Depression*.

[35]In 1928 Niebuhr published his *Does Civilization Need Religion?*, the first of many important works really on this theme; in 1954 Mumford began his series of

If there was an increased awareness of the concept of culture and its implications as well as a growing self-consciousness of an American Way or a native culture of value, there were also forces operating to shape that culture into a heightened sensitivity of itself as a culture. The development of systematic and supposedly scientific methods of measuring the way "the people" thought and believed is certainly one important example. The idea of public opinion was an old one (it can be traced back at least to de Tocqueville) and the political, social, and even economic consequences of such opinion had been studied by a number of serious students: Lowell, Lippmann, and Bernays, to point to the most obvious examples. The Creel Committee of World War I days had already paid careful attention to the advantages and special techniques of manipulating such opinion. But it was not until 1935, when George Gallup established the American Institute of Public Opinion, that "polling" became commonplace in American life. Now Americans had "empirical" evidence of how they felt and thought regarding the major issues of the day and generally shared attitudes and beliefs. It was easier now to find the core of values and opinions which united Americans, the symbols which tied them together, which helped define the American Way. It was not just the discovery of techniques that might be manipulated by experts to produce desired results, although this was a part of what happened; the polls themselves became a force, an instrument of significance, not only for the discovery and molding of dominant cultural patterns, but also for their reinforcement.[36]

Other technological developments played an even more vital role. The decade of the thirties was a most dramatic era of sound and sight. It is impossible to recall the period without recourse to special sounds: the "talkies," the machine-gun precision of the dancing feet in Busby Berkeley's musical extravaganzas, the "Big Bands," the voices of Amos and Andy, to say nothing of the magic of Franklin Roosevelt's Fireside Addresses. For our immediate purposes, examples of the consequences of a new age of sound can best be found by looking briefly at some of the effects of national radio networks. Through their radio sets a

four volumes pleading for a harnessing of science and technology in the interest of a better life for man with his *Technics and Civilization*. The series as a whole is called *The Renewal of Life*. The decade saw the publication of the *Dictionary of American Biography* as well as the *Encyclopedia of the Social Sciences, Recent Social Trends* and *Recent Economic Trends*. Many of these works had been begun, of course, during the 1920's. But the 1920's and the 1930's produced an enormous body of literature on the nature of history, culture, and the social sciences as well as the gathering of significant data about our history and society. See Merle Curti, ed., *American Scholarship in the Twentieth Century* (Cambridge, Mass.: Harvard University Press, 1953).

36For a brief introduction to this whole subject treated historically see Stow Persons, *American Minds* (New York: Holt, Rinehart & Winston, Inc., 1958), chapter 21.

unique view of the world, and a way of interpreting it came to the American people. Nothing more dramatically illustrates the power of this new-found sound medium than the response of the Orson Welles Mercury Theater dramatization of H. G. Wells' story of a supposed Martian invasion. Using the recently developed news broadcasting techniques expertly Welles' company made thousands accept (as they were used to accepting) the rhetoric of a radio show as a description of reality; the resulting panic is famous.[37] Sound helped mold uniform national responses; it helped create or reinforce uniform national values and beliefs in a way that no previous medium had ever before been able to do. Roosevelt was able to create a new kind of presidency and a new kind of political and social power partly through his brilliant use of the medium.

The photograph and the film, too, changed the nature of cultural communication in America. Unlike the printed word in newspapers and books, the photograph affected even those who could not or would not read. The thirties brought home the impact of the image created by the photograph in a more universal way. *Life*, founded in 1936, can perhaps be credited with the invention of the "picture essay"; however, it is but one example of the novel way Americans could experience the world. Luce's extraordinary empire also produced "The March of Time," the most brilliant of the newly developed newsreels which provided a fresh way of understanding events. The whole idea of the documentary—not with words alone but with sight and sound—makes it possible to see, know, and feel the details of life, its styles in different places, to feel oneself part of some other's experience.[38]

We are not yet in a position to evaluate the full consequence of these events. But certainly it is possible to suggest that the newly developed media and their special kinds of appeal helped reinforce a social order rapidly disintegrating under economic and social pressures that were too great to endure, and helped create an environment in which the sharing of common experience, be they of hunger, dust-bowls, or war, made the uniform demand for action and reform more striking and urgent. The unity provided deserves some special role in the story of the 1930's. Whatever else that might be said about the New Deal, its successes and its failures, it is obviously true that it was a sociological and psychological triumph. From the very outset of his presidential campaign in 1932, Franklin Roosevelt showed himself fully aware of the importance of symbols. "Let it be symbolic," he told the

---

[37]Hadley Cantril has provided us with a social-psychological study of this affair in *The Invasion from Mars* (Princeton, N.J.: Princeton University Press, 1940).

[38]Beaumont Newhall provides a good starting point for further analysis in *The History of Photography* (revised and enlarged edition) (New York: Doubleday & Company, Inc., 1964), chapter 10.

Convention that had nominated him, in his acceptance speech made after an unprecedented flight to Chicago to receive personally the leadership bestowed upon him, "that I broke the tradition. Let it be from now on the task of our Party to break foolish traditions."[39] The history of the ill-fated N.R.A. offers a series of examples of a brilliant sense for the symbolic in the administration itself: the Blue Eagle, the display of flags, the parades. Roosevelt on radio was to reach out to each American in his living room and make him feel that the Administration was thinking specifically of him, that he had a place in society. The film and the picture-essay brought the figures of power, in every aspect of their activity, personal as well as public, into the immediate experience of most Americans.

Even the lowly soap opera, the most frequently mocked of radio's innovations, played a role in reinforcing fundamental values and in providing the intimate experience of other people's lives so that millions of housewives knew they were neither alone nor unique in their problems. Timeless and consistent in portraying patterns of crisis and recovery, they provided a sense of continuity, assuring the triumph of generally shared values and beliefs, no matter what "reality" in the form of social and economic conditions might suggest.[40]

It is possible to see in the notorious "soaps" the operation of what might be called the force and power of myth. In his famous American Writer's Congress address in 1935, Kenneth Burke analyzed the function of myth in society. He argued that a myth was "the social tool for welding a sense of interrelationship by which the carpenter and the mechanic, though differently occupied, can work together for a common social end."[41] He was concerned, it is true, in this paper with the role of revolutionary myths and symbols. But an analysis of the 1930's reveals how significant a role the new media played in providing a huge public with a body of symbols and myths. In this sense it might not be unfair to consider the extraordinary mythic role the absurd soap opera played. The form may appear ridiculous to some today, but then so do many myths once socially operative which are nonetheless later discarded.

The photograph, the radio, the moving picture—these were not new, but the sophisticated uses to which they were put created a special community of all Americans (possibly an international community) unthinkable previously. The shift to a culture of sight and sound was of

39Quoted in T. V. Smith, "The New Deal as a Cultural Phenomenon," in F. S. C. Northrop, ed., *Ideological Differences and World Order* (New Haven, Conn.: Yale University Press, 1949), p. 212.

40The best analysis of the "soaps" is still the delightful series James Thurber did for the *New Yorker*, reprinted in his *The Beast in Me* (New York: Harcourt, Brace & World, Inc., 1948) as "Soapland."

41Kenneth Burke, "Revolutionary Symbolism in America," in Frederick J. Hoffman, ed., *Perspectives on Modern Literature* (New York: Harper & Row, Publishers, 1962), p. 181.

profound importance; it increased our self-awareness as a culture; it helped create a unity of response and action not previously possible; it made us more susceptible than ever to those who would mold culture and thought. In this connection it is possible to see how these developments also heightened a growing interest among social and political thinkers in the role of symbol, myth, and rhetoric. Kenneth Burke's study of the significance of Hitler's rhetoric and of the importance of the careful development of revolutionary symbolism in the U.S. showed how important such factors were in shaping cultures, the vast power (and therefore dangers) involved in language and symbol.[42] The major works of Thurmond Arnold, one of the more original thinkers of the period, deal with political life not in terms of ideology or the rational implementation of philosophies, but in terms of the role of "folklore" and symbols.[43] And perhaps the leading academic student of political life, Harold Lasswell, developed a whole school of political analysis dealing with psychological and sociological factors barely touched on in previous periods.[44] While a Progressive generation was much interested in problems of communications and even made small but significant use of the photograph, the painting, the cartoon, it is not possible to compare this with the developments in the 1930's, when an unusual sense of sight and sound, a peculiar interest in symbol, myth and language, created a novel kind of community, breaking down barriers, creating often new common experiences for millions. For no matter how great its interest in communication, how deep its concern for the social role of the arts, the Progressives relied primarily and most profoundly on the written word, the rational argument on the printed page. They were a generation of writers who produced an enormous political literature; but they did not and could not make their appeal to the ear and eye, with a sense of symbol and rhetoric that compared to the stunning techniques and effects developed during the 1930's. One significant difference between the two eras is this: the Progressives were people of the book; the children of the 1930's were people of the picture and the radio.

In a stimulating essay on "The New Deal as a Cultural Phenomenon,"

---

[42]Burke, "The Rhetoric of Hitler's 'Battle,' " reprinted in his *The Philosophy of Literary Form* (Baton Rouge, La.: Louisiana State University Press, 1941). This is an important collection of pieces for purposes of this essay.

[43]Arnold, *The Folklore of Capitalism* (New Haven, Conn.: Yale University Press, 1937). I have a reprint edition which indicates that at least ten printings of the work occurred between 1937 and 1941. There is an extended analysis of the work in Richard Hofstadter, *The Age of Reform* (New York: Random House, Inc., 1959), pp. 317–22. Previously, Arnold had published *The Symbols of Government* (New Haven, Conn.: Yale University Press, 1935).

[44]Lasswell's career began with a study of *Propaganda Technique in the World War* (New York: Alfred A. Knopf, Inc., 1927). In 1930 he published *Psychopathology and Politics* and in 1936 *Politics: Who Gets What, When, How.*

T. V. Smith suggests that "sportsmanship is the key to contemporary American life." Speaking of the American way of life itself, Smith argues:

> the *game* is a fitting symbol. Long before baseball came to furnish the chief metaphor of American life there was (and there remains) another game—a game of cards: 'poker' it is called—in which 'to deal' was but to initiate a cooperative activity that could be its own exciting reward, even to those who 'lost their shirts' in its honor. Politics is in common American parlance a game, and in expert parlance it is 'the great American game.' Moreover, the symbolism carried over into business: a deal is a trade, any transaction for gain from which both sides are presumed to profit. Thus the very name of the Rooseveltian movement in question raises connotative echoes in the culture organic to America, in its full multi-dimensionality.[45]

In this passage Smith has done more than to suggest additional evidence about the cultural responsiveness of the New Deal in its selection of symbols. For culture is reflected in and shaped by its games, something analysts writing in the 1930's themselves understood.[46] Most social historians take great pains to point out the significant increase in popular participation in sports, the development of new games and fads, the enormous increase in various forms of gambling in the period.[47] Too often, once again, these facts are explained as the search for escape —a truism to be sure—when they demand more fundamental analysis in terms of the *kind* of escape they propose. The dramatic increase is in special types of gaming, games of competition and chance, games frequently involving cooperation and carefully arranged regulations and limits. The "democratization" of golf and tennis in the 1930's provides a special outlet for the competitive spirit the traditional values of the culture demands and which cannot easily be satisfied in the "real" world of economic and social life. The Parker Brothers' fantastically successful board game "Monopoly" enables would be entrepreneurs to "make a killing" of the kind the economic conditions of the times all but prohibited. Dance marathons, roller derbies, six-day bicycle races, flagpole sitting contests, goldfish-swallowing competitions—these are not just foolish ways out of the rat-race, but rather alternative (if socially marginal) patterns duplicating in structure what institutionalized society

---

[45]"The New Deal as a Cultural Phenomenon," in Northrop, ed., *Ideological Differences and World Order*, p. 209.

[46]It was in 1938 that the distinguished Dutch cultural historian J. Huizinga published his landmark study of play and civilization, *Homo Ludens*.

[47]In addition to the Bird volume already cited (fn. 15), see the excellent social history of Frederick L. Allen, *Since Yesterday; The Nineteen-Thirties in America* (New York: Harper & Row, Publishers, 1940), chapter 6. There are some illuminating suggestions in Robert M. Coates' "Afterword" to the Horace McCoy novel previously cited (fn. 13). See also Foster Rhea Dulles, *A History of Recreation* (New York: Meredith Press, 1965), a revised edition of his *America Learns to Play*.

demanded and normally assumed it could provide. Thus the bank-nights and the Bingo games, the extraordinary interest in the Irish Sweepstakes, the whole range of patterns of "luck" and "success" offered on the fringes of social respectability but certainly within the range of social acceptance —these provided a way to maintain and reinforce essential values, to keep alive a sense of hope. Roger Caillois, in his brilliant book *Man, Play and Games,* suggests that there are "corruptions" of games as well as cultural forms found at the margins of the social order: resort to violence, superstition, alienation and even mental illness, alcoholism and the taking of drugs.[48] Certainly there is evidence that among some elements in the population such corruptions could be found in the 1930's. Yet the striking fact remains that the increase in the particular kind of games that did dominate that aspect of life in the 1930's tended to provide significant social reenforcement. Even the dances of the period marked a return to an almost folk-style pattern of large-scale participation and close cooperation. The holding of block parties which took place even in slum areas of large cities indicates special qualities of life in the 1930's, a fact not overlooked by those whose memory of the period is colored by nostalgia.

As Caillois tells us:

> Any corruption of the principle of play means the abandonment of those precarious and doubtful conventions that it is always permissible, if not profitable, to deny, but arduous adoption of which is a milestone in the development of civilization. If principles of play in effect correspond to power instincts . . . , it is readily understood that they can be positively and creatively gratified under ideal and circumscribed conditions, which in every case prevail in the rules of play. Left to themselves, destructive and frantic as are all instincts, these basic impulses can hardly lead to any but disastrous consequences. Games discipline instincts and institutionalize them. For the time that they afford formal and limited satisfaction, they educate, enrich, and immunize the mind against their virulence. At the same time, they are made fit to contribute usefully to the enrichment and the establishment of various patterns of culture.[49]

Commentators are right then, to indicate the importance of the kind of games played in the 1930's.

There is also the widespread and continuous use of the game metaphor—not only in the business and politics of the period—useful to writers in indicating the meaning or the meaninglessness of life. When Robert Sherwood sought an appropriate image for the fatuous and yet

---

[48]Roger Caillois, *Man, Play and Games* (New York: The Free Press, 1961), especially chapters 3 and 4.

[49]Caillois, *Man, Play and Games,* p. 55.

vicious forces of nationalism and international business, he too selected a game of cards. In his pacifist assault on those forces, insensitive to the human condition and hell-bent on destruction, he allows his heroine to speak of God:

> Yes...We don't do half enough justice to Him. Poor, lonely old soul. Sitting up there in heaven, with nothing to do, but play solitaire. Poor, dear God. Playing Idiot's Delight. The game that never means anything, and never ends.[50]

And from another perspective entirely, William Saroyan built his sentimental tribute to the gentle, innocent, and good American people out of a whole series of games and toys. Most memorable, perhaps, is the pin-ball machine that the bartender assures Willie he cannot beat. Willie undertakes to try; he

> stands straight and pious before the contest. Himself vs. the machine. Willie vs. Destiny. His skill and daring vs. the cunning and trickery of the novelty industry of America, and the whole challenging world. He is the last of the American pioneers, with nothing more to fight but the machine, with no other reward than lights going on and off, and six nickels for one. Before him is the last champion, the machine. He is the last challenger....

In the last act of *The Time of Your Life* Willie finally beats the machine. Saroyan tells us "the machine groans." And then

> the machine begins to make a special kind of noise. Lights go on and off. Some red, some green. A bell rings loudly six times....An American flag jumps up. Willie comes to attention. Salutes. 'Oh boy (he says) what a beautiful country.' A loud music-box version of the song 'America.' (Everyone in the barroom rises, singing). 'My country, 'tis of thee, sweet land of liberty, of thee I sing.' Everything quiets down....Willie is thrilled, amazed, delighted. Everybody has watched the performance of the defeated machine....[51]

The analysis of the structure that underlies an historical picture of the 1930's suggests some tentative conclusions at this point. First, there was in the discovery of the idea of culture and its wide-scale application a critical tool that could shape a critical ideal, especially as it was directed repeatedly against the failures and meaninglessness of an urban-

---

[50]Robert Sherwood's *Idiot's Delight* (1936) is conveniently reprinted in Harold Clurman, ed., *Famous American Plays of the 1930's* (New York: Dell Publishing Co., Inc., 1959). This passage appears on p. 253. Quoted by permission of Charles Scribner's Sons.

[51]William Saroyan's *The Time of Your Life* (1939) is also reprinted in Clurman, ed., *Famous American Plays of the 1930's*. The passages quoted appear on pp. 388 and 463. Quoted by permission of William Saroyan.

industrial civilization. Yet often it was developed in such ways as to provide significant devices for conserving much of the existing structure. A search for the "real" America could become a new kind of nationalism; the idea of an American Way could reinforce conformity. The reliance on basic culture patterns, stressed by further development of public opinion, studies of myth, symbol, folklore, the new techniques of the mass media, even the games of the period could and did have results far more conservative than radical, no matter what the intentions of those who originally championed some of the ideas and efforts.

Other studies bear out this conservative trend—no matter what memory may tell us about disorganization and a Red menace. The Lynds' return to Middletown in the 1930's led to the discovery that the schools of that community, for example, had had their heyday of freedom in education in the 1920's; by 1935 "the culture was tightening its grip on the schools to insure that 'only the right things' were being taught."[52] And perhaps the most significant experiment in higher education in the decade under Robert M. Hutchins at the University of Chicago can be considered an effort to reassert traditional values and standards in a retreat from the educational philosophy of the supposed followers of John Dewey. An important study of white acceptance of jazz documents the fact that when such music left the confines of the smaller Negro subculture and achieved wide-scale circulation and popularity in the larger national community through radio, records, and the "Big Bands" of the period, the lyrics of older jazz and blues as well as new works created tended to lack the bite and social criticism found in the jazz of the 1920's and earlier. In fact, lyrics tended to be bland, mouthing even more forcefully the commonplace and accepted values and beliefs, personal and social.[53]

In no field, however, was the consequence of the new approach stressing the role of existing patterns of culture to be as significant and striking as in the realm of popular psychology, or in that strange combination of religion and psychology that frequently ruled in the 1930's as a substitute for liberal protestantism, as Donald Meyer has brilliantly shown.[54] Any student of the 1930's cannot but be impressed with the enormous body of literature designed to instruct and inform on ways

[52]Robert S. and Helen Lynd, *Middletown in Transition* (New York: Harcourt, Brace & World, Inc., 1937), pp. 233–34 and Robert Lynd, *Knowledge for What?*, pp. 236–37.

[53]Neil Leonard, *Jazz and the White Americans* (Chicago: University of Chicago Press, 1962), chapter 6.

[54]A good deal that follows is based on Meyer's superb analysis in *The Positive Thinkers* (New York: Doubleday & Company, Inc., 1965), certainly one of the most important recent studies in the field of American civilization. See especially chapters 14, 18, and 19.

to succeed.[55] It was the great age of the "How-to-do-it" book. But what is most unusual about all such literature, in view of the enormous critical assault on capitalism and even the widely held assumption among many, right, left, and center, that capitalism was doomed, is its initial principle: failure is personal, not social, and success can be achieved by some adjustment, not in the social order but in the individual personality. Dale Carnegie's *How to Win Friends and Influence People* was the best seller of the period, and its publication in 1936 is a landmark for the study of American popular culture. In simplest terms, Carnegie called for adjustment to the existing order. Everyone wanted to feel important; the way to get ahead was to *make* other people feel important. Smile! In the same year Henry C. Link published his best selling *The Return to Religion*. In it religion joined hands with psychology "to promote not ego strength but surrender." Urging people to "behave themselves" rather than to "know themselves," Link reemphasized the importance of work and of just keeping busy (even by dancing, playing cards or joining clubs). Most important of all was the development of personality. Link's work in psychological testing led him to invent a method of "testing" personality, a way of measuring "Personality Quotient." PQ was clearly more important than IQ. Make people like you; fit in; develop habits and skills "which interest and serve other people." Here again the radio soap operas played their reinforcement role. They repeated the line of Carnegie and Link: "Just Plain Bill" kept smiling and "Ma Perkins" kept busy. Everyone tried to fit in and be well liked. The wisdom of the sages of the soaps—and few were without their wise man or woman—follow closely the patterns of advice suggested by the Carnegies and the Links and the Norman Vincent Peales who offered similar proposals during the decade. The stress on personal reasons for success and failure is also typical. New business ventures, relying heavily on the new methods of advertising made possible by the new media, proposed a host of products to help individuals guard against failure and perhaps even achieve success. New "diseases" could be countered with new remedies: bad breath, body odor, stained teeth, dish-pan hands. Advertising also assured us that a host of new mail-order courses might help us achieve success by home study; all we needed to do was improve our spelling or our vocabulary, learn how to develop our personalities, develop our talent for drawing or writing.[56]

[55]Hart, *The Popular Book*, pp. 255–56, is excellent here. Carnegie's book sold 750,000 copies by the end of its first year in print. By 1948 it had sold over 3,250,000 copies in all editions. Also popular were Pitkin's *Life Begins at Forty* and Dorothea Brande's *Wake Up and Live*, among the hundreds of best-selling do-it-yourself books devoted to self-help.

[56]All the social historians comment on this point. Caroline Bird, *The Invisible Scar*, p. 277, has some especially interesting material.

All this stress on conforming to what was demanded by society around us, all this emphasis on "fitting in," had its more sophisticated counterpart in the newly emerging field of human relations management. In his important work in the 1930's, Elton Mayo urged adjustment to the patterns of industrial organization from the perspective not of the worker, aiming to "get ahead," but from that of the manager anxious to provide an effective and happy work force.[57] Mayo speaking from a post at Harvard Business School is certainly a more learned and sophisticated student of human affairs than Dale Carnegie or Henry C. Link and yet his work strangely seems of a piece with theirs insofar as it seeks adjustment to the existing and ongoing patterns of cultural development. Other intellectuals not influenced by development in popular culture might find, interestingly enough, something at least analogous happening in other areas of professional psychology in the period. For the intellectual community the emergence of what has been called American Neo-Freudianism is undoubtedly the most important development. It may well be that in the thirties no representative work of the group was more widely read and influential than Karen Horney's *The Neurotic Personality of Our Time* (1937). Her analysis of the problem of anxiety argues that it is the contradictions within culture itself that bring about specific neurotic patterns in individuals. The attitudes that prevail within the culture to which we relate provide us with the basic conflicts that create our neuroses and our culture itself is patterned by the very nature of our anxieties, providing institutionalized paths of attempted escape from anxiety. The neurotic personality reflects the conflicts within the culture; the culture provides the mechanisms to escape from anxieties. It is not without reason that the Neo-Freudian position has often been accused of advocating an adjustment to the patterns of culture as a way of curing more serious problems of anxiety, and it is not completely unfair to read Neo-Freudianism in this aspect as a high brow translation of what we have already suggested marked the mainstream of popular psychology in the 1930's.[58]

If the idea of culture and the self-awareness of cultural involvement play crucial roles in a structuring of the history of the 1930's, another

[57]Mayo deserves more serious treatment than I have given him. He influenced Harold Lasswell's studies, for example, and his books *The Human Problems of an Industrial Civilization* (Cambridge, Mass.: Harvard University Press, 1933) and *The Social Problems of an Industrial Civilization* (Cambridge, Mass.: Harvard University Press, 1945) are important works. Meyer discusses Mayo briefly in his book, cited above (fn. 54), and Loren Baritz has an important analysis in *The Servants of Power* (Middletown, Conn.: Wesleyan University Press, 1960).

[58]Clara Thompson has a brief analysis of the Neo-Freudians in the last chapter of her *Psychoanalysis: Evolution and Development* (New York: Hermitage House, 1950), and there is a stimulating critique of the movement in the Epilogue to Herbert Marcuse's *Eros and Civilization* (Boston: Beacon Press, 1955).

idea—not unrelated as we shall see—also cannot be overlooked: the idea of commitment. A commonplace of contemporary language, the idea and its current forms came to significant fruition in the 1930's.[59] Hemingway's heroes of the 1920's had a sense of obedience to a code, to be sure, but perhaps nowhere in our fiction is the basic idea brought so much to the center of consciousness as in the mystery writing of the 1930's. This genre was extraordinarily important in the period; more significant (in quality and in number of volumes published) detective fiction was produced in the decade than in any previous period.[60] Unfortunately, too few historians have followed up Prof. William Aydelotte's superbly suggestive article on "The Detective Story as a Historical Source."[61] Here we cannot detail all the consequences of the popularity of the form in the 1930's. But we can look at an early and archetypical detective hero of the period and see the form the idea of commitment begins to take. Sam Spade first appears in Dashiell Hammett's masterpiece of 1930, *The Maltese Falcon*, and was immortalized in Humphrey Bogart's portrayal in John Huston's film version of the novel. Few who have read the book or seen the film can forget Sam's last great speech to Brigid O'Shaughnessy, the woman he loves, the woman who offers him love and money (both of which the culture values highly). Yet Brigid is a murderess and Sam vows to surrender her to the police. His argument forms a whole new cultural stance for several generations:

> Listen. This isn't a damned bit of good. You'll never understand me, but I'll try once more.... When a man's partner is killed he's supposed to do something about it. It doesn't make any difference what you thought of him. He was your partner and you're supposed to do something about it. Then it happens we were in the detective business. Well, when one of your organization gets killed it's bad for business to let the killer get away with it.... Third, I'm a detective and expecting me to run criminals down and let them go free is like asking a dog to catch a rabbit and let it go. It can be done, all right, and sometimes it is done, but it's not the natural thing. ... Fourth, no matter what I wanted to do now it would be absolutely impossible for me to let you go without having myself dragged to the gallows with the others. Next, I've no reason in God's world to think I can trust

---

[59]The word was perhaps not widely used in the decade; certainly, not as widely used as it was to become in the 1940's and 1950's. It did not quite gain the currency that the word "culture" did. But the idea was a concept important to the period. On the whole question of the word, its origins and meanings in contemporary discussion, see Edmund Wilson, "Words of Ill-Omen," in his *The Bit Between My Teeth* (New York: Farrar, Straus & Giroux, Inc., 1965), pp. 415–16.

[60]Hart, *The Popular Book*, p. 259, points out that nearly a quarter of all new novels published in the decade were detective-mystery stories. Only 12 books of this type appeared in 1914; only 97 in 1925. By 1939 the production of new titles (to say nothing of reprints) had reached 217.

[61]*Yale Review*, 39 (September, 1949), 76–95.

you and if I did this and got away with it you'd have something on me that you could use whenever you happened to want to.... Sixth,... since I've got something on you, I couldn't be sure you wouldn't decide to shoot a hole in *me* some day.... It's easy to be nuts about you.... But I don't know what that amounts to. Does anybody ever? But suppose I do? What of it? Maybe next month I won't.... Well, if I send you over I'll be sorry as hell—I'll have some rotten nights—but that'll pass.... If that doesn't mean anything to you forget it and we'll make it this: I won't because all of me wants to—wants to say to hell with the consequences and do it—and because—God damn you—you've counted on that with me the same as you counted on that with the others.... I won't play the sap for you.[62]

This is a remarkable passage and it is in its way especially a passage that could have come only out of the 1930's: hard, yet romantic (Spade will wait for Brigid until she is released from prison); pragmatic, yet with rigid adherence to a special code of belief and values; commonplace, yet strangely elevated in mood. Most remarkable of all, Sam expects Brigid to understand and accept, and Hammett expects his audience to understand and accept. It represents a remarkable effacement of the desires of the ego and yet its adherence to a particular scheme of values (meaning at the same time the rejection of still other things of value) allows for survival itself.

The very nature of the period and of the new dominant approach in the idea of culture created special problems for the individual. To be sure, the problems suggested by "individualism" as early as the 1830's, when de Tocqueville coined the expression, was whether or not the individual could survive in an age of mass civilization and industrialization. But the effort could be made nonetheless: witness the frequently wild antinomian spirit that infected so many of the young intellectuals of the 1920's with their hopes of asserting the supremacy and persistence of their unique personalities and the survival of their own egos. But the "cultural" approach of the 1930's seemed (even as it resisted the claims of "civilization") to pose still further problems rather than easy solutions. As John Dewey explained,

> The function of culture in determining what elements of human nature are dominant and their pattern or arrangement in connection with one another goes beyond any special point to which attention is called. It affects the very idea of individuality. The idea that human nature is inherently and exclusively individual is itself a product of a cultural individualistic movement. The idea that the mind and consciousness are intrinsically individual did not even occur to any one for much the greater part of human history.[63]

---

[62]I am using the Dell paperback reprint (New York: Dell Publishing Co., Inc., 1966), pp. 188–89. Copyright by, and quoted by permission of, Alfred A. Knopf, Inc.
[63]John Dewey, *Freedom and Culture* (New York: G. P. Putnam's Sons, 1939), p. 21.

Thus individualism can exist only if the culture permits it, that is, if it can have a necessary function within the structure of culture itself.

There was a deep current of pessimism in the thirties about the possible survival of individualism. In 1935 Robert Sherwood gave Broadway audiences *The Petrified Forest*, a play in which the rootless, wandering poet-intellectual and the fiercely independent gangster both represent types doomed to extinction by society, types as dead as the trees of the Petrified Forest itself. The drive for unity and conformity (ideals often reenforced by the concept of culture itself) that appears such a striking fact in the history of the period—no matter how noble and desirable the end—threatens the survival of individualism. Karen Horney's discussion of solutions to the problem of anxiety nowhere suggests a rebuilding of the ego so it can stand alone.[64] Yet the hunger for such survival of "I" remains; the search for immortality persists as an acute source of anxiety.

Observe Edward G. Robinson's memorable characterization of the title role in *Little Caesar*, the film of 1931. In an early scene he explains to his friend why he must have a major career in crime. He is not fighting back against social injustices done him; he is not trying to escape from the ghetto and the slum. The women and the money fail to attract him and he expresses no interest in the excitement of a contest between law and outlaw. He is Ricco, he announces proudly, and "I want to *be* someone." In the film's final scene, lying shot and dying under a billboard, he exclaims almost without belief, "Mother of Mercy, is this the end of Ricco?"

Thus, too, the "movements" and "ideologies" of a period—and certainly of the 1930's—helped people to "be" somebody. Malcolm Cowley comments on the special advantages Communist Party membership afforded:

> There was an enormous prestige at that time for people who belonged to the party. They were listened to as if they had received advice straight from God; as if they weren't quite inspired prophets, but had been at meetings where the word was passed down from Mount Sinai. . . . So they had a sort of mana that surrounded them. . . .[65]

One of the few novels written in the period that could be called political, Tess Slesinger's *The Unpossessed* (1934), treats with considerable

[64]Karen Horney, *The Neurotic Personality of Our Time* (New York: W. W. Norton & Company, Inc., 1937), p. 47ff. It is interesting, in passing, to note how much Prof. Lynd makes use of Horney's analysis in his own book *Knowledge for What?* previously cited.

[65]In "Symposium: The First American Writers' Congress," *American Scholar,* 35 (Summer, 1966), 505.

satiric effect the social and psychological uses to which middle-class intellectuals and writers put their involvement in the political Left.

Yet status and prestige represent only one part of the story of the survival of the ego. The period was one in which social anxieties heightened personal anxieties. Cowley, commenting on the large number of breakdowns among intellectuals, expresses his own belief that Party membership provided a way of helping "these people with psychological problems [who] were looking for some cure outside themselves."[66] Certainly the method could easily fit into one or more of the "dodges" Karen Horney tells us we build into our culture in our effort to escape our anxieties. Katherine Anne Porter, writing in 1939, saw the political tendency since 1930 as:

> to the last degree a confused, struggling, drowning-man-and-straw sort of thing, stampede of panicked crowd, each man trying to save himself—one at a time trying to work out his horrible confusions... I suffer from it, and I try to work my way out to some firm ground of personal belief, as others do. I have times of terror and doubt and indecision, I am confused in all the uproar of shouting maddened voices.... I should like to save myself, but I have no assurance that I can....[67]

"I suspect that it was the question of my own fate that took me to Spain as much as it was any actual·convulsion going on in that country," Josephine Herbst shrewdly comments.[68]

There is, of course, a significant difference between becoming a gangster and joining the battle against fascism, no matter what a crusader against the Red Decade might think. But the act of commitment itself had a psychological and sociological significance often unrelated to the specific nature of the profession or movement. For some the act itself could be defined in ways that made it sufficient in itself. For Ernest Hemingway, the Spanish War presented an easy and positive answer for the individual (Miss Herbst tells us that Hemingway was "at home" in Spain and that she was not). For him the war offered,

> a part in something which you could believe in wholly and completely and in which you felt an absolute brotherhood with others who were engaged in it.... Your own death seemed of complete unimportance; only a thing to be avoided because it would interfere with the performance of your duty.

---

[66]*American Scholar*, 35, 500.

[67]In her reply to the *Partisan Review* questionnaire "The Situation in American Writing," first published in 1939 and reprinted in William Phillips and Philip Rahv, eds., *The Partisan Reader* (New York: Dial Press, Inc., 1946), p. 617.

[68]Herbst, "The Starched Blue Sky of Spain," *The Noble Savage 1* (Cleveland, Ohio: The World Publishing Company, 1960), p. 78.

But the best thing was that here was something you could do about this feeling and this necessity too, you could fight.[69]

The simplicity of such an act of commitment almost overwhelms, especially in Hemingway's rhetorical flight. This act Hemingway describes is simple, clear, direct; it is obvious and essential.

Yet not everyone could find such immediate satisfaction in his act of commitment. The act might be necessary but there still remained in fact, new dilemmas developed as a consequence of the act itself. Compare Miss Herbst's response with Hemingway's:

I was probably trying to find some answers to the confusions in my own mind. The thirties had come in like a hurricane. An entire young generation had been swept up in a violent protest against the realities of events. But the answers were numbing. The slogans were pieces of twine throttling something that was struggling. Phrases like 'the toiling masses' did not answer terrible questions. There were always people, real people, each was an individual spirit with its own peculiar past. The Spanish War was doubtless the last war in which individuals were to enter fully with their individual might. But what a welter of conflicting views this implies! The soldier is not only fighting *against* an enemy but also *for* some beyond.[70]

The special dilemma for the intellectual that this passage reveals is central to any serious study of the 1930's, but Hemingway's contemporary response was perhaps more characteristic of writers of the times.

How important the ability was to make some commitment, to associate with some idea of culture may best be seen if we look briefly at those who lacked it. Frederick J. Hoffman tells us

The age of the Great Depression . . . was of course the time of the marginal man *malgre lui*. Time and again, he moves by necessity from place to place, vainly seeking employment, dreadfully aware of his lack of status, his emotional reaction varying from extreme despair to extreme anger.[71]

The 1930's had its forced wanderers, its vagabonds, its tramps. Indeed, such "marginal men" became the subjects of a literature which has

[69]From *For Whom the Bell Tolls* (1940), quoted in Norman Holmes Pearson, "The Nazi-Soviet Pact and the End of a Dream," in Daniel Aaron, ed., *America in Crisis* (New York: Alfred A. Knopf, Inc., 1952), p. 337. *For Whom the Bell Tolls* was originally published by Charles Scribner's Sons.

[70]Herbst, "The Starched Blue Sky of Spain," *The Noble Savage 1*, pp. 79–80.

[71]Introduction, *Marginal Manners* (Evanston, Ill.: Harper & Row, Publishers, 1962), p. 7. This excellent anthology of Prof. Hoffman's has an important section on the 1930's: "The Expense of Poverty: Bottom Dogs," pp. 92–126, with material reprinted from Dos Passos, Steinbeck, Dahlberg, and Maltz and very intelligent headnotes by Hoffman.

emerged as a special legacy from the period. Such marginality is not desired or accepted voluntarily; life on the road is not romanticized, nor is it a source of any genuine pleasure or special wisdom. It is not a journey that ends in discovery or explanation. There is little to suggest the appeal of any particular ideology (even anarchism, so popular in the literature of marginal men in previous periods, is almost strikingly absent). Seldom can the wanderer find alleviation of distress and anxiety by adherence to a group or a community of any lasting kind. Marginal men do not participate in any culture, real or imagined. They do not listen to the radio, go to the movies, or read *Life* magazine. They do not participate in sports or play traditional games. Here, rather, among the marginal men we find those corruptions of games of which Caillois speaks; here is the violence (sometimes personal, sometimes social, but generally in the end without meaning), the alienation, the drunkenness, the unacceptable and anti-social forms of "play." Even the strike takes on this aspect; it seems almost a perversion of sport without purpose or meaning, since it is generally lost or blunted. It can provide, for the moment, common purpose and brotherhood, the suggested beginnings of a pattern of belief or a way of life—as other events or acts also can do on occasion—but such common action is too easily dissolved and the individual marginal man is on the road again, the road to nowhere. He has no commitments and no culture (in the sense these words are used here). The phenomenon produced a strong body of literature: Edward Dahlberg's *Bottom Dogs* (1930), Jack Conroy's *The Disinherited* (1933), and Nelson Algren's *Somebody in Boots* (1935), are among the very best. These works, however, have become more admired and treated with fuller critical seriousness in our time than they were in the thirties.

Only one novel that might be said to be of the same genre was greeted with considerable enthusiasm when it appeared, John Steinbeck's *The Grapes of Wrath* (1939). Yet it is a novel of the enforced wanderings of marginal men with a difference, in fact with several crucial differences. Marginal man here was not alone; the strength and power of the family as a unit went with him. Frequently on the road he shared with other travellers a strong sense of common purpose and destiny, even the incipient form of a culture. There was an end in view: sometimes a romantic agrarian utopia, sometimes at least a sense of revolutionary enthusiasm and optimism. And the Joad family most especially, therefore, had what can be defined as a sense of commitment.

Thus it was characteristic in the 1930's for the idea of commitment itself to merge with some idea of culture and to produce, at least for a time, participation in some group, community, or movement. The 1930's was *the* decade of participation and belonging. This is obvious on almost every level of cultural development. The 1920's saw a growth of spectator sports; the 1930's mark a new era in sports participation. The 1920's found the intellectuals in revolt *against* the village; the 1930's witnessed the intellectuals in flight *to* the village. Such generalizations are obviously extreme, but they do suggest a basic truth about the decade: the need to feel one's self a part of some larger body, some larger sense of purpose. Harold Clurman's excellent memoir of the Group Theater and the thirties, *The Fervent Years* (1945) makes clear that it was not only the excitement of new plays and new theater ideas, or even a new sense of social purpose that made the venture memorable. It was the sense of working together, sharing ideas and beliefs, the sense in fact of being a "group."

It is not possible to come away from wide reading in the literature of the period without some sense of the excitement—even the enthusiasm and optimism shared by many. They *were* "fervent years." A participant in the intellectual life of the decade comments that there was an "almost universal liveliness that countervailed universal suffering."[72] The historian must wonder whether the "facts" warranted such enthusiasm. Depression problems were not solved during the period, although they were considerably alleviated. Yet even while political events at home suggested some grounds for hope (although surely no grounds to anticipate any "revolutionary" triumph of the workers), abroad the international order was rapidly collapsing and the menace of Fascism constantly growing. One explanation for this mood may very well be found in the additional "fact" of increased participation: in groups, in movements, in what appeared to be the major action of the time.

Political "participation" has most consistently attracted the attention of scholars and citizens who revisit the 1930's. The growth of the Communist Party and its position as a rallying point, at least for a time, of considerable numbers of outstanding American intellectual and artistic figures, helped create the image of the decade as heavily political. Such political participation has received excellent scholarly treatment recently; we are now able to understand such activity more fully than ever before. Yet, the historian analyzing the culture of the thirties must attempt to appraise this activity in terms of the total record. There were political tracts; there were petitions and manifestoes. The Communist Party did receive considerable political support, especially in 1932, from leading intellectuals. But somehow there also seems to have been a paucity of political ideas and, more significantly, an inability to maintain effective political stances except on negative issues: against Franco, against the menace of Fascism, against the dehumanization of Depression America. When it came to vital issues of political involve-

[72]Herbst, "Moralist's Progress," *Kenyon Review*, 28, 776.

ment as distinct from commitment to ideas and often vaguer ideals, that is, issues of power, strategy, and organization which are the lifeblood of actual political movements, the Party soon found itself divided; each issue of genuine political importance brought not only division into factions but actual withdrawal of increasing numbers of intellectuals from the Party itself.[73] It was easy, as Miss Herbst suggested, to be against; it was harder by far to look beyond for something.

The genius of the Communist movement of the 1930's was its ability to use the obvious social and psychological needs of the period. It re-cruited effectively individuals who had no other place to go and who sought to belong and to do, those who had a commitment to ideals shared by those in the Party if not complete knowledge or understand-ing of its ideology. There were sentiments and values which united members; there was in those remarkably confused and complicated times little political knowledge and intelligence among intellectuals whose training and preparation usually left them ill-suited to face the political realities of a collapsing capitalist order. And the Party offered more than political participation: there were its camps, its discussion groups, its magazines, even its dances and social affairs, its lecturers, its writers' congresses. For the first time in the twentieth century the Party had attempted to organize writers and intellectuals, and to bring them to-gether to exchange views, political and aesthetic, to feel themselves an important part of the American scene. This was an important develop-ment—and a major contribution of the Party—for writers who had grown up in the 1920's with the view that America offered no place for the artist and the intellectual. (The New Deal, of course, in this area offered considerable competition with its own projects in the arts, in the theater, and in the Federal Writers' Project.) There was, furthermore, great satisfaction for many in

> the idea of uniting themselves with the mass or the group, and being not leader, but just one in the ranks of the great army that was marching toward a new dawn. If they could forget themselves, they could solve their psycho-logical problems. So there was a great deal of almost religious feeling going on at the same time among people you would never suspect of having it, and who tried to hide their religious feeling in talk of Marxian dialectic.... The feeling was there.[74]

It is all too facile to describe the commitment to the Left as a religious surrogate and yet it is a fact of some importance that American Protestantism was itself suffering in the 1930's. Liberal Protestantism

---

[73]The article by Norman Holmes Pearson, "The Nazi-Soviet Pact," is excellent on this whole question. It is an important piece on the intellectuals and the Left in the 1930's. The works of Daniel Aaron previously cited (fns. 6 and 8) are basic.

[74]Malcolm Cowley, "Symposium," *American Scholar*, 35, 500.

had tended to disintegrate into a strange breed of mind-cure and positive thinking; the Social Gospel found itself usurped by the political magic and action of the New Deal; and the mighty search for "political realism" among intellectual leaders of Protestantism was just itself in process.[75] The rise of Neo-Thomism at the University of Chicago and the efforts of the Southern Agrarians in the period offer additional evidence of an effort to make religion and religious values relevant to society. It is therefore not far-fetched to see for some in the movement to the political left quasi-religious motives.

In a sense, Granville Hicks came to communism through youth groups of the Universalist Church, theological school, and the teaching of Bible at Smith College. But there was perhaps something even more important, as a reviewer of his memoir of the period has observed:

> His native feeling for the decentralized, for the communion of the small group, for collective action coming from individuals drawn together for a common purpose, acting out their parts of a common aim, is thoroughly consistent with his life pattern as it is revealed to us in *Part of the Truth*.[76]

Thus Hicks' participation in the communist movement of the 1930's seems somehow related to his later enthusiastic efforts to make the *Small Town*[77] an operative factor in American culture.

Mary McCarthy selected a most apt image when she called her novel about the 1930's *The Group*. In addition to the Communist Party itself, the various groups within it, and the leagues of authors, there were the Southern Agrarians who issued a group manifesto, *I'll Take My Stand*, in 1930 and joined in yet another, *Who Owns America?* in 1936. Allen Tate indicated his desire to participate in more genuine and meaningful group life than offered by industrial capitalism: a producers' capitalism, the peasant community, the religious community, or a sense of regional community.[78] Ralph Borsodi was not only a widely read critic of modern urban living who urged a *Flight from the City* (1933), but he also organized Homestead Units, one of many communitarian ventures in the period. Arthur Morgan, of Antioch College and the T.V.A., founded in 1939 an organization designed "to promote the interests of the community as a basic social institution and con-

[75]On this whole subject Donald B. Meyer has produced a key book in our understanding of the 1930's with his *The Protestant Search for Political Realism* (Los Angeles, Calif.: University of California Press, 1960).

[76]Herbst, "Moralist's Progress," *Kenyon Review*, 28, 777.

[77]Granville Hicks, *Small Town* (New York: The Macmillan Company, 1946). This is the autobiographical account Hicks has given us of his involvement in his New York community after his break with the Communists.

[78]Allen Tate, in his answer to the 1939 *Partisan Review* questionnaire, reprinted in *The Partisan Reader*, p. 622.

cerned with the economic, recreational, educational, cultural and spiritual development of its members."[79]

In part this was a continuation of a tradition well established during the Progressive Era, and perhaps traceable to the mid-nineteenth century movements, but there is little question that the 1930's saw a general revival of communitarian concern. Stuart Chase's description of the Mexican village has already been cited. Lewis Mumford looked forward to the creation of a new, human city while he looked back with considerable enthusiasm to the achievements of the medieval city.[80] Black Mountain College, which opened in September of 1934, advanced a special communitarian ideal of college living. There was an unusual equality between students and faculty; they built the institution together, literally sharing even tasks of physical construction. The students developed a strong tradition of native arts and craft work as a part of their college experience.

Thorton Wilder's sentimental hit of 1938, *Our Town*, provided a far different picture of village life than, for example, Sherwood Anderson's *Winesburg, Ohio*, his "book of grotesques" published in 1919. Clifford Odets treated the idea of the strike almost as ritual; *Waiting for Lefty* (1935), his vision of labor solidarity and common action, also created a sense of audience participation in a special community with the workers in the play. The unions themselves were or tried to be more than economic institutions: union membership meant group consciousness and the union supplied important social functions, sometimes even cultural ones; for example, *Pins and Needles* (1937), the International Ladies Garment Workers' marvellous theatrical review which delighted audiences of the 1930's and once again audiences in the 1960's. The MacDowell Colony, a long-time center affording artists the opportunity to work and live away from the demands of jobs and other kinds of social pressures, seemed to some almost a communitarian dream come true in this period. And Miss McCarthy was to satirize in *The Oasis* (1949) the kind of communitarian venture attempted by some intellectuals in the 1930's. There was a whole new interest in "the folk society" which led to a whole reappreciation of Indian life and most especially pre-Columbian Indian Life despoiled by the coming of European civilization.[81]

[79]Morgan is quoted here from a pamphlet published by the organization, "About Community Service Incorporated," n.d.

[80]*The Culture of Cities* (New York: Harcourt, Brace & World, Inc., 1938), the second volume in the already cited *The Renewal of Life* series (fn. 35). Mumford had begun his career in the 1920's with a study of various Utopias men had devised through the ages.

[81]See Edward Dahlberg's interesting piece on the communitarian tradition reprinted in *Alms for Oblivion* (Minneapolis, Minn.: University of Minnesota Press, 1964), "Our Vanishing Cooperative Colonies," pp. 91–103. Dahlberg as well as Hart

Individual acts of commitment led to particular visions of culture, often through participation in specific groups or movements or hoped-for participation in ideal ones. This search often involved a new emphasis on tradition. Mention has already been made of the special search for an American tradition. But the movement went beyond this. Robert Penn Warren has said, "The past is always a rebuke to the present,"[82] and the 1930's indeed demonstrated this special use of history, so different from the uses to which history had been put in the Progressive period or in the debunking 1920's. Not only did the Agrarians attempt to create a picture of the pre-Civil War south as an aid to the development of their twentieth-century Agrarian stand; even those of left-wing persuasion found much in the past—miniature class wars, slave revolts, revolutionary heroes—as V. F. Calverton shows in his *The Awakening of America* (1939). Gilbert Seldes' *Mainland* (1936) found much to praise in our past; as a work it stands in sharp contrast to his depressing and negative report on Depression America, *The Year of the Locust* (1932). The professional historians' more favorable assessment of previously-despised Puritanism led to a reassessment of our whole intellectual past. And the work of Mumford, once again, sees much in early history destroyed by the coming of modern technology and urban civilization.

The idea of tradition itself—and most especially the supposed tradition of civilization in the West before the Industrial and the French Revolutions—becomes increasingly important in the period. Not only was there an appeal to the Southern Agrarian tradition and various versions of an American tradition. The Humanists, Irving Babbitt and Paul Elmer More, offered a lively source of debate in the early 1930's and were widely read in intellectual circles.[83] T. S. Eliot, long interested in "The Tradition and the Individual Talent," placed considerably more of his attention on The Tradition in the thirties, especially in *After Strange Gods* (1934) and *The Idea of a Christian Society* (1939). At the University of Chicago, Robert M. Hutchins not only reorganized the institution but also produced a significant defense of his version of *The Higher Learning in America* (1936). His work was a direct confrontation to the previous work of Thorstein Veblen and a specific challenge to the Pragmatists. He would use the tradition to help shape and reenforce the culture.

Crane and Archibald MacLeish became interested in pre-Columbian Indian life and its extinction by the Conquest. William Carlos Williams may have led the way in his *In The American Grain* as early as 1925. At the end of the Dahlberg essay cited he asks, "Is the solitary American superior to the communal Indian?"

[82]Quoted in Louis Rubin, Jr., "Introduction" to the Harper Torchbook reprint of *I'll Take My Stand* (New York: Harper & Row, Publishers, 1958), p. xiii.

[83]See Malcolm Cowley's critique, "Angry Professors," written in 1930 and reprinted in *Think Back on Us*, pp. 3–13.

In general education we are interested in drawing out elements of our common human nature; we are interested in the attributes of the race, not the accidents of individuals.... We propose permanent studies because these studies...connect man with man, because they connect us with the best that man has thought, because they are basic to any further study and to any understanding of the world.... Real unity can be achieved only by a hierarchy of truths which show us which are fundamental and which subsidiary, which significant and which not.[84]

The Pragmatists, already under attack in the 1920's, found themselves fighting for their intellectual lives under the heavy assault of the traditionalists and the antinaturalists.[85]

Even the writing of the period, diverse and different as it was in form and content, shared a common commitment, no matter what the individual participation, in various movements. The Marxist critics may have tried to mold a special kind of proletarian writing but they did not succeed, even among Party members; the movement was surprisingly brief in spite of all the attention paid to it. However, Joseph Freeman's interesting introduction to the anthology *Proletarian Literature in the United States* (1935) is worth examination:

Art, then, is not the same as action; it is not identical with science; it is distinct from party program. It has its own special function, the grasp and transmission of experience. The catch lies in the word 'experience.'[86]

That is indeed where the catch did lie. Even John Dewey had defined art as experience and the word "experience" had been a crucial one for the Progressive generation. Freeman himself argued for the virtues of the *avant-garde* in America from the poetic renaissance of 1912 to the economic crisis of 1929. In this period American writers had repudiated "eternal values" of traditional writers and had emphasized immediate American experience.

The movement has its prophet in Walt Whitman, who broke with the 'eternal values' of feudal literature and proclaimed the here and now. Poetry abandoned the pose of moving freely in space and time; it now focused its

---

[84] Robert M. Hutchins, *The Higher Learning in America* (Chicago: University of Chicago Press, 1936), pp. 73, 77, and 95.

[85] Gail Kennedy, ed., *Pragmatism and American Culture* (Boston: D. C. Heath & Company, 1952) is an excellent anthology with a good bibliography to help the reader trace this development. One of Dewey's own best answers appeared in 1943 in the *Partisan Review*: "Anti-Naturalism in Extremis." It is reprinted in *The Partisan Reader*, pp. 514–29.

[86] *Proletarian Literature in the United States*, ed. by Granville Hicks *et al.* with a critical introduction by Joseph Freeman (New York: International Publishers Co., Inc., 1935), p. 10.

attention on New York, Chicago, San Francisco, Iowa, Alabama in the twentieth century.[87]

The next stage was to be a rendering of the experience of the class struggle itself as it emerged to consciousness with the depression of 1929 and finally and hopefully there would come a literature of The Party.

But literature in general—no matter what the political allegiance of individual writers might be—did not generally respond to the demands of political leadership. There was a new sense of a widening range of experience dramatically brought home because of the events of the era and their wide-spread transmission by the media. Jack Conroy was associated with Party activities, but *The Disinherited* is not an ideological novel. As Conroy himself remarked, "I, for one, considered myself a witness to the times rather than a novelist. Mine was an effort to obey Whitman's injunction to 'vivify the contemporary fact.'"[88] Allen Tate was a Southern Agrarian, but as he has suggested, "The success or failure of a political idea is none of my business; my business is to render in words the experience of people, whatever movement of ideas they may be caught up in."[89] And Alfred Kazin, recalling his own *Starting Out in the Thirties*, declared,

> What young writers of the Thirties wanted was to prove the literary value of our experience, to recognize the possibilities of art in our own lives, to feel we had moved the streets, the stockyards, the hiring halls into literature —to show our radical strength could carry on the experimental impulse of modern literature.[90]

But in many cases this aim, this search for experience and ways to record it (some interesting new forms were produced, especially the "documentary" techniques characteristic of the period, not only in Dos Passos' *U.S.A.*, but in various Federal Theater productions and works like Agee and Walker's *Let Us Now Praise Famous Men*) was related to the discovery of significant myths, symbols, and images from the culture itself that might also serve as a basis of reenforcement or indeed the re-creation or remaking of culture itself. The efforts of William Faulkner in the South and of Hart Crane to build his *The Bridge* (1930), self-consciousness striving to use our history and even our technology mythically and symbolically as Faulkner in a sense was

[87]Freeman, *Proletarian Literature*, p. 19.

[88]Jack Conroy, in his contribution to "The 1930's, a Symposium," *The Carleton Miscellany*, 6 (Winter, 1965), 39.

[89]In his answer to the 1939 *Partisan Review* questionnaire, reprinted in *The Partisan Reader*, p. 622.

[90]From *Starting Out in the Thirties* by Alfred Kazin, by permission of Atlantic-Little, Brown and Co. Page 15. Copyright © 1962, 1965 by Alfred Kazin.

attempting to, stand out. The most persistent symbol to emerge from the bulk of the literature of the period, however, was "the people." It was the theme of Burke's lecture on "Revolutionary Symbolism in America." In 1936 Carl Sandburg insisted, at extraordinary length and with much sentimentalism *The People, Yes*. Others pointed to the "workers" (Burke's preference for "people" rather than "workers" created something of a literary battle at the First American Writers' Congress[91]), to brotherhood or even to Man (always capitalized).

This self-conscious interest in myth, symbol, and image (to become in succeeding decades a special branch of criticism and philosophy, if not a cult among writers and scholars) was in the 1930's, a way in which literature could once again relate experience to culture, not necessarily to political action. Herbert Agar, in his introduction to *Who Owns America* (1936), declared that the social and economic system in America was on the rocks. There was a need to "build a better world" and to provide some picture "in human terms" of what this would be like. Reformation was necessary, but social and economic theories were not enough: "if a reformation is even to begin, it must be based on an ideal that can stir the human heart."[92]

In an age demanding an image—or a myth or symbol—did the social and political movements provide one effective enough? Josephine Herbst has asked whether a phrase like "toiling masses" is enough and Edward Dahlberg, a former "proletarian novelist" himself at one time associated with left-wing politics, was to write devastatingly in 1941 of the failure of the Left to provide meaningful symbols and myths. The mystery of the Mythic Strike, for example, was not enough. "The strike fails as tragic purification, as psychic ablution; the strke is barter, a pragmatic expedient, not a way of seeing." Thus he demanded of ideology more than it can provide, indicating in his extraordinary and special rhetoric a dissatisfaction with communism and fascism that may have led others out of the kinds of political involvement they sought earlier in the 1930's. "The drama of Bread can never be a substitute for the Wine and the Wafer, because man must not only have his loaf of bread, but he must also have an image to eat. Communism and fascism fail as awe and wonder. They are weak as image-making sources."[93] Dahlberg demands what others in this decade so interested in myth, symbol, and image tried to find in a variety of ways. Perhaps in the long run, too, the New Deal succeeded even in its limited way because it, rather than

[91]The story is told by Burke in his comments in the Symposium on the First American Writers' Congress, *American Scholar*, 35, 506–8.

[92]Herbert Agar, *Who Owns America* (Boston: Houghton, Mifflin Company, 1936), p. vii.

[93]Edward Dahlberg, "The Proletarian Eucharist," in *Can These Bones Live* (New York: Harcourt, Brace & World, Inc., 1941), pp. 73–74.

the artist or the intellectual, the Communist Party or other political and social movements like Technocracy, commanded the set of images, symbols, and myths with most meaning for the bulk of the American people.

At least two recent critics of the 1930's have argued that one of the great failures of the period, especially on the Left, was the effort to associate itself with the "folk" rather than the "intellectual" tradition in America, that is, with "mass culture."[94]

> The most important effect of the intellectual life of the 30's and the culture that grew out of it has been to distort and eventually to destroy the emotional and moral content of experience, putting in its place a system of conventionalized 'responses.' In fact, the chief function of mass culture is to relieve one of the necessity of experiencing one's life directly.[95]

William Phillips has suggested that the writers of the Concord school mark the first appearance of an American intelligentsia. In their revolt against commercialism and the Puritan heritage, he suggests, "they set out consciously to form, as Emerson put it, 'a learned class,' and to assimilate the culture of Europe into a native tradition."[96] In the 1930's, it might be argued, the self-conscious American intelligentsia set out to become 'an unlearned class,' to assimilate the culture of the "people" into the inherited European tradition, perhaps especially those ideas and forms brought back from long stays abroad in the 1920's.

Whether the criticisms voiced above constitute a valid perspective on the period or not, the fact remains that there is in much of the literature and thought of the period a kind of sentimentalism, a quality of intellectual softness all too often apparent: Saroyan's "gentle people," the extraordinary messages of hope with which Odets so frequently ended his plays, and for which the content of the plays themselves provided no warrant, Carl Sandburg's positive nod to "the people," MacLeish's hymn to Man. The idea of commitment frequently led, when combined with the idea of culture, not to revolution but to acquiescence.

Significantly, there emerged in the decade of the thirties two other voices from two other rooms, but they achieved full cultural voice and power primarily in the post-depression period. One may be called the commitment to irresponsibility as a cultural stance; extreme antinomian-

[94]William Phillips, "What Happened in the '30s," *Commentary*, 34 (September, 1962), 204–12; Robert Warshow, "The Legacy of the '30s," reprinted in his *The Immediate Experience* (New York: Doubleday & Company, Inc., 1962).

[95]Warshow, *The Immediate Experience*, p. 7.

[96]Phillips, "The Intellectuals' Tradition," reprinted in *The Partisan Reader*, p. 489. This essay originally appeared in 1941.

ism, glorying in the experiences of the self and saying to hell with every-thing else. At first in a kind of underground of the literary world, Henry Miller emerged in 1934 with *Tropic of Cancer*. George Orwell, home from the Spanish War, was to hail Miller in 1940 as "the only imaginative prose-writer of the slightest value who has appeared among the English-speaking races for some years past."[97] Miller was neither a defeatist nor a yea-sayer. "Where Miller's work is symptomatically im-portant," Orwell explains,

> is in its avoidance of any of these attitudes. He is neither pushing the world-process forward nor trying to drag it back, but on the other hand he is by no means ignoring it. I should say he believes in the impending ruin of Western Civilization much more firmly than the majority of 'revolutionary' writers; only he does not feel called upon to do anything about it. He is fiddling while Rome is burning, and, unlike most of the people who do this, fiddling with his face toward the flames . . . . he feels no impulse to alter or control the process that he is undergoing. He has performed the essential Jonah act of allowing himself to be swallowed, remaining passive, *accepting*.[98]

Miller's is an act of commitment in which the act itself is the most important thing. There is no need for "participation," no sense of "belonging" as a part of a group or a culture, real or imagined. If he is part of a tradition, it is personal tradition picked up among frag-ments left behind in history. In Miller there is little sense of history; there is a religious sense, but again antinomian and highly personal. His work attempts a direct expression of his own experience, unstructured by philosophy, ideology, society, by traditional myths or symbols. There is no glorying in the "folk" or special interest in the culture of the "people." American history means no more to him than European, and the America that interests him is only the America of his own experience. Miller's special stance belongs to the cultural history of the thirties: it represents an important modification of the idea of commitment, and one that was to become increasingly important in later decades. For Orwell, Miller's writing is symptomatic: "it is a demonstration of the *impossibility* of any major literature until the world has shaken itself into its new shape."[99]

The other room might be called "Kierkegaardian" in its décor (and it is important to note that this Danish philosopher was translated for the first time into English in the 1930's; although, it is not proper to

[97]George Orwell, *A Collection of Essays*, p. 256 in the Anchor paperback edition. Quoted by permission of Harcourt, Brace & World, Inc., and Miss Sonia Brownell and Secker & Warburg, Ltd.

[98]Orwell, *A Collection of Essays*, pp. 248 and 249.

[99]Orwell, *A Collection of Essays*, p. 256.

say that the movement under discussion depended upon his thinking). In 1932 Reinhold Niebuhr "loosed his bombshell on individualistic and utopian social thinking, *Moral Man and Immoral Society.*"[100] From this time on Niebuhr and other like-minded theologians (generally called Neo-Orthodox) developed a position which was to eventually rule advanced Protestant thinking and ultimately to supply many intellectuals in America with an important world view.

Any generalized picture of the basic structure of the Neo-Orthodox position necessarily risks becoming a parody. But it is fair to suggest that it demanded of man a most difficult commitment. He must live in the world but not be of the world; man is both creature and creator; he is involved in history and yet transcends it. Restoring the doctrine of original sin to a central position once again, Niebuhr asked man to continue to participate in the job of political reform knowing full well that his limitations would make it impossible for him to succeed fully. He dramatized the distinction and the tension that must exist between the Biblical view of history and the "modern" or "progressive" view. Life was a paradox that must be taken with due seriousness. Sydney Ahlstrom offers this summary of the major features of the movement that emerged as the Protestant Neo-Orthodoxy sought some alternative to the types of cultural surrender implicit in both Liberal Protestantism and Social Gospel Protestantism:

> its critique of group, class and personal complacency; its demand for personal appropriation of Christian truth; its insistence that man's moral obligation under the Gospel cannot be stated in terms of legalistic precepts; its warning against the dangers of rationalizing the great Biblical paradoxes; its emphasis upon a radically personalistic understanding of the self, and of God; above all, the reality, the objectivity, and the sovereignty of God and His judgments.[101]

The fundamental role of Christ was, in effect, to stand in opposition to culture. Man was somehow caught in between. Christ was to offer a constant criticism of life in the world, of culture; yet man must continue to operate within the culture with a more realistic sense of the situation. There was no essential morality in any group, party, or class. Ultimately, man was alone in his struggle within culture and had to rely on his commitment, his belief in Christ to sustain him.

[100]Sydney E. Ahlstrom, "Theology in America," in James Ward Smith and A. Leland Jamison, eds., *The Shaping of American Religion*, Vol. I (Princeton, N.J.: Princeton University Press, 1961), p. 312. Copyright © 1961 by Princeton University Press.

[101]Ahlstrom, in *The Shaping of American Religion*, pp. 315–16. Meyer's *Protestant Search* is again a crucial study here.

Thus by the end of the decade two new general positions emerged from the confusions of the period and from the idea of culture and the idea of commitment itself, two positions implying significant criticism of the other views of culture and commitment that had characterized the period. With the growing acceptance of these positions by American intellectuals during the Second World War and after, the thirties came to an end.

Yet, in our effort to achieve an honest understanding of what the decade did achieve, a post-script is called for. In 1941 James Agee and Walker Evans finally published their extraordinary book (begun in 1936) *Let Us Now Praise Famous Men*. It may be the decade's great classic, for the book represents much of what was characteristic of the thirties' finest contributions. It is, of course, a "documentary"; it deals in intimate detail, not with "the people," but with specific members of three families of sharecroppers in the American South. Brilliantly combining photographs and texts, it responds especially to the demands of an era of sight and sound. Significantly, Agee tells us the text was written "with reading aloud in mind . . . it is suggested that the reader attend with his ear to what he takes off the page: for variations of tone, pace, shape, and dynamics are here particularly unavailable to the eye alone, and with their loss, a good deal of meaning escapes."[102] The text was intended to be read continuously "as music is listened to or a film watched." He wishes he did not have to use words at all, but could put together pieces of cloth, lumps of earth, bits of wood and iron, phials of odors, plates of food and of excrement.

"Above all else; in God's name don't think of it as Art." For Agee struggles to achieve a direct confrontation, by his audience, with the experience of these people themselves, their style of life, their very being. The true meaning, he argues, of a character in his work is that he *exists* "as you do and as I do and as no character of the imagination can possibly exist. His great weight, mystery, and dignity are in this fact."[103] Thus the concentration on the direct experience and the re-creation of the total cultural environment in rich detail marks the work. It is a work of passion, a work that involves a fundamental act of commitment by its authors, a belief in the meaningfulness of the lives of such people, a belief in human dignity. There is a moral intensity, albeit without a particular "social" or "political" lesson to teach or doctrine to preach. There may be, as Lionel Trilling suggests, a refusal to see any evil in the universe and thus a moral flaw in the work, but the passion and the innocence are also ways of seeing, perhaps characteristic ways of seeing in the best of the work of the 1930's, ways

[102]James Agee and Walker Evans, *Let Us Now Praise Famous Men* (Boston: Houghton Mifflin Company, 1941), p. xv.

[103]Agee and Evans, *Let Us Now Praise Famous Men*, p. 12.

of seeing that we may forget are part of a genuine and valuable legacy of the decade.[104] Later critics were to hail the end of innocence—that lack of a sense of personalism, the sentimentalism, the failure to see complexity and inherent evil in the world, the optimistic faith in simple solutions to all human problems. These same critics greeted a newer "realism" with considerable enthusiasm. The innocence of the period can be documented; that it was all weakness, perhaps not so easily. The decade was also to be criticized for its commitment to "ideologies," but alas we cannot comment on this charge because there is so little evidence that such a commitment existed. Rather, what appears to have been the stunning weakness of the decade was that innocence *replaced* all ideological sense, when *both* may in fact be essential.

The thirties this essay has attempted to portray and understand may not correspond to the decade as it exists in myth and memory. It had more than its share of grave weaknesses. But the fact remains that the era made a significant contribution to our development in the acculturation of the idea of culture and of the idea of commitment. Later decades would determine whether better use could be made of these discoveries.

[104]The Trilling criticism comes in his excellent review of the work which appears in *The Mid-Century*, Number 16 (September, 1960), 3–11, on the occasion of the appearance of the newly revised edition. On the subject of the various attacks on American "innocence" in recent American scholarship and criticism see the interesting article by Robert A. Skotheim, " 'Innocence' and 'Beyond Innocence' in Recent American Scholarship," *American Quarterly*, 13 (Spring, 1961), 93–99.

CUSHING STROUT

Cornell University

individuals

well

organized

Americans are characteristically curious about themselves, a puzzle to each other as well as to visitors. This national self-fascination has made the American scene a sociologist's happy hunting ground. Our age is rich in his labels—mass society, mass culture, the organization man, the lonely crowd, the power élite, alienation. While "individualism" is still a theme of public oratory, in sober social science, as Prof. Robert A. Nisbet has noted, "the individual has been replaced by the social group as the central unit of theoretical inquiry and ameliorative action," and "there is a dominant interest in themes and patterns of cultural integration, in ritual, role, and tradition, and in the whole range of problems connected with social position and social role."[1] On the popular level readers of nonfiction seem to prefer not the "soap-opera" formula of a tragedy with a happy ending, but the new convention of a social documentary with a sad conclusion. If the language of these documentaries is loosely drawn from the social sciences, their

---

[1] *Quest for Community* (New York: Oxford University Press, 1953), pp. 28–29.

spirit is more like a jeremiad on the wrath of God, disguised as an omnipotent vengeful Society. In this light many Americans have learned to see themselves as lost in an impersonal world of dehumanizing technology and large organizations.

Popular sociology has its counterpart in the pretentious pessimism of some European philosophers of history who blend Hegel, Marx, and Freud to diagnose the tragic "alienation of modern man." These provocative and learned works, neither history nor philosophy but arbitrary hybrids of both, are gloomily fascinating Gryphons inhabiting the higher regions of our intellectual life.[2] In Wonderland the Mock Turtle sighed, "Once I was a real Turtle," and the skeptical Gryphon assured Alice, "It's all his fancy, that: he hasn't got no sorrow, you know." Our Gryphons sigh with the Turtle and tell us that we have no real happiness. Their abstractions confirm in the end the popular shudders of horror at the Hidden Persuaders, the Status-Seekers, the Waste-Makers, and the Brain-Washers. The expatriate's romantic rage against what Henry Miller called "the air-conditioned nightmare" of his country seems to have turned into a commonplace by a mass of readers who feel that through sociology they have acquired the "lowdown" on the national character.

Perhaps a historian of ideas, though he cannot settle sociological problems, can point to changes in the social scientist's perception of American society from Tocqueville to our own time, which has rediscovered the great Frenchman's work in the light of his ominous prophecy of a coming "democratic despotism." It is true that Tocqueville envisioned a future in which men, absorbed in their "petty and paltry pleasures," would draw apart into a private circle of family and friends, leaving the public order to a highly centralized government, "absolute, minute, regular, provident, and mild." But his fears for America were carefully limited because he knew that the United States differed from his abstract model of "the image of democracy itself" by inheriting from England a tradition of local self-government and by enjoying the beneficial circumstances of continental resources, popular churches, and conjugal felicity. Above all, the Americans protected themselves from his ominous prophecy of a "perpetual childhood" under a vast "tutelary power" by their admirable capacity for forming voluntary associations for commercial, religious, moral, or intellectual purposes. This pluralism was the safeguard of liberty in a society threatened by a potential "tyranny of the majority." By this civic energy democratic men could also protect themselves from the political apathy induced by a "virtuous materialism" that would lead them to regard "every new theory as a

2See, for example, Herbert Marcuse, *One-Dimensional Man* (Boston: Beacon Press, 1964), and the criticisms of its unhistorical generalizations by Julius Gold in "The Dialectics of Despair," *Encounter*, 23 (September, 1964), 68–74.

peril, every innovation as an irksome toil, every social improvement as a stepping stone to revolution." There was a lesson for Europe in the American case. "My aim has been to show," he explained, "by the example of America, that laws, and especially manners, may allow a democratic people to remain free."[3]

Modern political sociologists tend to look at America neither in the light of his fear nor of his confidence. In one respect they are more sanguine than he was, because they discount political majority tyranny by pointing out that American politics generates policies which reflect the interests of a variety of *minorities* within the bounds of a consensus set by the important values of the politically active members of society.[4] It is not the great Leviathan of centralized government which alarms them; it is instead the bureaucratic world of large-scale private organizations with oligarchic power to influence the lives of men to whom they are not made responsible:

> The demand of traditional pluralist theory for individual participation in the policy-forming process through primary groups has been made sentimental by modern organizational conditions. When we accept these conditions, it becomes meaningless to exhort individuals to share in making the decisions of their organizations. What, after all, are "their" groups in a highly industrial, hierarchically organized, thoroughly interdependent, and preeminently urban society? Few are the neighborhoods which successfully contain the individual's manifold interests, and those few which remain are increasingly more quaint and less viable.... When public policy is made at all, it emerges from the quite concerned participation of competing oligarchies.[5]

Alexis de Tocqueville's insight into the associative activity of Americans remains a wise warning against accepting loosely drawn and horrifying pictures of atomistic man adrift in mass society, but modern social scientists are likely to look at this happy pluralism with a more skeptical eye. Today, they say, most people do not have the vested interest, nor

[3]*Democracy in America*, Phillips Bradley, ed. (New York: Alfred A. Knopf, Inc., 1945), I, 329. Tocqueville's fears of the inertia and centralization which will afflict "coming generations" are summed up in *Ibid.*, II, 262–63; 318–19.

[4]Robert A. Dahl, *A Preface to Democratic Theory* (Chicago: University of Chicago Press, 1956), from which the crux of his argument against "Tyranny of the majority" in the American case is reprinted in Leonard J. Fein, ed., *American Democracy: Essays on Image and Realities* (New York: Holt, Rinehart & Winston, Inc., 1964), pp. 123–30.

[5]Henry S. Kariel, *The Decline of American Pluralism* (Stanford, Calif.: Stanford University Press, © 1961), p. 182. Kariel cites Tocqueville's description of the future "tutelary power" as if he were talking about managerial cadres rather than government. Kariel's analysis of the threats to pluralism is distinguished by its clarity, historical sense, and constructive spirit.

the tradition of responsibility, which lead to participation. They orient themselves instead "towards evening, week ends, and vacations, which they spend *en famille* looking at television, gossiping and eating with friends and kin, and cultivating the garden."[6] Nor do sociologists share Tocqueville's enthusiasm for local government, which upon close inspection appears to be an indiscriminate, overlapping jungle of jurisdictions and governments interposed between the citizen and the state. No one was a warmer friend of private rights and procedural forms than Tocqueville, yet the town meeting, which he idealized, is now seen as usually indifferent to anything but the adjustment of government to the provincial peculiarities of the local area and the personal esteem of the influencial citizens.[7]

Much more relevant today is Tocqueville's prophecy that if democracies were to preserve a respect for due process of law and the rights of individuals, the judiciary power would have to grow more extensive and stronger. Under Chief Justice Warren the Supreme Court, particularly in the area of equal protection of the law for Negroes, has fulfilled this prediction in spite of bitter protest. Freedom of association in modern America has suffered attrition from Cold War anxiety about "subversive" organizations and the deep South's violent efforts to stamp out Negro movements. Mass communications, inspired by the populistic slogan of "the right to know," can also sabotage the orderly processes of law, and history cruelly proved the point to thousands of TV watchers in November, 1963, when the local authorities and the national press corps in Dallas, Texas, jeopardized Lee Harvey Oswald's right to a fair trial and virtually invited his murder in the jail itself. Even so, due process is now better established in most of the states outside the deep South than in Tocqueville's time, when newspaper criticism of the War of 1812 could lead to mob violence in Baltimore, and neither militia nor jury would restrain or convict the guilty.

Much of the modern interest in Tocqueville's ideas has fixed upon his complaint that he discovered "less independence of mind and real freedom of discussion" in America than in any constitutional state of Europe. In the great example of a free country you could not speak freely of anything "except, perhaps, the climate and the soil; and even then, Americans will be found ready to defend both, as if they had concurred in producing them."[8] But Tocqueville was mainly thinking of a national vanity and irritable patriotism which demanded adulation for the great experiment being conducted in the New World. Just be-

[6]Scott Greer, "Community—and Modern Urban Society," in Fein, ed., *American Democracy*, pp. 85–86. First published in *Approaches to the Study of Politics*, ed. Roland Young (Evanston, Ill.: Northwestern University Press, copyright 1958).

[7]Robert C. Wood, "Suburbia: The Miniature Reexamined," *Ibid.*, pp. 87–93.

[8]*Democracy in America*, I, 244. See also *Ibid.*, I, 263–65.

cause the New World's mission was defined in polar opposition to the Old World's monarchy and aristocracy, a member of France's *petite noblesse* was particularly sensitive to this youthful American gasconade. Beyond this tendency of the eagle to scream, there was, Tocqueville noticed, a "singular stability of certain principles" in the United States. What appeared to be conformism was, in fact, a kind of political and moral consensus on ideology. If Tocqueville missed a "manly candor" of opinion in America, he was, on the other hand, impressed with the political value of the American consensus. It meant, after all, that the majority recognized limits on its own behavior, thus disarming Tocqueville's fear of its potential despotism in democratic countries:

> But the power of the majority itself is not unlimited. Above it in the moral world are humanity, justice, and reason; and in the political world, vested rights. The majority recognizes these two barriers; and if it now and then oversteps them, it is because, like individuals, it has passions and, like them, it is prone to do what is wrong, while it discerns what is right.[9]

This feature of American politics was a salutary reproof of European radicals, who imagined that a republic meant the rule of a vanguard acting in the name of the people without consulting them, just as it also deflated the European reactionaries, who were sure that democracy meant perpetual and anarchic unrest. The contemporary fashion of appealing to Tocqueville in discussions of American "conformity" has badly blurred the actual context of his analysis.

Yet conformity is an old American issue for our own social critics, ever since James Fenimore Cooper returned home from seven years in Tocqueville's Europe to complain that "in morals, habits and tastes, few nations have less liberality to boast of, than this."[10] But this gentleman-Democrat, a country squire from upstate New York, the New World's Tocqueville, did not blame democracy, but rather the provincial circumstances and religious sectarianism of the early settlers. By the 1920's home-grown critics, like H. L. Mencken, Sinclair Lewis, and Van Wyck Brooks, had inflated a caricatured Puritanism into a massive explanation of American deficiencies. Our cultural rebels of the twenties first glimpsed the world of mass production, mass culture, and the organization man, and they turned to Europe for refuge. Their images—puritanism, Babbittry, Main Street—still color our popular talk about

---

[9]*Ibid.*, I, 416. Tocqueville is rather ambivalent about the "singular stability" of certain principles in America; they press too heavily on the individual. See *Ibid.*, II, 257–61.

[10]*The American Democrat*, 3rd ed. (New York: Alfred A. Knopf, Inc., 1956), p. 72. Cooper found a tendency to mediocrity in democracy but he expected that in time "the influence of masses" would prove to have "a generally beneficial effect."

"conformity" long after they have lost any realistic relevance to our problems.

The rebels of the twenties turned to Europe with mixed motives—the search for a more tolerant individualism, for a livelier and more ardent feeling for art, for an earthier, less artificial sense of pleasure. Van Wyck Brooks struck the note of a generation of criticism when he blamed "puritanism" for making a disastrous split between "highbrow" and "lowbrow" in American life. Puritanism was, he argued, the philosophy of both pioneer and businessman who had together thwarted the growth of native culture. These three negative symbols were set against the positive virtues of a country like France where the court had kept alive the nonacquisitive conception of life and the pit had kept the cultivated class in touch with primitive emotional life, thus fostering an "organic" culture.[11] On a more popular level, Sinclair Lewis merged two myths by appealing to both the American frontier and the Old World as the means of redemption in a world where all the towns were becoming like New York, "traffic jams and big movie theaters and radios yapping everywhere and everybody has to have electric dishwashers and vacuum cleaners and each family has to have not one car . . . but two or three—and all on the installment plan!"[12] In *Dodsworth* (1929) his businessman hero, through the good offices of both earthy and cultured Old World women, sheds his puritanism to discover his true character as a pioneer. At the end of the novel Dodsworth, having learned a respect for culture and "the good vulgarity of earth," returns to America full of pioneer zeal for building mobile homes and garden suburbs, the modern equivalents for Lewis of Conestoga wagons and the old homestead. The First World War shattered Brooks's image of a unified European culture, and today what Lewis mocked as the American "God of Speed" is worshipped more devoutly in the streets of Paris or Rome than in Los Angeles. History has played another ironic trick: Dodsworth's dream of a garden suburb has become the sociologist's nightmare of dreary conformity, and Brooks's wish for a unifying genial middle ground has been sardonically fulfilled in the form of a bland, homogenized "middle-brow" culture, now the despair of literary critics.[13]

Before the twenties had ended, the expatriates themselves discovered that making Europe a foil for America yielded diminishing returns. American popular culture of machines, jazz, and advertising were

[11]See *Letters and Leadership* (New York: E. P. Dutton, 1918), reprinted in *America's Coming-of-Age* (New York: Doubleday Anchor, 1958), especially pp. 94, 104–5, 132–34.

[12]*Dodsworth* (New York: Modern Library, by arrangement with Harcourt, Brace & World, Inc., 1947), pp. 162–63.

[13]For a concise analysis of "middle-brow" culture see Clement Greenberg, "The Plight of Our Culture," *Commentary*, 15 (June, 1953), 558–66.

artistically fashionable among many European intellectuals, and fascism increasingly put the freedom of Europe in a baleful light. Malcolm Cowley's mocking sketch, drawn in 1922, of the European-oriented intellectuals who dreamed of "Sunday baseball in Pittsburgh (or better, Sunday cricket); open urinals and racetrack gambling; the works of Freud and Boccaccio and D. H. Lawrence sold at newsstands openly," has lost its point.[14] Contemporary legal interpretations of obscenity have lifted Joyce, Lawrence, and Miller out from under the counters into the drugstore racks, and even *Fanny Hill* has been made an honest woman. The tone of popular culture now is so anti-"puritan" that psychiatrists worry about the bad influence of erotic comic books. If we can judge by the newsstands, America is a pornographer's paradise. There are sad hearts at the discothèque, but it is the melancholy of the after-hours hedonist.

The cultural Bible Belt, which provided H. L. Mencken with so many gleeful opportunities to score against the "boobs" and the yokels, has also lost its shape. "The traditional flight, from west and south to New York," as Peter Viereck has remarked, "still was essential for the creativity of a Hart Crane in the 1920's. Today such a flight to the east seems outdated ... philistia and anti-philistia are no longer regional (if ever they were) but evenly diffused over most of the continent, both of them too protean and intermingled for easy labelling."[15] However Americans spend their leisure—and apart from TV watching no single activity enlists the support of as much as half the population—the diffusion of paperback books, records, and magazines offers a spectrum of quality broader than at any other time. If Main Street is much less remote from the urban mainstream, so also is Babbitt much less of a philistine. Even the Beatniks, those "imaginary rebels" who violently advocate a nonconformism they already possess (as Daniel Bell has noted), find their enemy, The Man in the Gray Flannel Suit, dissolving into an Upper Bohemian for whom their own nonconformism has become culturally chic. Thus a Chicago financier, with Picasso, Monet, and Pollock paintings on his walls, threw a party in 1959 for Allen Ginsberg and fellow-poets, wearing blue jeans and lumberjack shirts.[16] Philistia, where is thy sting?

[14]"Young Mr. Elkins," *Broom*, 4 (December, 1922), 55.

[15]Peter Viereck, *The Unadjusted Man* (New York: Capricorn Books, 1962), p. 15. Reprinted by permission of the Beacon Press, copyright © 1956 by the Beacon Press.

[16]"America as a Mass Society: A Critique," in Daniel Bell, *The End of Ideology* (Glencoe, Ill.: The Free Press, 1960), p. 34. On the variety of leisure-time pursuits see "Careers and Consumer Behavior," in David Riesman, *Abundance for What and Other Essays* (Garden City, N.Y.: Doubleday & Company, Inc., 1964), p. 136. Riesman challenges the connection usually drawn between mass production and consumer uniformity and looks to the scientist for pioneering in the arts of consumption and leisure.

226 _Individuals Well Organized_

Today Europe can no longer be, as it was for Tocqueville, Cooper, and the critics of the 1920's, a touchstone for valuable perspective on American conformity if only because "anti-Americanism" is so often a projection of Europe's fears, envy, or self-righteousness. European intellectuals often displace their resentment at the popularity of drugstores, jukeboxes, movies, and supermarkets in their own countries by blaming the insidious tempters from the New World. The old American legend told of the native innocent tempted by the artificial pleasures of old Europe; the new European fable has reversed the leading roles. "The Americans make us uneasy," Jeanne Hersch explained in 1954 at an international forum in Geneva, "because, without wishing us ill, they put before us for our taking, things which are so ready to hand and so convenient that we accept them, finding perhaps that they satisfy our fundamental temptations."[17] European pundits, ever since Georges Duhamel's _America the Menace: Scenes from the Life of the Future_ (1931), are prone to indulge in the fantasy of the United States as a vast Technocracy blinded by the magic of machines to which the citizenry pay a superstitious homage. In this piece of social science fiction the United States is a robot inspired by the enthusiasm of Tom Swift and driven by the ambition of Henry Ford. (Ford's dream of an efficient, low-priced car for the people, instead of an elegant plaything for the idle rich, was as American as his sentimental nostalgia for folk music and square dancing; what he entirely lacked was that esthetic awe and mystique of the machine often found in fact among European intellectuals.) Europeans forget that the technocratic rationalism which they fear as an American obsession is much more evident in the architecture of "the international style" of Le Corbusier, Gropius, and Mies Van der Rohe than in the more romantic individualism of Frank Lloyd Wright; not an American, but a Swiss designer living in France, fathered the slogan, "a house is a machine to live in."

European horror of American conformity found its monster in the McCarthyite demagoguery of irresponsible and unscrupulous "anti-communism," but Americans did not need to go to Europe to learn the scurrility of his genius for turmoil and confusion. If nearly half the population supported him, the polls did not foretell how quickly and decisively he lost power and prestige after censure by conservative Senators. Hyper-patriotism, as political sociologists have observed, is endemic in a society with vast influxes of rapidly assimilated immigrants. In their anxiety to retain ties with their homeland and yet be accepted

[17] _The Old World and the New World: Their Cultural and Moral Relations_ (Basle: UNESCO, 1956), p. 198. I have discussed European myths of America in "America, the Menace of the Future: A European Fantasy," _Virginia Quarterly Review_, 33 (Autumn, 1957), 569–81, and American myths of Europe in _The American Image of the Old World_ (New York: Harper & Row, Publishers, 1963), pp. 271–73.

as unquestioned Americans, they are strongly tempted to make their ancestral enemies the nation's, or to assert the proof of their American-ism by their sensitivity to the "un-Americanism" of others. Too im-patiently and suspiciously watched by old-stock Americans, the melting pot, in times of crisis, tends to boil over with a loud hiss of steam.[18] The McCarthy mania reflected as well the American need for learning to see the outer world of other nations in realistic perspective, disen-thralled from the illusions generated by so many years of isolated security from "Old World" wars. The ancient tradition of thinking of ourselves as injured innocents in a naughty world has made us all too vulnerable to feeling betrayed whenever we experience international setbacks, and the disillusionment breeds the search for scapegoats. Thus, from a sentimental underestimation of the Communist danger during the last years of the second World War, public opinion swung with violent force to an exaggerated concern for that threat in the 1950's, and former isolationists, true believers in the special immunity of the New World, desperately grasped the devil-theory of American reverses which McCarthy bountifully provided.

The menace of conformity loomed especially large in the 1950's when, in addition to the "witch-hunting" mentality dramatized by Arthur Miller's *The Crucible*, widely read sociologists stimulated anxious discussion of "other-direction" and "the organization man." The upper-middle-class educated American became a fascinated *voyeur* of his own victimization. A deterministic and nostalgic haze hung over these new catchwords. Did a society in a stage of "incipient population decline," with a corresponding development of the "tertiary" sector of the economy —trade, services, and communications—necessarily make obsolete old-fashioned "inner-directed" pioneer individualists? In the new corporate world of the large company and the package suburb, with their emphasis on social adjustment and "well-roundedness," had individual inde-pendence, as celebrated in the old American Dream, necessarily given way to an ideology more relevant to contemporary realities? Neither David Riesman in *The Lonely Crowd* (1950) nor William H. Whyte, Jr., in *The Organization Man* (1956) explicitly held up 19th century rugged individualism for admiration, and both writers warned against reading their analysis as a self-fulfilling prophecy of a dismal tide of history which could not be reversed. It is, however, very doubtful that many readers were much impressed with these cautions.

Even for careful readers the texts were scarcely encouraging. Whyte discounted talk of counter-trends as putting "a rather heavy burden on providence," described individual assertion against the organization as

---

[18]This theme is illuminatingly developed in Edward A. Shils, *The Torment of Secrecy: The Background and Consequences of American Security Policies* (Glencoe, Ill.: The Free Press, 1956), with Great Britain as a contrasting case.

"excruciatingly difficult," possible only "a few times in organization life," and concluded by recommending cheating on company personality tests as the main weapon against the new Leviathans.[19] Riesman (who has in a revised edition abandoned his demographic categories for determining social character) constructively argued for a rational utopianism against shortsighted "realists," but he largely abandoned the area of work as a place to achieve meaningful satisfaction and personal autonomy, modestly dismissed his own suggested reforms as "paltry," and attributed to social character, "with all its intractabilities and self-reproducing tendencies," the power to "largely dictate the way ideas are received."[20] It is not surprising that a popular ideology of "nothing can be done about it" should have found its slogan in the image of "the rat race," particularly among those who were living in it. The suburbanite could find his epitaph in Mr. Whyte's observation: "It is not despite the success of their group life that Park Foresters are troubled but partly because of it, for that much more do they feel an obligation to yield to the group. And to this problem there can be no solution."[21] The relish with which so many academics devoured these depressing images of American society reflects a blend of self-congratulatory relief for not having "gone into trade" and self-accusing recognition of their own fate in the struggle for tenure and grants in the affluent "multi-versities."[22]

It is useful to recall that in 1909 a leading Progressive and apostle of a new individualism should have looked with hope toward the growing process of organization in business, labor, and government. In *The Promise of American Life* Herbert Croly, scandalized by the neglect of the public interest and the demoralizing maldistribution of wealth produced by "rugged individualism," pleaded on behalf of the "boss," the big capitalist, the trade union, and the strong executives in politics for their efforts to bring coherence into modern life. "A national struc-

---

[19]William H. Whyte, *The Organization Man* (New York: Doubleday Anchor, 1956), pp. 9, 10, 14. Quoted by permission of Simon & Schuster, Inc., and Jonathan Cape Ltd.

[20]David Riesman, Nathan Glazer, and Reuel Denney, *The Lonely Crowd: A Study of the Changing American Character* (abridged ed., Garden City, N.Y.: Doubleday Anchor, 1953), p. 347. Riesman and Glazer extensively revised their conclusions in "The Lonely Crowd: A Reconsideration in 1960," in Seymour Martin Lipset and Leo Lowenthal, eds., *Culture and Social Character: The Work of David Riesman Reviewed* (Glencoe, Ill.: The Free Press, 1961), rejecting, among other things, their emphasis in 1950 on the linkage of social character with population trends.

[21]*The Organization Man*, p. 400.

[22]Harold Rosenberg wittily discusses what he calls "the Orgamerican Phantasy" in terms of post-radical nostalgia and the guilt of intellectual employees who have achieved prosperity and prestige in his *Tradition of the New* (New York: Horizon Press, 1959), pp. 269–85. The explanation is too *ad hominem*, but the essay brilliantly criticizes a mood engendered in many people by reading both Riesman and Whyte.

ture which encourages individuality as opposed to mere particularity," he wrote, "is one which creates innumerable special niches, adapted to all degrees and kinds of individual development." The organization could "accomplish more than can a mere collection of individuals, precisely because it may represent a standard of performance far above that of the average individual."[23] Croly looked forward to a future in which specialized training, rather than a pioneer's amateurism, would provide opportunities for the forging of mental independence through disciplined work. In the light of modern sociology Croly's enthusiasm is hard to recapture, but the reader of contemporary indictments of the organizational life, as the psychoanalyst Erik H. Erikson has remarked, should not be blamed for sympathizing with Socrates who, as he drank the cup of hemlock, "calmly watched the numbness creep upon him and asked his friends to give an offering to Asclepius, the god of medicine, since it was only in being poisoned that he expected to be cured."[24]

The poison has had its beneficial effects. The worker has gained bargaining power and self-respect; the farmer has found protection from arbitrary weather, exploiting middlemen, and absentee bankers. Positive government has regulated industrial and financial power, curtailed the worst swings of boom and bust, and cushioned the shocks of unemployment and old age. University teachers have found new opportunities and higher prestige than ever before. "Intellect," as Lionel Trilling declared in 1952, "has associated itself with power, perhaps as never before in history, and is now conceded to be in itself a kind of power."[25] New agencies of government have played a contributing role in the remarkable revival of Western Europe as a confident growing region of democratic peoples. What Croly did not foresee was the dangerous development of what President Eisenhower called "the military-industrial complex," with its vested interest in the Cold War; yet military power has also supported the United Nations in Korea, protected Western Europe, and kept Soviet missiles out of Cuba, thus paving the way, despite intense opposition from the Air Force lobby, for the negotiated ban with the Soviet Union on nuclear testing in the atmosphere. The impersonality of the big universities and companies may have depersonalized life, but they have also freed many from the all-too-personal conformity of the small town and offered them a kind of freedom which lies "betwen the intersections among the interstices," the opportunity for specialized competence.

[23]*The Promise of American Life* (New York: Macmillan, 1909) pp. 414, 408. I have analyzed Croly's themes in an introduction to the Capricorn reprint of 1964.

[24]*Childhood and Society* (New York: W. W. Norton & Company, Inc., 1950), p. 368.

[25]"The Situation of the American Intellectual at the Present Time," in Trilling, *A Gathering of Fugitives* (Boston: Beacon Press, 1956), p. 66. Reprinted by permission of the Beacon Press, copyright © 1956 by Lionel Trilling.

Large organizations propose difficult challenges to the demand for making power socially responsible as they do for the need to find integrity in work, but these problems are only obscured by fantasies about the social machine, a monster out of Dr. Frankenstein by Vance Packard, Mr. Everyman's sociologist. One of the dangers implicit in social science is that its findings tend to be vulgarized in a sociological age. The popularity of sociology as a mode of national self-scrutiny, in contrast to the moral or ideological discourse of an earlier day, is itself support for Riesman's thesis about the urban educated man for whom "other figures in the landscape—nature itself, the cosmos, the Deity—have retreated to the background."[26] But nostalgic readers tended to edit out of his book his concern for "autonomy," rather than for the rigid posture of the "inner-directed" character who merely internalizes parental precepts, just as they also ignored his warning that deliberately constructed ideal types should not be taken as historical, whole persons.[27] The social psychologist Kenneth Keniston has remarked on the feeling of powerlessness among postwar American youth: "The world is seen as fluid and chaotic, individuals as victims of impersonal forces which they can seldom understand and never control."[28] Such students are portrayed as pessimistic about their chances of influencing the organizations for which they will work, or of finding more satisfying jobs outside them. Simplistic reading of sociological texts must have played its part in confirming these self-fulfilling fears.

The organizational world of "other-direction," as Riesman defined it, does not focus in Tocqueville's sense on the issue of conformity or nonconformity in behavior or opinion; rather it raises new questions about how to find pleasure in play, meaning in work, and commitment in politics. The convinced heretic who has traditionally aroused liberal sympathies did not doubt himself; the new sufferer, now appearing on the psychoanalytic couches, wonders who he is, what it all means, and if it is worth it. No doubt rootlessness has been accelerated by the organizational life of moving out in order to move up, with all the attendant anxieties of displacement, but in this respect it has something in common with the formative experiences of the Westward movement and immigration from Europe, which have played such a large role in

[26]"The Study of National Character: Some Observations on the American Case," in *Abundance for What?*, p. 601. Carl N. Degler has challenged the thesis of a change in American social character but at the price, in my judgment, of making a "straw man" out of Riesman's argument. See Degler, "The Sociologist as Historian: Riesman's *The Lonely Crowd*," *American Quarterly*, 15 (Winter, 1963), 483–97. For my reply see "A Note on Degler, Riesman, and Tocqueville," *American Quarterly*, 16 (Spring, 1964), 100–102.

[27]*The Lonely Crowd*, p. 48.

[28]"Social Change and Youth in America," *Daedalus*, 91 (Winter, 1962), p. 137.

making the migratory American.[29] The ultimate questions asked by men "alienated" by their participation in society have a religious flavor, and traditionally in America the strain of mobility has been eased by the portage of religion as a portable form of community. The rise in church membership from some 36 percent of the population in 1900 to 63 percent in 1958 may reflect the growth of more impersonal organizations and more transient homes. A majority of Americans have come increasingly to identify themselves as Protestant, Catholic, or Jew.[30] The religious meaning of this revival is much in doubt, as witnessed by the enormous popularity of Norman Vincent Peale's *The Power of Positive Thinking* (1952) with its reduction of belief to believing in believing. Yet the "crisis theology" of the divinity schools and the seminaries, like the heroic nonviolent resistance movement of Martin Luther King, have given some Americans religious resources for the courage of commitment, while the intellectual leaders of all major faiths have challenged the blandness of popular religion and called for a dialogue to destroy stereotypes and to discover integrity in difference. The vitality of associative life in suburbia may well depend upon the mooted power of the churches to engage their members with the larger problems of the world.

Religious and social pluralism is both an impressive fact and a precarious achievement. The election of a Catholic President in 1960 was unthinkable in the 1920's. If the enemies of pluralism, once dominant in the age of the Klan, the immigration restriction laws, and the Fundamentalist "monkey trial" in Tennessee, are no longer a majority power, they are still an influential minority force to be reckoned with, especially in the South and West. Fundamentalist suspicion of immigrants, cities, unions, Negroes, intellectuals, and Europe connects at many points with the Radical Right and the small-town sentiments of Goldwater Republicans.[31] Overwhelmed nationally at the polls in 1964, this ethnic parochialism still has a tenacious grip on the Republican party. If the New Deal era washed large numbers of Americans into the world of organizations, social pluralism, and international involvement, it left behind a host of followers of King Canute who have set

[29]On the migratory nature of Americans see George W. Pierson, "A Restless Temper," *American Historical Review*, 69 (July, 1964), 969, 89.

[30]That socio-religious groups are replacing ethnic groups in the sociologist's picture of the American status system raises problems of its own. It may sharpen political disputes between them and move American society towards a "compartmentalized" indifference to those outside the fold, as Gerhard Lenski warns in *The Religious Factor: A Sociologist's Inquiry* (rev. ed., Garden City, N.Y.: Doubleday Anchor, 1963), pp. 365–66. The recent movement of change in the Catholic Church, however, works against this development.

[31]See David Danzig, "Conservatism after Goldwater," *Commentary*, 39 (March, 1965), 31–37, an ethnic analysis of the 1964 campaign.

their bitter faces against the tide. President Johnson's landslide victory over Senator Goldwater expressed a healthy widespread fear of the Arizonian's reckless impatience of prudent restraint in foreign affairs, but Goldwater could later claim that the Administration's acceleration of the war in Vietnam and intervention in the Dominican Republic stole his own thunder. The huge electoral victory of the Democrats merely showed that they had become the guardians of the interests of the major organized groups beyond the borders of the old Confederacy.

Tocqueville correctly predicted that democracy would err on the side of conservatism rather than of radical change, but he did not foresee how much radical élan reactionary conservatism could show. The extremist temper of the Radical Right has forced its opponents into a defensive position of "moderation." Daniel Bell exposed the deflated temper of modern liberalism when in 1959 he emphasized the exhaustion of nineteenth century ideologies in the post-war period. This deflationary mood led Bell to praise the pragmatic give-and-take of American politics in contrast to the damaging tendency "to convert concrete issues into ideological problems, to invest them with moral color and high emotional charge."[32] Attacking both socialists and the Radical Right, he implied that democratic politics prohibited anything but the conventional higgle-haggle of organized interest-groups. Justifiably critical of fundamentalist attitudes toward ideas, morality, and rhetoric, he unjustifiably conceded to the Know-Nothings a monopoly on the politics of principle, morality, and emotional appeal.

The deflation of ideology in the world of large-scale organization had begun with the New Dealers whose pragmatic style, however, had been vigorous, buoyant, and inventive. Looking backward in 1941, it seemed as if in one sense they had "reduced a rich heritage of hopes and dreams to the bare endeavor to make the system work"; but, as Edgar Kemler argued in his "ethical guide for New Dealers," *The Deflation of American Ideals*, this perspective was possible only because moral ideology had become the doctrinaire style of Hoover Republicans, who proposed no institutional changes to meet American domestic problems and who resorted in foreign policy to pious rhetoric rather than to a realistic concern for national security.[33] The war itself accelerated the tendency for pragmatic distrust of ideology to become linked with accomodation to the status quo and a weary disdain for principled politics. For the average soldier, naturally enough, ideals were tarnished by their association with the rhetoric of military propaganda. "Though the level of intelligence in the average man might justly be considered

[32]"Status Politics and New Anxieties," in *The End of Ideology*, p. 110.

[33]*The Deflation of American Ideals* (Washington: American Council on Public Affairs, 1941), p. 71.

low," as James Gould Cozzens wrote in *Guard of Honor* (1948), "in very few of them would it be so low that they accepted notions that they fought, an embattled band of brothers, for noble 'principles.' "[34]

Guard of Honor itself marked the growing conservative implications of a general attack on principled interpretations and actions. Although Cozzens makes a valid protest against the distortions of experience which ideology can produce in self-righteous radicals or naïve moralists, the dry tone of his wisdom often has the ring of a tired acquiescence in "the portentous truth, full of comfort though so melancholy, touched with despair yet supportable, that nothing, not the best you might hope nor the worst you might fear, would ever be very much, would ever be very anything." With this knowledge his characters can act sensibly because their feelings have become "more temperate—really, more indifferent."[35] Since "the Nature of Things abhors a drawn line and loves a hodgepodge, resists consistency, and despises drama," then politics can only be the art of the possible, "a balance of disguised bribes and veiled threats."[36] Appropriately, therefore, the issue of racial segregation in the novel is reduced to a problem of public relations, smoothed over by bestowing a medal on an aggrieved Negro officer. Cozzens liberates us from the myth of invulnerable leaders running a ruthlessly efficient machine by showing us in rich detail how the military organization at an Army Air Base works through personal loyalties among vulnerable men who know how to protect each other for the sake of the organization's mission and reputation. But while his irony directed at "the West Point Benevolent and Protective Association" of officers is sympathetic, the irony he uses against the radical intellectual, who poses as a defender of "the dignity of man" against the "brass-hats," is contemptuously hostile. The disparity of tone betrays a bias—with a future.

The increasingly fashionable rejection of ideology for conservative reasons found its own theorist in 1953 when the historian Daniel J. Boorstin sang the praises of "the genius of American politics" for having taught Americans "the meaning of conservatism" by stressing traditional institutions rather than "outspoken values." Boorstin sought to enlist Tocqueville in his own campaign against European intellectuals by citing the Frenchman's observation that Americans had not seized upon general ideas with "the passionate energy" or "blind confidence" of the *philosophes*; but Boorstin betrayed his own ideological bias by ignoring Tocqueville's conclusion that in politics general ideas and practical experiment need and support each other. Far from elevating practice over theory, Tocqueville, in fact, admired the New World politically because

---

[34]*Guard of Honor* (New York: Harcourt, Brace & World, Inc., 1948), p. 275.
[35]*Ibid.*, p. 573.
[36]*Ibid.*, pp. 572, 395.

"in America the two things constantly balance and correct each other."[37] In the age of large-scale organization this complex truth was in danger of being lost in a mindless cult of moderation for which the Eisenhower Administration was a historical symbol.

Since Bell's declaration of the end of ideology, there has been a shift in the mood of American criticism. Critics have rediscovered poverty in the midst of "the affluent society," Negroes have eloquently demonstrated the social value and effectiveness of associated action and moral protest, and students have recaptured their initiative in taking the offensive against arbitrary administration. The class of 1955, as David Riesman sketched it on the basis of reports from *Time*-commissioned interviews with 184 seniors, seemed to be on an air-cushioned escalator to big-company and large-family security.[38] Now, for some at least, there is a world to win. The new spirit has appeared in social science itself. Thus a political scientist warned his colleagues in 1961:

> That men are not autonomous, that societies develop along predetermined lines, that governments reflect the unfree will of individuals—these are propositions we have been conditioned to accept as true. But we must remain alert to that perverse but honorable quality in man and his organizations which, at least so far, has always cheated a naturalistic social science of its success, just as it has always challenged every totalitarian autocracy.[39]

Thoreau has become our national symbol of the anti-organization man, but he left Walden Pond after two years because he had other lives to lead. The point of his experiment was to work down "through the mud and slush of opinion, and prejudice, and tradition, and delusion" until he came to a firm place where a man might "found a wall or a state, or set a lamp-post safely." These symbols of civilization point away from the Pond toward the work that needs to be done to fulfill what Croly called, in the unembarrassed idiom of a more sanguine day, the promise of American life.

The modern world, as Tocqueville saw, offers new benefits for its losses and forces us to seek our own form of greatness and happiness. In warning of the future growth of a "manufacturing aristocracy" he prefigured the large-scale organizations which have become influential oligarchies and whose power now needs to be reconciled with the American constitutional tradition of setting procedural standards to make all organized power responsible. He clearly saw that if men were to remain civilized, or to become so, "the art of associating together"

---

[37]*Democracy in America*, II, 18, quoted by Boorstin, *The Genius of American Politics* (Chicago: University of Chicago Press, 1953), pp. 171–72.

[38]"The Found Generation," in *Abundance for What?*, pp. 309–23.

[39]Kariel, *The Decline of American Pluralism*, p. 300.

would have to grow and improve. There is no guarantee that men will not meanly lose their opportunities. But there is, in Tocqueville's phrase, "a salutary fear which makes men keep watch and ward for freedom" rather than indulge in "that faint and idle terror which depresses and enervates the heart."[40] We can, at least, insist on his distinction in order to keep the future open.

Postscript

I wrote the above essay in its main outlines during the early months of 1965. Since then a great Negro leader, a distinguished Senator, and the civility of a major city have all been slain. The disingenuous conduct of an undeclared war for the control of Vietnam has polarized the country, posing the threat of a popular repressive reaction, stimulated by the fear of sporadic anarchy. Tocqueville was most worried about the future fate of Europe. His fears for America were very long-range— the power of the presidency was potentially dangerous, the white man's refusal to grant the black man his civil rights would lead to violence, and small property owners would be tempted to indulge in an obsession with order at the expense of liberty. The more we see ourselves in the light of his fears the more we must have lost those valuable safeguards against "democratic despotism" that made America for him the most persuasive example of how a democratic people could be free. He thought that American republicanism was deep-rooted, congenial to the American people's "natural state." Now it has become for us as precarious as he knew it was for Europeans. Sufficient unto the day is the darkness thereof. We are all Cassandras now, and we have our reasons. Even so, "faint and idle terror" is not what animates those who are most engaged in keeping "watch and ward for freedom," and in that fact alone perhaps there are, in Jefferson's phrase, "grounds of hope for others," including historians and sociologists.

[40]*Democracy in America*, II, 330. On the value and limitations of prophecy, as Tocqueville saw them, see Edward T. Gargan, "Tocqueville and the Problem of Historical Prognosis," *American Historical Review*, 68 (January, 1963), 332–45.